Ian W. Shaw resides in Canberra where he and his wife look after a number of pets, a number of children and an increasing number of grandchildren.

A social historian, Ian writes about those things which have been used to define the Australian 'character'; sport, wartime bravery and, now, bushrangers. All are subjects that both unite and divide Australians, subjects that allow a wider discussion on what place heroes and villains have in our history.

In between bouts of writing, Ian continues to ply a trade as a security consultant while balancing the demands of family, friends and an unrequited love for the Sydney Swans.

Also by Ian W. Shaw

*The Bloodbath
On Radji Beach*

GLENROWAN

IAN W. SHAW

First published 2012 in Macmillan by Pan Macmillan Australia Pty Limited
1 Market Street, Sydney

Reprinted 2012

Copyright © Ian Winton Shaw 2012

The moral right of the author has been asserted.

All rights reserved. No part of this book may be reproduced or transmitted by any person or entity (including Google, Amazon and similar organisations), in any form or by any means, electronic or mechanical, including photocopying, recording, scanning or by any information storage and retrieval system, without prior permission in writing from the publisher.

National Library of Australia
Cataloguing-in-Publication data:

Shaw, Ian Winton.
Glenrowan.

ISBN 9781742610986

Subjects: Kelly, Ned, 1855–1880.
Byrne, Joe, 1856–1880.
Kelly, Dan, 1861–1880.
Hart, Steve, 1859–1880.
Glenrowan Inn (Glenrowan, Vic.) – Siege, 1880.
Sieges – Victoria – Glenrowan – History – 1851–1891.
Bushrangers – Australia.
Glenrowan (Vic.) – History.

364.154099455

Every endeavour has been made to contact copyright holders to obtain the necessary permission for use of copyright material in this book. Any person who may have been inadvertently overlooked should contact the publisher.

Typeset in 12/16 Fairfield LH 45 Light by Post Pre-press Group
Printed in Australia by McPherson's Printing Group

Papers used by Pan Macmillan Australia Pty Ltd are natural, recyclable products made from wood grown in sustainable forests. The manufacturing processes conform to the environmental regulations of the country of origin.

To the next generation of Kelly Hunters – Hannah, Darcy, Eli, Clementine and Violet (the Shaws) and Billy Winton Fowlie.

CONTENTS

Cast of Characters   ix

Prologue: The Long Drop   1

1   Ned Kelly, Son of Red Kelly   10
2   Outlaws   26
3   The Killing of Aaron   43
4   Ann Jones's Glenrowan Inn   67
5   Saturday Night and Sunday, 26/27 June 1880   75
6   The Dark Hours: 27/28 June 1880   99
7   The Police Special   119
8   First Blood   138
9   Reinforcements   158
10   The Siege   171
    i. 03:00–05:00 Monday   171
    ii. 05:00–07:00 Monday   183
    iii. The Man in the Mist   196
    iv. The Trophy   210
    v. 07:00–11:00 Monday   217
    vi. 11:00–15:00 Monday   228
11   Last Rites   237
12   Midwinter Afternoon, Glenrowan   255
13   Aftermath   261
14   The Reckoning   275
15   The Legacy   289

Notes   309
Bibliography   323
Acknowledgements   328
Index   330

CAST OF CHARACTERS

Outlaws
Ned Kelly, *charismatic 25-year-old leader of the Kelly Gang.*
Joe Byrne, *23-year-old friend and companion of Ned.*
Dan Kelly, *nineteen-year-old brother of Ned.*
Steve Hart, *21-year-old, superb horseman and close friend of Dan.*

Police
Commissioner Frederick Standish, *aristocratic Chief Commissioner of the Victoria Police.*
Superintendent Frank Hare, *ambitious protégé of Standish. Led first police to Glenrowan.*
Superintendent Charles Nicolson, *conservative senior policeman first charged with catching the Kellys.*
Superintendent John Sadleir, *local senior policeman in 'Kelly Country'.*
Sergeant Arthur Steele, *opinionated and driven senior officer at Wangaratta.*
S/C Charles Johnston, *quietly spoken officer from Violet Town.*
S/C John Kelly, *experienced but unambitious Benalla policeman. One of Hare's party at Glenrowan.*
Const. Robert Alexander, *based at Sherrit's hut and later at Glenrowan.*
Const. Harry Armstrong, *also at Sherrit's hut and later at Glenrowan.*
Const. James Arthur, *Benalla policeman, one of Hare's party who performed very well at Glenrowan.*
Const. Daniel Barry, *another of Hare's original party at Glenrowan.*
Const. William Canny, *with Hare's party at Glenrowan.*

CAST OF CHARACTERS

Const. Thomas Dowling, *at Sherrit's hut and later at Glenrowan.*
Const. William Duross, *also at Sherrit's and Glenrowan.*
Const. James Dwyer, *Wangaratta officer whose performance at Glenrowan was patchy.*
Const. Patrick Gascoigne, *native-born officer who performed well at Glenrowan.*
Const. Patrick Healey, *Wangaratta police reinforcement at Glenrowan.*
Const. Patrick Kelly, *Benalla reinforcement at Glenrowan; 'that fat bastard'.*
Const. Thomas Kirkham, *one of Hare's party. Sociable and very mobile at Glenrowan.*
Const. Robert McHugh, *one of the Beechworth reinforcements at Glenrowan.*
Const. William Moore, *one of the Wangaratta reinforcements at Glenrowan.*
Const. William Phillips, *least experienced officer in Hare's party at Glenrowan.*
Const. Patrick Walsh, *one of the Wangaratta reinforcements at Glenrowan.*

Queensland Native Police

Sub-Inspector Stanhope O'Connor, *well-connected and well-performed Queensland policeman.*
Barney.
Hero.
Jacky.
Jimmy.
Johnny.
Moses.
Spider.

CAST OF CHARACTERS

Prisoners
Const. Hugh Bracken, *sole officer in charge of the Glenrowan police station.*
Tom Cameron, *fifteen-year-old visiting Glenrowan when the Kellys took over.*
Martin Cherry, *60-year-old labourer at Glenrowan quarry and district pioneer.*
Jean Isobel Curnow (commonly called Isobel), *delicate wife of the Glenrowan schoolmaster.*
Thomas Curnow, *young schoolmaster of the Glenrowan primary school.*
John Delaney, *one of three teenaged brothers visiting friends in Glenrowan.*
Patrick Delaney, *brother of John and William.*
William Delaney, *brother of John and Patrick.*
Robert Gibbons, *local farmer who boarded with the Reynolds at Glenrowan.*
Ann Jones, *owner and publican of the Glenrowan Inn.*
Jane Jones, *fourteen-year-old daughter of Ann Jones.*
John Jones, *twelve-year-old son of Ann Jones.*
James Kershaw, *quarry labourer who resided at Glenrowan.*
John Lowe, *Benalla road-building contractor who resided at Glenrowan.*
Jock McHugh, *quarry labourer who resided at Glenrowan.*
Catherine Mortimer, *sister of Isobel Curnow, who lived at Glenrowan.*
Dave Mortimer, *brother of Isobel and brother-in-law of Thomas Curnow.*
Alphonse 'Louis' Piazzi, *foreman of the quarry labourers, resident at Glenrowan.*
James Reardon, *railway worker, lived with his wife and family at Glenrowan.*
Margaret Reardon, *wife of James.*

CAST OF CHARACTERS

Michael Reardon, *eighteen-year-old son of James and Margaret.*
Alexander Reynolds, *eight-year-old son of Edward.*
Edward Reynolds, *prominent Glenrowan famer and property owner.*
Tom Rowan, *local farmer visiting Glenrowan.*
Matthew Ryan, *local farmer, lived with his wife and three children near Glenrowan.*
William Sandercook, *quarry worker resident at Glenrowan.*
John Stanistreet, *Glenrowan stationmaster, lived with his family near the station.*
Dennis Sullivan, *railway worker from Benalla staying in Glenrowan.*

Others
George Allen, Daily Telegraph *reporter from Melbourne.*
Thomas Carrington, Australasian Sketcher *reporter and artist from Melbourne.*
Jesse Dowsett, *railway guard based at Benalla.*
Reverend Fr. Matthew Gibney, *Catholic priest from Perth visiting eastern Australia on a fundraising trip.*
John McWhirter, *Melbourne* Age *reporter.*
Joe Melvin, *Melbourne* Argus *reporter and would-be policeman.*
Charles Champion Rawlins, *Benalla grazier and friend of Frank Hare.*

PROLOGUE
THE LONG DROP

For someone they had demonised for so long and were now preparing to kill, the authorities who ran the Crown Colony of Victoria in 1880 were certainly going out of their way to make his last few hours of life as comfortable as they could. The light would remain on in his cell that last night, but it had been left on every night since he was condemned to death and didn't appear to interfere with his sleep anyway. The leather collars the warders had placed on his leg irons prevented chafing, an important consideration given the pain that he was in when moving about, but then, he would not have much more moving about to do. There were just two trips left to make, one was quite short, probably less than 50 metres, and the second even shorter; no more than ten steps.

The prisoner had been neither violent nor uncooperative in his last few days, and several who had met him for the first time had trouble reconciling the calm and gentle young man with the bloodthirsty monster the government and the papers had made him out to be just a few months earlier. He seemed to face his fate unflinchingly and with a kind of natural dignity. Authorities were not certain though, whether his family and friends would respond in the same manner. In recent days they had sent 162 revolvers, 89 shotguns and 29 carbines to the police now reinforcing the prisoner's home town and the surrounding countryside. It was November, the prisoner's name was Ned Kelly and he was about to hang for murdering a policeman two years earlier.

* * *

Ned was scheduled to die at 10 o'clock on the morning of Thursday, 11 November, and barring a last minute miracle, all the planning and preparation undertaken by the state was directed to that end. On the morning of Wednesday, 10 November, John Buckley Castieau, Governor of the Metropolitan Gaol (as Melbourne's oldest gaol was officially called), informed Ned that all possibilities of official intervention had been exhausted, and he should now prepare himself to die the following day. As the authorities made their final preparations, so did Ned.

One of the condemned prisoner's last requests was that his photograph be taken as a keepsake for his family and friends. That afternoon, Charles Tettleton, the official gaol photographer, took two formal photographs of Ned.

Both were carefully posed in the gaol courtyard, with Ned putting as much thought into them as Tettleton. The first was a full length portrait in which Ned struck the pose that best disguised the injuries he carried from his last clash with the police. The second, a simple head and shoulders shot, showed him gazing past the camera and photographer, a smile forming at the edge of his eyes.

PROLOGUE

That afternoon, a number of people were allowed to visit and farewell Ned. His mother Ellen, his sisters Maggie and Kate and his brother Jim, and his cousins Kate and Tom Lloyd were admitted into his cell. Maggie and Kate were both very emotional during the meeting, while young Jim told Ned that he was sorry he had not been there to help at the last fight. Ned thanked him and told Jim that it was now up to him to look after their mother and sisters. It was at this meeting that Ellen told her son to 'die like a Kelly'.

Later in the evening, Governor Castieau brought his thirteen-year-old son Godfrey to meet Ned, a gesture the condemned man seemed to appreciate. Catholic chaplain Doraghy and visiting priest Father O'Hea also made professional calls on Ned, with O'Hea promising that he would be with Ned in the morning. Finally, nine-year-old John Castieau, the youngest of the governor's sons, also made an unexpected visit during the evening. There was no special reason for the visit other than young John's somewhat ghoulish fascination with death.

Ned's last meal was roast lamb and peas, accompanied by a bottle of claret. After all the visitors had been and gone and the remains of the meal removed, Ned went to bed. He seemed to have trouble falling asleep, sitting down then getting up before finally stretching out on his bunk at 1.30 am. He did not fall asleep straightaway, but lay quietly for an hour or so before finally drifting off.

Ned was awake at 5 am and got up and prayed – on his knees and alongside his bunk – for twenty minutes before lying down again. He finally rose at 8 o'clock, dressed and sang a few songs. They were his favourites and he sang them quietly to himself. He finished with a song he had sung on most nights before he slept; the warders recognised it as 'The Kelly Song':

> Farewell to my home in Greta,
> My loved ones fare thee well.
> It grieves my heart to leave you,
> But here I cannot dwell.

When he finished singing, the warders also noted that the prisoner looked contented.

At 8.45 am, a blacksmith arrived to remove Ned's leg-irons. Ned had declined the offer of breakfast, explaining that he had wanted to use the time instead to speak to the chaplain. Father Doraghy, who was Dean of St Paul's Cathedral as well as a gaol chaplain, had accompanied the blacksmith and after Ned's irons were off and the man had left, Ned and Doraghy were alone in the cell. The priest heard Ned's final confession and then administered the last rites of the church. Shortly after this, Father O'Hea arrived and the three men spoke quietly in Ned's cell. At 9.30 am, the formalities began.

A group of warders entered Ned's cell, explained what was about to happen, and escorted Ned and the clergymen out of the cell. The group left the old wing of the gaol, where Ned had been held, and crossed the small internal courtyard to the main building containing holding cells for the condemned, and the gallows. As they crossed the courtyard, Ned pointed to some flowers in a garden bed and said to Edward Adams, one of the warders he had befriended, 'They look beautiful,' and then sighed. Still in pain and hobbled by his wounded foot, Ned's progress was slow, his escorts going at his pace and staying with him.

Crossing the courtyard, Ned may also have noted a handcart outside the door to the execution chamber. It was there to carry his body back to the mortuary. He may also have heard the murmuring of the crowd outside the gaol's main gates, a crowd that would grow to 5000 people as the hour of execution approached.

PROLOGUE

When the group entered the main building and approached the holding cell, they saw a number of priests already there, chanting prayers as the little group arrived.

* * *

Not only did justice need to be done, it had to be seen to be done, and so 27 official witnesses were invited to attend Ned's execution. Most were senior members of the Melbourne establishment – judges, lawyers and doctors – but there were also policemen and newspapermen, including the young journalist and future Australian Prime Minister, Alfred Deakin. The official witnesses all had tickets, which they presented at a wicket gate set in the iron-studded main gates of the gaol facing Victoria Street. After their tickets were checked, they were admitted to a small courtyard normally reserved for people who had committed a contempt of court.

There, the group stood and talked and perhaps smoked until they were joined by the official party comprising the Sheriff, the Under-Sheriff and the Governor of the gaol. That official party then led them to the other end of the courtyard and into the main building. After passing through an iron-grated gate, they walked down a corridor to another iron-grated gate. Beyond that were the gallows.

It was a quiet and sombre walk – the corridors and execution chamber dampened with coir matting laid down for the occasion – and what confronted them in the chamber discouraged conversation. Looking to the northern end, they could all see a huge wooden beam stretching across the chamber from wall to wall. A rope had been coiled around it several times. This rope, as thick as a man's thumb, had a running noose at its end. The witnesses could also see a ten kilogram weight attached to a rope which ran through a pulley at the rear of the gallows' platform. That rope was connected to the trapdoor to prevent it swinging back and striking the hanged man.

The lower end of the noose hung down below the lever which operated the trapdoor. To witnesses who had not previously seen an execution, the mechanism looked very similar to the levers used by the railways to switch trains from one track to another. On either side of the platform were holding cells which opened onto the platform, itself part of an iron walkway which extended all the way around the first level. The cells closest to the gallows were occupied; one by the condemned man and his entourage, the other by the executioner, a convicted felon named Elijah Upjohn.

* * *

A few minutes before 10 o'clock, the formal process began when the Sheriff, Colonel Robert Rede, and Governor John Castieau climbed a set of stairs to the first level and took up positions on the platform. When they were ready, Rede turned to Castieau and in a clear voice demanded the body of the condemned felon, Edward Kelly. Castieau replied by requesting the warrant authorising the Sheriff to make such a demand. Castieau then accepted the warrant document that Rede offered, gave a little bow, and turned to knock on the door behind him, on the right-hand side of the platform.

The cell door opened, and executioner Upjohn stepped out. For the witnesses, this was their first look at Upjohn. A powerful and powerfully ugly man, he had close-cropped white hair, short white whiskers and a hugely carbuncled nose. He was dressed in prison uniform, prompting one of the journalists to write that, 'Altogether the man's appearance fully sustains the accepted idea of what a hangman should look like.'

Upjohn strode straight past the officials and through the open

PROLOGUE

door of the holding cell on the other side. There he quickly pinioned and tied Ned's arms using a heavy leather strap he carried. He said not a word nor showed any interest in Ned as anything but an object to be handled and moved. His attitude prompted a gentle rebuke from Ned: 'There's no need for tying me.' Upjohn then placed a small white cap on Ned's head and Ned, preceded by the priests praying aloud in Latin, walked the short distance to the gallows, to the spot where Upjohn indicated he should stop, within the boundaries of the trapdoor and directly below the massive wooden beam.

The witnesses on the lower level now focused their attention on the platform. One of them, a man named Henry White, had noted Ned's firm step and apparent lack of timidity or fear. He also noted that Ned seemed pale, as did several of the other witnesses. While some believed they heard Ned say, 'Ah well, I suppose it had to come to this', others would always recall Ned's last words as, 'Such is life'. When they looked up, Ned glanced down, his face expressionless.

Standing upright and now staring straight ahead, Ned winced a little when the thick rope noose was passed over his head, but then he angled his head to one side to assist Upjohn in adjusting the knot to the correct position. There was a pause. As this was Upjohn's first execution, the placement of the noose and the knot, and the length of the drop were all discreetly checked by a doctor – Dr Baker – and then it was all over in a rush.

Upjohn reached up to the white cap on Ned's head and pulled the sides down, forming a white hood which covered the outlaw's face. The hangman then stepped back from Ned and, in one movement, half-turned and pulled the lever which held the trapdoor's bolt in place. The trapdoor crashed open; Ned dropped straight through and fell almost two metres before being snapped upright with an audible crack as the rope reached its full length.

Ned's body, at first still, convulsed and the legs drew up towards the body, an action that slowly repeated itself several times over before the legs straightened down and were still. Just on four minutes had passed since Ned left the cell. The witnesses felt they could now breathe again.

* * *

Those witnesses were then escorted out, many heading for a stiff drink before going somewhere else to talk or write about what they had just seen.

Back in the gaol, the law was being followed to the letter, with Ned's body left suspended half a metre above the flagstone floor for 60 minutes after it had stopped moving. It was examined and Ned pronounced dead by Dr Edward Baker, the official doctor appointed for just that task. The body was then lowered to a group of attendants who carried it to the handcart and wheeled the cart across the courtyard to the mortuary. In an act of pettiness, the government ordered that the black flag normally flown to signify an execution be left furled.

Before the execution, men of medicine and science and learning had issued orders and requests now rapidly put into effect. In the mortuary, these men and their assistants were quickly at work, shaving and cutting, slicing and measuring, all in the name of advancing man's knowledge of his fellow man. Ned was different to other men, Ned was special, and so Ned's earthly remains would receive all the treatment science could offer. Yet, those present and those who followed never did include in their learned writings what may have been the most significant aspect of what they found when they removed the outlaw's head. His skull, its brain removed for further examination, would reside in various government offices until it finally disappeared a century later. Various skulls of dubious provenance occasionally reappear, all claimed to be Ned's.

PROLOGUE

Ned had left this life wearing a look of contentment, almost satisfaction, on his face, as if he had done all that he could as well as he could, and could now do no more. Wherever he had gone, he had gone with his eyes wide open, perhaps now looking forward to whatever lay beyond. Or perhaps looking back to what had gone before.

CHAPTER 1

Ned Kelly, Son of Red Kelly

Ned Kelly's future was always going to be determined by his past. At his birth, Ned not only inherited genetic characteristics – size, colouring, personality traits – from his biological parents, he also inherited a set of social characteristics almost as immutable as his genes. Ned was always going to be the son of Irishmen and women, he was always going to be Catholic and he was always going to be the son of a transported convict. In a society dominated by Protestant Englishmen of independent means, this inheritance put Ned at an immediate disadvantage.

Ned's father, John 'Red' Kelly, was a native of County Tipperary in Ireland where he was convicted of the theft of two pigs in 1841 and sentenced to seven years' transportation. Red was just 21 years of age. He was sent to Van Diemen's Land where he was, if not a model prisoner, at least one who seemed to have learned from his earlier mistake. Granted a Ticket-of-Leave in July 1845 and a Certificate of Freedom in January 1848, Red sailed across Bass Strait a month later to make a new life in the Port Phillip District.

People who knew Red from this and subsequent periods of his life would always regard him as a generally quiet man, a peacemaker who always had an acute awareness of man's inhumanity to man. As an emancipated convict in the Port Phillip of that time, those characteristics would have been sorely tested. Red found employment as a splitter and fencer on the outskirts of the growing port town of Melbourne. He felled trees, split the timber, and used the posts and rails he made to construct fences for the smallholdings just north of the town. While working at his trade, he met a vivacious young Irish emigrant girl named Ellen Quinn.

Ellen was one of eight children of James and Mary Quinn, natives of County Antrim who had migrated to Australia in 1841. They were 'bounty immigrants', free settlers whose passage to the Port Phillip District was subsidised by the colonial authorities of New South Wales. After their arrival, James and the older Quinn children took whatever work they could find in and around Melbourne. They worked hard and they were thrifty, and were soon able to lease a small dairy farm on the Moonee Ponds Creek near Brunswick.

Ellen grew into a beautiful young woman in Melbourne. A hard worker and always a superb horsewoman, she enjoyed some new found freedoms when the Quinn family moved to Wallan, some 45 kilometres from Melbourne, in 1849. There, James Quinn leased a 260-hectare farm and it was to that farm that a tall, red-haired fencer named Red Kelly came sometime in early 1850, just as the Port Phillip District was in the process of becoming the Crown Colony of Victoria. There was an attraction between the teenaged Ellen and the 30-year-old emancipated convict. It was an attraction that James Quinn both noted and discouraged, but it was also an attraction that grew to the point where, in November 1850, the couple chose to elope.

Red Kelly and Ellen Quinn travelled just down the road – Sydney Road – to Melbourne where they married at St Francis' Church in Elizabeth Street. They were young and in love.

Ellen Kelly, as she would be known for the rest of her life, was just seventeen years old when she married. She was also pregnant. Five months after the wedding, the couple welcomed their first child, a girl they named Mary Jane. Their daughter lived for just a few weeks, however. Two years later a second daughter, Annie, was born, and a further two years on, in 1855, their first son, a boy they named Edward, was born. He took his name from his father's oldest brother, half a world away in Tipperary.

Almost like clockwork, a Kelly child would be produced every second year. If the child was male, it would be named after one of Red's brothers; if female, after one of Ellen's sisters. Thus, in 1857 Maggie was born, followed by Jim (1859), Dan (1861), Kate (1863) and finally Grace (1865). For Ellen, her daughters' names reminded her of the family that lived just down the road. For Red, the boys' names were a reminder of a family far away. While the growing Kelly family barely had enough for themselves – the children grew up in poverty and semi-squalor – Red always sent any extra money he had back to Ireland to help finance his brothers' plans for emigration. His dreams of a family reunification were partially realised in 1857 when his brothers arrived in Melbourne. While the arrival of his brothers ought to have eased the financial strain on Red, their arrival coincided with a decline in Red's health, meaning less work and therefore less income; the downward spiral continued.

Red, Ellen and their children lived on several smallholdings on the northern outskirts of Melbourne. Theirs was a life without frills, an ongoing struggle to put food on the table and to keep a roof over their heads. They lived in a succession of timber shacks; split slab walls, bark roofs and stamped earthen floors with one or two rooms separated by hessian curtains. The furniture, when they had any, was whatever Red could cobble together plus hand-me-downs from friends and relatives. Clothing, too, was patched and patched again and worn until it could be worn no more at which point it would be handed down or cut up to provide patchwork for other hand-me-downs.

From Wallan to Beveridge to Avenel, Red, Ellen and their growing family moved slowly north from smallholding to smallholding, their struggles growing with each move. The children all started school and maintained attendance whenever they could. All did well enough when there to suggest they had both a native intelligence and an interest in learning. Ned was neither at the top nor the bottom of his class, and was rated as competent in Reading, Writing and Arithmetic, and was regarded as being functionally literate by the time he completed fifth grade.

It was at Avenel that a small degree of regularity came into the Kellys' lives. During the week, three or four of the children would head off across the paddocks to school, collecting other kids along the way, and on Sundays they might walk with some of the parents to church. The Roman Catholic parish priest, based at Avenel, was Father Charles O'Hea and he baptised several of the Kelly children in his little church. As well as his duties as priest in a large rural parish, the avuncular Father O'Hea was a visiting priest at Melbourne Gaol and the newly constructed Pentridge Prison.

Avenel was also where the young Ned Kelly first came to the attention of a public audience beyond his immediate family and friends. One of his schoolmates was a young boy named Shelton, the offspring of one of the district's more prominent families. Young Shelton tried to cross a flood-swollen creek on a slippery log and fell in. Ned plunged into the water and dragged the boy to safety. A grateful Shelton family presented Ned with a two metre green cummerbund, with gold trim and gold tassels at both ends. For the rest of his life, Ned would regard the cummerbund as his own good luck charm.

It was at Avenel, too, that Red Kelly's life finally unwound. As a freed convict, he was always going to struggle to find rewarding employment and the social mobility that this sometimes offered. He probably made the right decision by choosing to raise his family in the country rather than the city, but country life could be as cruel as any inner-city slum. Red's farms were always small and were always someone else's. A few hectares may have been enough for a couple of work horses, some milking cows and a brood of chickens, but were never going to support a large and growing family.

Timber felling and fencing occasionally provided an income, but both were jobs for fit young men, and Red was getting old before his time. The rigours of bush life and the pressures of providing for a young and growing family took a physical toll. He sought alternatives and found few. The best farming land was locked up by the squatters, large scale pastoralists who had firstly occupied large properties and then had that occupation formalised by conservative colonial governments. The goldfields were increasingly dominated and controlled by large mining companies. Red had walked on the other side of the law before and chose to do so again. One of his emigrant brothers, James, was well on the way to becoming a hardened criminal, but this was a path he actively sought out. Red was an almost reluctant criminal, selling some sly grog here, lifting a calf or a sheep there, all to keep his family together.

Irrespective of causes or scale, the activities were criminal and the outcome inevitable. There were warnings and close shaves before finally, in 1866, imprisonment in Kilmore Gaol for stock theft. Not a well man after years of alcohol, freezing nights and broiling days with marginal nutrition, Red was released from a relatively short incarceration in time to spend Christmas 1866 with his family. He became ill – dropsy – and died on 27 December. He was buried in a plain, home-made coffin without a requiem. He was 45 years old when he died. His widow, Ellen, was 34 and his oldest son just eleven. When his father died, Ned was at an age where that father was still very much an idealised figure. He died before a teenaged Ned could see him in perhaps a different light. Red certainly imprinted a strict set of values on Ned, with 'family' being both the first and the most important of these. Throughout his life that son would introduce himself as, 'Ned Kelly, son of Red Kelly'.

* * *

Red's death cut Ellen and the children adrift, and Ellen looked north again, this time to the high country of north eastern Victoria where her parents had bought a large property on the headwaters of the King River. There would eventually be considerable intermarrying between three families – the Kellys, Quinns and Lloyds – and Ned would be able to count 77 relatives by blood and marriage in the region. While Ellen chose to live near her family, she also chose not to live with them, taking up a small selection at Greta West, then on the main road between Benalla and Wangaratta. As selectors, the Kellys were now at the bottom of the scale of rural workers. Most of the good land had been taken up a generation previously. Those who had seized the land – the squatters – and those who supplied the needs of those on the land were well above them. But land meant security for Ellen, and land, no matter how poor, she now had. At Greta West, the family moved into a five-roomed, slab-walled hut with an earthen floor.

The Kelly children came of age living in that slab hut at Greta. In April 1869 the sixteen-year-old Annie Kelly married the 27-year-old Alexander Gunn, a local Scottish-born selector who was trying to eke out a living on the land. At sixteen, Ned's favourite sister Maggie also married, and her husband was another neighbour, the 24-year-old Bill Skillian. Neither marriage would last, and both would end in the type of tragic circumstances that were beginning to plague the Kelly family.

Annie Gunn died of complications after giving birth to her first child in 1872. She was alone at the time as Alex Gunn was serving three years' hard labour in prison after being found guilty of horse theft in Beechworth in August 1871. Her brother Ned had been given the same sentence for his part in the offence. The circumstances were complicated, with the father of Annie's child believed to be a ne'er-do-well policeman named Ernest Flood. Ned would never forgive Flood for the seduction of his sister or for his desertion of her when the results of their intimacy became apparent.

As a young widow Ellen Kelly was, by any definition, still an attractive woman, one who kept both her looks and her brains as she moved through her thirties and into middle age. It was her judgement that occasionally let her down. Another doomed relationship led to another child, a daughter also named Ellen, in 1871. The child fell dangerously ill with diarrhoea in 1872. Dr John Nicholson of Benalla travelled out to Greta to see what he could do but was unable to save the little girl. Ellen senior did finally marry again, wedding George King, an American adventurer many years her junior, at Benalla in February 1874. One of the witnesses was Ellen's son Ned; he had been released from prison just two weeks earlier.

* * *

Both family and friends regarded the teenaged Ned as impulsive and there were a number of stories used to support this assessment. In one of these stories, Ned and his younger brother Dan had a major falling out, and Dan – feeling intimidated and threatened – went to live with one of their cousins. After a couple of days, Ned went to visit him and the brothers made up, primarily because they recognised the necessity of staying together. In this story lie most of the elements of what was to come: Ned's need to dominate, his mercurial temperament, and the family's proclivity to stick together when push came to shove. Unfortunately, criminality was another aspect of the family story. By 1880, thirteen members of the Kelly/Quinn/Lloyd extended family had racked up 57 arrests and 37 convictions.

* * *

Ned's first run-in with the law occurred when, as a fourteen-year-old, he was accused of assaulting and robbing a Chinese hawker named Ah Fook. It was a confused set of circumstances, and the magistrate quite correctly dismissed all charges outright. The second run-in had a similar result – Ned was never charged with an offence – but this time it is probable that he was indeed involved in a number of criminal acts. These acts were in support of an ageing bushranger named Harry Power, a gentlemanly highwayman who preyed on wealthy travellers on the isolated roads of north-east Victoria. Power was eventually captured, not too far from the elder Quinn's homestead, and returned to Pentridge, his more regular home. In both instances, the youthful Ned voluntarily engaged in criminal behaviour, probably aware of the consequences that such behaviour could bring. Rather than demonstrating any inherent criminality though, these early brushes with criminality are indicative of the narrow range of options that life offered Ned after leaving school upon the death of his father. He was on his way to a potential life of crime, certainly, but primarily because that kind of life may well have seemed to be the best of a number of unattractive options the teenager faced.

Ned's first conviction and incarceration came as the result of a vicious fist fight prompted by, variously, a pair of competing hawkers, a bogged wagon, a childless marriage and a set of bull's testicles. One of the hawkers was close to the Kellys, the other – a married man named McCormick who had a childless marriage – was not. Ned inflamed a minor dispute between the two by despatching the testicles to the childless couple, with a note outlining their possible use. Ned won the subsequent and inevitable fight with McCormick but the sixteen-year-old was sentenced to six months' imprisonment to be served at Beechworth prison. When he entered, Ned's vital statistics were recorded: 5 feet, 10 inches (178 centimetres) tall and 11 stone, 4 pounds (75 kilograms) in weight, with dark brown hair, hazel eyes and a sallow complexion. Nine scars adorned his head and body.

Just a few short weeks after his release from Beechworth Ned was back in court, this time facing the serious charge of horse theft. Ned, his brother-in-law, Alex Gunn, and an acquaintance named Isaiah Wright had all been involved with a horse that was earlier reported stolen, although it appears that only Wright knew that the horse had been 'borrowed'. The various charges the three faced appeared questionable at the time and downright spurious in hindsight. More disturbingly, the arresting officer – a Constable Hall – tried to shoot Ned while arresting him. There was also a harshness to the sentences. Wright was given eighteen months' imprisonment for horse theft, while Ned and Alex Gunn were found guilty of the same offence and each given three years' hard labour at Pentridge.

Ned did his time without obvious problems. He served it

in Pentridge and on a hulk moored in Port Phillip Bay, and he served it in a way that allowed the authorities to grant him some remission of his original sentence. The Ned Kelly who left Pentridge was not, however, the Ned Kelly who had entered. He had been an overgrown boy when he came in but he departed a man in both outlook and appearance. The beard he grew as a prisoner would not be shaved off in his lifetime.

Ned returned home to the north-east and to Greta. On the surface little had changed but underneath everything was different. From now on Ned would believe strongly, sometimes with justification, that he and his family were increasingly the victims of a system that favoured the rich and which slowly but inexorably drove him and his confederates into a life of crime. The Kelly family were in the sights of the local police but could not avoid being involved in criminal acts. Jim Kelly was gaoled as a fourteen-year-old for alleged involvement in horse theft. Released four years later, Jim and his mates, perhaps realising that the writing was on the wall at Greta, left the district for farm work in the Riverina. The youngest son, Dan, was first arrested when he was just ten years old and then again at fifteen.

But it was Ned who was the talisman for his family, as he was for a growing group of young men in the Greta district. Ned was young and hard, fearless and forceful, and many were prepared to follow the lead he offered. At first that lead stayed within the fringes of the law. He took up employment as a timber worker after his release from prison, and Ned was a good enough worker to be promoted to overseer. However, the temptations to stray proved too strong and as he came to the end of his teenage years, Ned returned to the horse and cattle 'trading' that he knew so well. He also started to build up an entourage.

* * *

Joe Byrne would become Ned's best friend, confidant and co-author of some of the most famous criminal acts in Australian history. The two had a lot in common. Joe, two years the younger, had a brother and four sisters, all younger than him. His father, Patrick Byrne, had been a miner and a bullock driver but died in 1870 when Joe was thirteen years old.

The Byrnes lived in the Woolshed area, a few kilometres north of Beechworth. There, the young Joe impressed those he met with his intellect and manners and his sunny disposition. He was an outstanding student at primary school and even though, like most of his class and generation his education was limited, every year that he attended school he finished at or near the top of his class. Joe apparently learned to speak rudimentary Cantonese from the dozens of Chinese gold fossickers who still lived in the Woolshed area and – if the rumours are true – he may also have picked up the habit of smoking opium.

The quiet and thoughtful boy that was Joe loved books and horses, and grew into the quiet and serious young man who started to have some run-ins with the local police. Joe had grown to a solid 178 centimetres, and was regarded as being handy at boxing and wrestling. He was a good horseman and a crack shot; with a pistol, he could hit coins thrown high into the air. His problems with the police were those endemic in the north-east: street fighting and, more commonly, suspected involvement in stock theft. More often than not, Joe had an associate in mischief-making, a school friend and neighbour named Aaron Sherrit.

No records exist of the moment Ned Kelly met Joe Byrne. It was possibly in the Beechworth prison, but equally could have been in a hotel or a shanty, or as part of a business transaction involving mutual friends and/or relatives and maybe even stolen stock. Equally there are no surviving recollections about how their friendship grew and developed, but it certainly did. The two shared many common characteristics – family, outdoor interests and a lifestyle that skated along the edges of legality – but in other respects the men were markedly different. Ned was always full of action and on the move, while Joe was quiet and thoughtful, at times almost philosophical. Both were pipe smokers and careful dressers, Ned flamboyant and Joe conservative.

Ned and Joe together made quite an impression: tall, strong native sons at home in the saddle, in the bush and with guns in their hands. They soon attracted a number of like-minded young men.

* * *

The larger towns of rural Victoria in the 1870s often contained groups of young men, given the sobriquet 'mobs', who generally did little more than annoy the more conservative elements of society. They were invariably dressed loudly and distinctively and entertained themselves (and others) with feats of horse-riding, fisticuffs and the occasional provocation of local police. In the north-east the best known was probably the 'Greta Mob', with their thin-soled riding boots with larrikin heels, tall and tapered and ideal for stirrups, and cabbage tree hats with wide, flat brims and chinstraps worn jauntily under the nose. They provided a natural constituency for Ned and Joe.

It was from these local mobs that a core of Kelly confederates emerged, and those confederates fell into inner and outer circles. Closest of all, at least to Ned, was his youngest brother Dan, born in 1861 and just approaching manhood when matters were coming to a head in 1878. Dan was shorter than Ned, yet of average height and strongly built. He was clean-shaven with a sallow complexion and thick, dark hair which had a reddish tinge. Those who knew the brothers well regarded Dan as quieter and less forceful than Ned. Both of them were fiercely loyal to and protective of their family, although Dan was reserved with people he did not know so well.

Dan brought into the inner circle his best friend, a flash young tearaway from Wangaratta named Steve Hart. Hart had been born in Beechworth in 1859 and grew up on the family's small farm near Wangaratta racecourse. After minimal schooling, Steve's first job was as a butcher's boy in nearby Milawa. The butcher's boy was always going to be dragged into Ned's orbit. Steve had an older brother, Dick who was good friends with Ned, a friendship cemented by Dick's membership of the Greta Mob and Ned's occasional romantic interest in Dick and Steve's sister, Ettie Hart.

Steve Hart was short – less than 170 centimetres – and of slight build, but he was a smart dresser, standing out in the Greta Mob partly because of it. He stood out even more when he was on horseback, for Steve Hart may well have been the best horseman in horse-obsessed north-east Victoria. As well as being one of the best rough riders the district had seen, Steve was also good enough to compete successfully against professional jockeys at the district's larger race meetings.

It was his love of horses that regularly got Steve Hart into trouble. Like so many of his mates, Steve was prone to 'borrowing' horses and only returning them when and if compelled to do so. Most of the Greta Mob did the same, including his closest friend, Dan Kelly, but it was Steve who felt the full force of the law when Wangaratta's senior policeman, Sergeant Arthur Steele, led the prosecution after Steve had been found in possession of a stolen horse. When found guilty, Steve Hart was sentenced to twelve months' imprisonment. Steele, who seemed to be personally affronted by every criminal activity that occurred within 'his' district, felt that the young horseman had merely received his just desserts.

After his release, Steve returned to his friends and their way of life. Those who didn't know him well regarded Steve as unremarkable and surly, while even those who did know him best, his brothers plus Ned, Dan and Joe, conceded that he could be erratic and even dishonest. Apart from his sharp dressing and superb horsemanship, Steve seemed to have few interests, and followed Dan and Ned and Joe, relying on them to make decisions that he would not or could not make. But he was one of them through and through by both birth and natural inclination, and had a number of skills the others admired.

Standing a little further back from the epicentre that was Ned was an inner circle of friends and confidants of the group, young men who shared most of Ned's values and many of his experiences, but who also led lives quite distinct from his. Ned in particular was always close to his cousin and neighbour, Tom Lloyd, a contemporary in both age and outlook, although a bit more cautious and deliberate than the Kellys. Ned was also close to his stepfather, George King, with whom he partnered in various stock handling schemes until King left Ellen Kelly, their child, and the north-east of Victoria without so much as a goodbye.

There were also friends who weren't relatives. First among these was probably Dick Hart, Steve's older brother and the second most senior figure in the Greta Mob. There were also two brothers, Isaiah and Tom Wright, members of the Mansfield Mob from south of Greta. Both brothers were best known by their nicknames. Isaiah was always known as 'Wild' Wright, for that was what he was, a large and well-built wild man always looking for either a fight or a challenge. He was also one of the district's toughest men whose first loss in the boxing ring came after twenty bloody, bare-knuckle rounds with a young Ned Kelly. Similarly, Tom Wright was always known as 'Dummy'; born profoundly deaf, he had never learned to talk.

A further step back was an outer circle of trusted friends and relatives who had more of a passing involvement in the lives of Ned and the others. In this category was Ned and Dan's brother-in-law, Alex Gunn. Gunn and Isaiah Wright would often go cattle droving together. Others were Bill Skillian and William 'Bricky' Williamson, neighbours, friends, and active suitors for the affections of the Kelly girls. Among this outer group were also the younger members of a number of local families, the Delaneys, Ryans and McAuliffes in particular. In this outer group, ties of age and outlook were often reinforced through courtship and marriage.

And then there was Aaron Sherrit. Joe Byrne's neighbour and schoolmate had grown into a complex man by 1878 and part of this complexity was his family background. Like most of those of that time and place, it was a large family; Aaron had two brothers and four sisters. Their father, though, was what set the Sherrits apart. John Sherrit was Irish, but he was an Irish Protestant and a former member of the Royal Irish Constabulary to boot. This meant that there would always be a question mark over their solidarity with neighbours from the poor, Catholic side of Ireland's dividing line. In Australia, as in Ireland, neither side was willing to completely forgive or forget decades of mutual enmity, and there was always bitterness between the two bubbling just below the surface. Aaron had a high estimation of his own abilities and intellect, an estimation that others did not always share. Yet, he was a superb bushman and a good rider and marksman. Usually well-dressed and always vain about his appearance, as 1878 unfolded he was courting Joe Byrne's sister, Kate, with a view to marriage.

Aaron Sherrit had taken up a 40-hectare selection near his father's property some ten kilometres north of Beechworth. There, in paddocks he fenced by hand with Ned and Joe, he ran a few cattle and horses, did some borrowing and trading on the side. He also worked at maintaining networks of contacts, people he thought may be of use to him in the future. To all of them he suggested either overtly or implicitly that he was a person of substance and knowledge, someone with a finger firmly on the pulse of the local society. He was close to but not an intimate part of the Greta Mob, friendly with them all but Dan Kelly. Aaron and Ned were friends yet there was always an element of rivalry in the relationship, as Aaron considered himself second only to Ned in terms of physical toughness. And Aaron disliked Dan, primarily because Dan treated him with suspicion and did not hide his contempt for the son of an Irish Protestant policeman.

Among this group were the architects of the tragedy about to unfold.

CHAPTER 2

Outlaws

Around mid-afternoon on Monday, 15 April 1878, Mounted Constable Alexander Fitzpatrick of the Victoria Police rode up to Ellen Kelly's slab hut outside Greta. He was on a one-man mission to arrest Dan Kelly for horse theft. There was also an outstanding warrant for Ned Kelly for the same offence, albeit in a different case, but the police thought that Ned was probably some distance from Greta. Fitzpatrick was not a good policeman; he was a serial womaniser who did his best to avoid real police work, and as a result he had been moved from station to station. Fitzpatrick perhaps saw this day as a chance to redeem his reputation. As he approached the Kelly hut, he was very nervous. His judgement was also affected by the alcohol he had drunk to quieten those nerves.

What happened next would be disputed for years afterwards. All those present, and even some who were not, would offer different and often contradictory accounts, and it is possible that all contained an element of truth. Ellen Kelly was definitely there, nursing her new baby, Alice. Dan, Bill Skillian – recently married to Maggie Kelly – and a neighbour named Bricky Williamson were a short distance away, working on a new house for Ellen. The younger children, John and little Ellen, were probably in the house, with the fourteen-year-old Grace and sixteen-year-old Kate there or thereabouts. It was the exact nature of the verbal and physical interplay between these characters that would forever be in doubt.

Whatever actually occurred took place within the confines of the Kelly hut. The Kellys had a general dislike of policemen, but held no particular grudge towards Fitzpatrick, and he would have been invited in as a matter of course. Those outside also moved inside, and the violence commenced. Kelly partisans claim that a drunken Fitzpatrick propositioned Kate Kelly while trying to pull her onto his lap for a kiss. Fitzpatrick and his supporters claim the Kellys and others present assaulted Fitzpatrick viciously as soon as he said that he was there to arrest Dan Kelly for horse theft.

One side would claim that Fitzpatrick was given a thrashing by young men defending the honour of a sixteen-year-old girl. The other would say that a felon trying to escape arrest attacked an officer of the law as he performed his duty. Even the details of the altercation would forever remain in dispute. The Kellys would claim that the issue was settled with fists, and that Dan's were the faster and more effective. Fitzpatrick, though, swore that a different kind of conflict had occurred, one that included Ellen Kelly assaulting him with a fire shovel and Ned suddenly appearing in the doorway to fire three shots at Fitzpatrick with a revolver, hitting him once in the wrist.

The stories agree again that when Fitzpatrick left the hut later that evening, he was in a much more dishevelled state than when he arrived. Travelling slowly, and stopping at least once at a tavern, Fitzpatrick rode back to Benalla police barracks where he reported to the senior officer, Sergeant James Whelan. Whelan was concerned enough by Fitzpatrick's story and appearance to send for Dr. John Nicholson. After examining Fitzpatrick and noting that he smelt strongly of brandy, Nicholson concluded that the wrist wound could have been caused by a bullet. That was enough for Whelan who drew up arrest warrants for all those involved in the 'attempted murder' of Constable Fitzpatrick.

Things were also happening at the Kelly home late that evening. Ned was probably there by then – if he had not been there during the afternoon – and he and his brother Dan packed bedrolls, clothes and supplies onto packhorses, made their farewells, and rode off into the dark accompanied by a third figure on horseback. Joe Byrne would join his best mate and his best mate's brother in whatever lay ahead.

* * *

On Tuesday, 16 April, arrest warrants were issued; Ned and Dan Kelly were now wanted for the attempted murder of Constable Alexander Fitzpatrick, while Ellen Kelly, William Skillian and Bricky Williamson were wanted for aiding and abetting the commission of that offence. That morning, details of the offences and the warrants were telegraphed to all police barracks in north-eastern Victoria. At the Wangaratta barracks, Sergeant Arthur Steele, Steve Hart's nemesis, decided to take matters into his own hands. Steele knew the Kellys well, having served at Greta when there was a police barracks there. He organised a small police party and rode at the head of that party to the Kelly home at Greta and arrested Ellen Kelly. Leaving her under guard in Greta, he returned to the Kelly farm before finding and arresting Skillian and Williamson at their properties nearby. Late that night, he took his catch to the police barracks at Benalla.

Although her family and friends were able to raise bail, Ellen and her tiny baby had to spend several weeks in either Benalla lock-up or Beechworth Prison. At the latter, she may even have seen Dan's friend Steve Hart, who was released during the time she was held there. Ellen returned to Beechworth in October 1878 to face trial alongside Bill Skillian and Bricky Williamson. A defence of sorts was attempted; Joe Ryan, a Lake Rowan farmer and relative, said that Skillian was with him when the offences allegedly occurred, but the result was never in doubt. The Kellys, their friends and relatives had been caught out time and time again in criminal activity. To many, this was simply the latest in an ongoing pattern of behaviour. Judge Redmond Barry sentenced both Skillian and Williamson to six years' imprisonment with hard labour. Turning to Ellen, he pronounced a sentence of three years' hard labour, before adding the gratuitous observation that if her son Ned had been present, Barry would have sent him down for at least fifteen years.

Those in the gallery who knew Ned knew also of his devotion to his mother. To them there was no doubt that Ned would make someone pay for the sentence that had just been handed down to her.

* * *

While their family and friends were being processed through the legal system of the Crown Colony of Victoria, Ned, Dan and Joe Byrne spent much of the winter of 1878 on a secret property they had established in the Wombat Ranges to the south of Greta. While not exactly an idyllic existence, their life was not without its charms. For days at a time they would be joined by their inner circle of trusted friends, and slowly they cleared and fenced the land, hoping that one day it would become the base for a thriving cattle and horse clearing operation. Gold sluicing in a creek that ran through their valley provided enough income for the supplies that family and friends occasionally brought in. The illegal still they built also brought in money and helped, no doubt, to keep out the cold at night.

One of those friends was Steve Hart. Released with a month to go on his twelve-month sentence for horse theft, Steve travelled from Beechworth to Wangaratta and took up where he had left off – casual labouring and horse breaking jobs – while keeping an eye out for the main chance. For decades locals would tell the story of how Steve was working on a local property, doing some job in which he had no real interest. A stranger rode up and told Steve that Dan was waiting for him in the Wombats, then rode off. Steve sat and thought for a moment, and then said to his workmates: 'Here's to a short life but a merry one!' He packed his belongings, saddled his horse and rode out of their lives forever.

Ned and Joe knew their interlude in the bush retreat was just that, an interlude, while colonial authorities planned their next move, and so they, too, made plans for the future. For now they were secure. They had friends who would tell them of police movements in the area, while Steve, Dan and their cattle dogs maintained a good lookout, day and night. The four men and their friends built a firing range and stockyards, and imagined various futures. But in their minds, sometimes at the front and sometimes at the back, they worried about the police and the confrontation they all knew was coming.

* * *

The Victoria Police, the force they would eventually confront, was not a happy service, with problems and fissures based on class and religion and ethnicity from its chief officer, Commissioner Standish, all the way down to its most junior constables. Commissioner Standish himself preferred to be known as 'Captain' Standish. The English born Frederick Charles Standish had served for a short time with the Royal Artillery and had kept his former rank as an honorific title. Shortly after arriving in Australia, his credentials and connections saw him appointed Commissioner of the Victoria Police in 1858.

It was those connections rather than any pre-existing or acquired credentials that saw Standish still in the position two decades later. He understood politics, and he understood how to make political patronage work for him. A committed bachelor and an inveterate gambler, Standish was considered to be something of a liberal in political circles. Despite that reputation, he moved most comfortably among the members of Melbourne's conservative establishment. He was one of the city's leading Freemasons and he literally resided within the walls of Melbourne's most conservative institution, the Melbourne Club in Collins Street. One of his closest friends there was Robert McBean, a wealthy squatter and Justice of the Peace who had extensive property holdings around Benalla.

Jockeying for position below Standish were a number of senior officers, most of whom seem to have had more ambition than ability. Within the rank and file of the Victoria Police, it was widely believed that Standish had a favourite subordinate and that, moreover, that particular officer had been promised the commissioner's job when Standish eventually retired. Francis Hare, the officer concerned, really did stand out from his rivals. Born in South Africa in 1831 and beginning his Victorian life on the diggings before joining the police, Frank Hare was a giant at just over 190 centimetres and 100 kilograms. Self-assured and confident to friends, egotistical to rivals, Hare possessed an unusual, high pitched and squeaky voice, physical courage, and a rampant ambition to succeed. As well as Captain Standish, Hare had powerful patrons in the Clarke family and often stayed at their property, 'Rupertswood', near Sunbury.

Hare's main rival as successor to Standish was Charles Nicolson. Like Hare, he was a superintendent in mid-1878, but that was where the similarities ended. The 49-year-old Scotsman had been with Hare at the capture of Harry Power, but where Hare was outgoing and confident, Nicolson was dour and at times irritable and prickly. While the tall, powerful Hare cut a dashing figure, Nicolson was of middling height, balding, and with a full spade beard showing streaks of grey. While not entirely disclaiming the politics of senior officerdom, Nicolson preferred to let results speak for themselves. He was an efficient and hard-working officer and one whose talents did match his ambition.

Another rival would emerge in the search for the Kellys. He was Superintendent John Sadleir and he had already racked up 25 years' service with the Victoria Police. Born in Ireland in 1833, Sadleir migrated in mid-1852 and joined the police force as a cadet later that year. The cadet scheme was then brand new, designed to attract better recruits and gradually raise the force's standards. Sadleir was a bit of a plodder, but a careful and methodical plodder who had worked hard to achieve his rank.

The force that these men commanded was also split along class and sectarian lines. In 1874, 82 per cent of the members of the Victoria Police were Irish-born and, if Catholic, they were most likely constables, while Protestants dominated the officers' ranks. And while none of the officers in the force were native-born, an increasing number of the rank and file were. Finally, members of that rank and file believed – with some justification – that the opportunities for promotions and rewards were much better in

Melbourne than anywhere else in the colony. The best policemen therefore tried to stay as close to headquarters as possible.

* * *

In July 1878, Superintendent John Sadleir took up the position of officer in charge of the newly created North East Police District. In the three months since the Fitzpatrick incident at Greta, nothing much new had happened. Stock still disappeared at an unacceptable rate and several of the dozen or so police informers in the district suggested that Ned, Dan and their friends were responsible for at least part of that activity. They also reported that the Kellys and their supporters moved through the district quite openly and were even more open with their opinions about the police's efforts to catch them. This intelligence was of little more than passing interest to Sadleir; his focus was increasingly on the reports that Ned and Dan, and possibly others, were holed up on a remote creek in the middle of the Wombat Ranges.

The methodical Sadleir put together a plan designed to force the Kellys from the safety of the bush and into the paths of mounted patrols that would soon criss-cross the open plains of the north east. Greta and Mansfield, 80 kilometres apart, represented the northern and southern extremities of what was becoming known as Kelly Country, with the Wombat Ranges between them. Sadleir would send two parties of heavily armed police from those towns into the ranges. Each party would be under the command of a sergeant and each party would comprise only experienced bushmen. The parties would be disguised as prospectors and equipped to kill or capture the renegades. They would live off the land for as long as it took to flush the Kellys out of their hiding place.

If the police had a dozen informers, the Kellys had hundreds of supporters and sympathisers, and if not privy to the specifics of Sadleir's plan, the Kellys certainly picked up on its broad outlines. Realising that it could pose a serious threat to their freedom, Ned and Joe continued to use their network to closely monitor police movements in and around Kelly Country.

The two police parties were to depart from their respective barracks on Friday, 25 October 1878. There were last minute changes to both. For the Greta party, it was a change of personnel; its leader, Sergeant Arthur Steele was required in court, so Senior Constable Michael Strahan assumed command while Steele was replaced by a junior mounted trooper. For the Mansfield party, the change was in the firearms they would carry.

A couple of days before the hunt began, a regular gold shipment from Wood's Point passed through Mansfield en route to Melbourne. The leader of the shipment's police escort, Senior Constable John Kelly, called in to see his friend, Sergeant Michael Kennedy, at the police barracks. Kennedy explained that he was about to lead a party out after the Kellys, but wished that his party were as well-armed as the gold escort. John Kelly was equipped with a Spencer revolving rifle and, after a bit of bartering, this weapon was swapped for a pistol. John Kelly also took the opportunity to catch up with another old friend who was part of Kennedy's party, Michael Scanlan. Some years before, when he had been posted to Beaufort in the Western District, John Kelly had encouraged a young Scanlan, then managing the local general store, to join the police. Escorting gold shipments while his friend hunted bushrangers reflected the differing characteristics of Michael Kennedy and John Kelly. While Kennedy was seen as a man of action, a policeman who could meet and defeat the bushrangers on their own terms and in their own territory, John Kelly was seen as a plodder by those whose opinion counted when it came to promotion. He was slow and somewhat stodgy. Kelly was good at organising things like gold escorts but it you wanted flair and imagination, you should probably look elsewhere.

Kennedy led his party north from Mansfield before dawn on that Friday morning. They made steady progress into the rugged mountain terrain and late in the day made camp at a place called Stringybark Creek near an abandoned goldmining works. Kennedy announced that this would be their base for the next few days as they searched the surrounding bushland. The tents were pitched and supper was prepared by Thomas McIntyre, there primarily for his cooking and camp skills. After the four policemen had eaten, Kennedy explained that he and Scanlan would leave early the next morning to start the search for the bushrangers.

The Kellys' secret camp was in the next valley over a ridge from the police camp. If the fugitives weren't aware of the police party's presence on the Friday, they were by Saturday. Kennedy and Scanlan departed just after dawn, disappearing into the dense bush in the general direction of the King River to the north. McIntyre and Thomas Lonigan, the fourth member of the police party, remained close to their campsite all day, readying it for what might be a lengthy occupation. Late in the afternoon, McIntyre lit a bonfire to guide the others back. Then he and Lonigan sat on a large log by that fire.

If the setting up of the camp did not alert the Kellys to the presence of strangers nearby, Lonigan's shooting during the day certainly did. A quick reconnaissance of Stringybark Creek revealed the campsite and the police, while the amount of stores and number of horses suggested the rest of the party was nearby. Ned led a brief council of war and made the decision to act. The police were getting too close to the Kelly's secret camp and needed to be forced further back from the Kelly heartland. Capturing and ransoming the four policemen could change the dynamic that seemed to be developing. Between them, the Kellys had only two weapons – a revolver and an old shotgun they loaded with bullets – so they would certainly lose any pitched battle with the police. Like many other settlers, the Kellys could not afford the luxury of buying ammunition whenever they needed it, and made do by manufacturing their own bullets, even if these were to be used in shotguns (often the only guns available). Guile would be their main weapon.

Thus it was that shortly after they had sat on the log to enjoy the warmth of the fire, McIntyre and Lonigan heard a voice call out, 'Bail Up!' and looked up to see four men advancing towards them through the bush. All appeared armed. McIntyre stood with his hands in the air but Lonigan leapt over the log, dropping behind it for cover and drawing his pistol. Looking back over the log, pistol in hand, a single bullet from Ned's old shotgun struck him in the eye, entering his brain and killing him instantly.

It was all over in less than twenty seconds, and was followed by a shocked silence. Ned moved quickly to fill the vacuum, reassuring McIntyre that he would be safe if he did not resist and telling him that Lonigan would still be alive had he not drawn his gun. He then questioned McIntyre closely as to the whereabouts of the other policemen. McIntyre, badly shaken, told Ned that Kennedy and Scanlan were due back at any moment and pleaded with Ned not to kill them. Ned responded that, if the police surrendered, no harm would come to anyone and once they had the police's weapons and horses, Ned and his friends would be on their way.

Dan was initially upset at the shooting of Lonigan but now, under Ned's direction, quickly searched the campsite, looking particularly for weapons and ammunition, plus anything else that might be useful in the flight they all knew must follow this episode. As usual, Dan was accompanied by Steve, who seemed to treat the whole thing with equanimity. At one point Dan went past the log where Ned was instructing McIntyre on what to do when the other police returned. Dan said McIntyre should be handcuffed; Ned replied that restraints would not be necessary.

At another point, Joe Byrne sat down alongside McIntyre. Joe, too, appeared disturbed by the killing of Lonigan, but his concerns were more of a moral than of a practical bent. Joe seemed to recognise that there was now probably only going to be one outcome to the challenge the killing of a policeman offered to the authorities. Things were now out of his hands. He brought a pannikin of tea he had just brewed to where McIntyre sat, and the two young men sat alongside each other on the log, drinking tea and smoking their pipes, flaking tobacco from McIntyre's plug. It was a moment that couldn't and didn't last. The sound of approaching horses was heard, and Ned swung into action.

As Kennedy and Scanlan entered the clearing, McIntyre stood and walked towards them, hands held away from his body. Speaking quickly, he told Kennedy that Ned Kelly and his gang were in the camp, had them surrounded, and that they must surrender to avoid bloodshed. As McIntyre finished his little speech, Ned stepped into the clearing, fired a warning shot into the air and ordered the two policemen to 'Bail Up!' The response was immediate. Scanlan fired at Ned from horseback, using John Kelly's Spencer rifle, shooting underneath his arm without unslinging the weapon. Ned returned fire as did Joe and the others who had emerged from their hiding places. A bullet to the body knocked Scanlan from the saddle and, as he tried to struggle to his feet, a second bullet struck the side of his chest under his right arm. Michael Scanlan pitched forward on his face, mortally wounded.

Michael Kennedy's horse had reared and snorted when the shooting started, and Kennedy had used its movements to ease out of the saddle, lower himself to the ground and draw his pistol. He and Ned then began a duel that took them away from the clearing and into the bush. Moving swiftly but carefully from tree to tree, the two exchanged shots until, stepping from cover to fire, Kennedy was hit in the body. As he raised his right hand, probably to surrender, a second bullet struck him in the armpit and he fell to the ground. Ned hurried over to where Kennedy had fallen. For the rest of his life, Ned would maintain that he saw at once that the policeman was dying, and dying in excruciating agony. Despite Kennedy's pleas for mercy, Ned took careful aim and, at point blank range, fired a shot through the wounded man's heart.

When Ned and Kennedy had moved away from the clearing, they left behind a scene of general confusion. Kennedy's horse was prancing backwards and forwards and, as it passed McIntyre – still standing in the centre of the clearing – on impulse he leapt aboard, lay low across its neck and urged it down the track between the trees and away from the camp. He was certain the men in the clearing fired in his direction, while the last thing he heard clearly before the bush swallowed up all sounds was Dan Kelly screaming almost hysterically, 'Shoot the bastard! Shoot the bastard!'

For the second time, something that felt like it had gone on for a long time was actually over in just a few minutes. Ned soon returned to the clearing and told the others that he had killed Kennedy; it had been a fair fight, he said, and the sergeant had been a brave man. Ned collected a cape from one of the tents and said he was going to place it over Kennedy to protect the body from animals. Learning that McIntyre had escaped, he told the others to collect everything of value and load it onto the police packhorses. When he returned from his short trip into the bush, he ordered that the police tents, plus any supplies and equipment they couldn't carry should be burnt.

The four then led the loaded horses into the gathering gloom and back towards their own camp where they would pack up everything of value and destroy whatever they couldn't take with them. They would not be coming back anytime soon. Before they left the site of the killings at Stringybark Creek however, there was a strange little interlude. Joe Byrne, who was still upset by what had taken place, removed rings from the dead fingers of Thomas Lonigan and Michael Scanlan. Joe placed one on his right hand and the other on his left. Both were dress rings and quite distinctive. He then joined the others as they rode slowly away.

* * *

When Thomas McIntyre fled from the Kellys on a dead man's horse, he had no plan about where to go and what to do. He only knew he had to get away. Five or ten minutes into his flight, the horse galloped under a low hanging branch and he was thrown off. Shaken, but not badly injured, McIntyre continued south on foot. There were times when he was sure that he was being followed, noises from behind that seemed to stop when he stopped, and so he took rudimentary precautions. At one point he discarded his boots as the tell-tale footprints they left would lead trackers directly to him. At another, he lowered himself into a wombat hole, knowing he would be all but invisible to passers-by. While hiding, he scribbled a few lines in a notebook about what had happened at Stringybark Creek.

After a night that he thought would last forever, McIntyre continued his lonely trek back to Mansfield. Daylight meant that he would be able to see any pursuers at a distance but the reverse was also true and as he came to more open farmland at the foot of the ranges, he stayed in the bush margins rather than travelling in the open. By early afternoon he was in settled country and took the chance of stopping at a farmhouse whose owners he knew. They helped revive him and drove him in their buggy to Mansfield where at the police barracks, he told the tale of Stringybark Creek and the deaths there of Lonigan and Scanlan. McIntyre's story was immediately sent by telegraph to Melbourne where it would be repeated and embellished in the days to come.

As the story was being sent over the wire, a combination search-party/posse was being organised at Mansfield, and the emotionally and physically exhausted McIntyre elected to join the group. Late that Sunday night, Lonigan and Scanlan's bodies were recovered, strapped lengthwise on either side of a packhorse, and carried back to Mansfield, the town they had left with such high hopes just three days before. The destruction of the police camp was noted, as was the absence of any sign of Sergeant Kennedy, although no-one was certain of just how this should be interpreted. It was also starting to rain and rain heavily, and the party had no choice but to return.

Events quickly developed their own momentum. In Melbourne, the government immediately introduced legislation aimed at the Kellys. Known officially as the Felon's Apprehension Act, it was more commonly known as the Outlaw Act. Under its provisions, the Kellys were ordered to surrender at a specified place by a specified time. Should they fail to do so, they would be declared outlaws and thereafter could be captured or killed by any member of the public, with or without warning. Anyone who assisted them in any way was also committing an offence and could expect to face the full force of the law.

Parliament passed the Act on Wednesday, 30 October, and it became law two days later when it was approved by the Governor of Victoria. On the day the Act was passed, a second search party returned to Stringybark Creek where it found the corpse of Sergeant Michael Kennedy. The body was pretty much as Ned had left it, and was still covered by the cloak. It did, however, show some signs of interference, with fingertips and ears nibbled by small animals. These injuries gave rise to a series of rumours which swept Melbourne. Each outdid the earlier in horror, culminating in a story that all the police had been ambushed and shot without warning, and that Kennedy's body had been mutilated. His ears were cut off and his eyes gouged out, so the story went, and no-one could be certain if he was alive or dead when these atrocities were committed.

The public's bloodlust was temporarily sated as the legal procedures rolled out. The Felon's Apprehension Act required Ned, Dan, and two unidentified men who had been involved in the Stringybark Creek killings to surrender to authorities at Mansfield before dusk on Tuesday, 12 November 1878. When they failed to do so, the provisions of the Act kicked in and three days later they were all declared outlaws, the first in Victoria's history. New South Wales had introduced an Outlaw's Act many years previously, but theirs' had been formulated to deal with experienced bushrangers like Ben Hall and Daniel 'Mad Dog' Morgan, hardened criminals. Ned was 23 years old and Dan just seventeen. Victoria now had four newly minted outlaws; the problem for authorities was that no-one knew where they were.

* * *

In the immediate aftermath of Stringybark, Ned led his companions north, aware of another police party heading south from Greta, and suspecting that many more would be out searching as soon as news of the killings spread. They visited family and friends at Beechworth and Greta before continuing on to the Murray River. Once in New South Wales, they could regroup and rethink; Ned and Joe knew there was an answer to their problems and they needed time and space to work out just what it was. The rain that thwarted the searchers at Stringybark also thwarted the fugitives when they reached the Murray. Rising floodwaters meant the secret crossing places could not be used, while police patrols meant that the usual punts and crossing points were too dangerous.

Two days of looking for somewhere to cross were two days wasted. Cold and wet and short of both rations and stockfeed, Ned turned the group around and led them south. They faced an uncertain future, but they would face it among family and friends in a country that they knew.

CHAPTER 3

The Killing of Aaron

At the policy level, the response of the Victorian government to the deaths of three policemen at Stringybark Creek was to pass the Felon's Apprehension Act, which effectively placed Ned and Dan Kelly, Joe Byrne, and Steve Hart beyond legal protection. It also effectively placed them outside society since any interaction with the four declared outlaws was likely to constitute a criminal act. To this stick was added the carrot of a £4000 reward, a figure that then represented 40 years' wages for most workers. At the strategic level, Robert Ramsay, the Colonial Secretary, agreed with the Police Commissioner that north-eastern Victoria needed a new and unique policing model. Commissioner Standish proposed a new operational group be established under Superintendent Charles Nicolson, and that the group be staffed by police from both Melbourne and country areas. Ramsay approved, and Nicolson moved to Benalla to be close to the action. Superintendent Sadleir would remain in charge of normal policing activities in the district.

Nicolson was ordered to capture or kill the Kellys, with the tactics left largely up to him. In conjunction with Sadleir's ongoing policing of the district, Nicolson added additional patrols to follow up leads, and also decided to expand and improve the existing intelligence network. The recruitment efforts ultimately led to 32 spies and informants spread across what most were now calling Kelly Country. They were briefed to report on sightings of and actions by Ned and Dan, their two confederates from Stringybark, their families and numerous friends, supporters and sympathisers in and around Greta. The quality of these informants – and their access to the Kellys – varied greatly, but Nicolson and his senior staff were increasingly interested in the reporting of one particular source; Aaron Sherrit, Joe Byrne's friend, a young farmer at Sebastopol, just outside Beechworth.

One version of the story has Aaron personally recruited by Commissioner Standish when the latter was on a flying visit to the area but it is equally likely that he was recruited by a Beechworth detective named Michael Ward. Ward, at this time, was busily establishing his own network of spies stretching from Beechworth to Benalla. Aaron's reasons for becoming a police informant are also open to speculation. He genuinely feared Ned, but equally seems to have been steadfast in his admiration for Joe Byrne, apparently trying to have his friend's life guaranteed by the police. In the end, it may have been simple greed. He might have been promised all the reward money should the Kellys be captured or killed due to information he supplied. As it was, the police paid him seven shillings a day and gave him a codename, 'Moses'.

* * *

THE KILLING OF AARON

Ned and Dan and Joe and Steve were not sitting down waiting to be overtaken by events as the police worked to ensnare and even kill them. Rather than establish just the one base camp as they had done near Stringybark Creek, they set up several while – when the coast was clear – spending time openly with family and friends. Ned and Joe also started tinkering with various plans. The two worked well together. The big ideas, the targets and tactics, were all basically Ned's, with Joe providing realism and sophistication to those ideas. Both knew that if they were to survive, they needed the time and space to make solid long-term plans. They also knew they needed money to buy that time and space.

* * *

From the distance of 130 years, the plan appears to have been a bit complicated, but the players knew their parts and in the end it was successful.

Shortly after midday on Thursday, 12 December 1878, Ned and his team took over Younghusband's Faithfull Creek station some seven kilometres from the small Victorian country town of Euroa, just on the edge of what Ned would consider his home range. Faithfull Creek was a large, working station and by sundown the Kellys held more than twenty prisoners in and around the farmhouse. Most were farm workers or domestic servants, although a number of passers-by were also detained. Ned and the others were quite open about who they were and made no attempt to hide the fact that they had 'business' to transact in Euroa.

Ned had a literally captive audience and was not prepared to let the opportunity slip. In the afternoon and evening he told the prisoners his truth – about the Fitzpatrick incident, the ongoing struggle for his family's very survival, and his account of what precisely had happened at Stringybark Creek. It was polemic, but it was polemic spoken with genuine passion. His explanations formed the basis of a letter that Ned dictated and Joe transcribed between dusk that evening and morning the next day. As was his wont, Joe toned down and added some whimsy to Ned's often harsh and abrasive language.

It was a language that Ned enjoyed using, explaining in graphic detail what he would personally do to anyone in his audience who cooperated with the police now or in the future. Several times he told them, 'Remember, we are outlaws and our orders must be obeyed!'

Early on Friday morning the real action began. Leaving Joe in charge of their prisoners, Ned led Dan and Steve, their horses and a hawker's cart into Euroa, stopping on the outskirts to chop down some telegraph poles. Euroa was a small town with a population of just 300, but it was home to a branch of the National Bank, and this was the gang's target. Steve, not yet identified as a member of the gang, had made a comprehensive reconnaissance of the town the previous day, and Ned's plan proceeded like clockwork. The bank was held up, bloodthirsty threats were made, and the manager and his family were brought in from their adjoining home: the manager to open the safe and strongboxes; his wife and children to focus his mind while doing so.

There was only one minor hitch when the maid at the manager's house, a young woman named Fanny Shaw, recognised Steve Hart as one of her classmates from years before. They exchanged brief greetings and reminiscences. Then more than £2000 was bundled into calico bags and the bank manager and family directed into a cart and a wagon. A procession formed and rode out to Younghusband's. There the gang gave the prisoners a brief but spectacular exhibition of horsemanship and Ned gave all the prisoners a lecture on the grisly fate of anyone who tried to leave the station in the next three hours. After a final flurry of whinnying horses they were gone, galloping towards the distant Strathbogie Ranges.

* * *

After Euroa, a legend began to grow around the 'Kelly Gang' – all four members of which had now been identified – and around Ned in particular. He was on the way to becoming a kind of superman, a better rider and a better shot than any policeman in the colony. To some in both city and bush he was also on the way to becoming a better man than the police. To those people, Ned represented what ability and common sense could bring, rather than birth and rank. They also believed that Ned had been forced into many of his deeds, and they began to make up songs and poems about him.

After Euroa, too, the pressure mounted on Nicolson and his police to get results. Nicolson's tactic of recruiting informers would take time to bear fruit, while his patrols would keep the gang on the move and away from their support and supplies. Yet, as those supporters kept a close eye on the police, this was never likely to succeed, and after a few weeks Nicolson decided on a new tactic.

Choosing to strike directly at those believed to be providing material support to the gang, Nicolson and the senior police drew up a list of over twenty persons in the north-east. Most were friends or relatives of gang members and came from right across the district – from Mansfield, Benalla, Greta, Wangaratta, Chiltern and the King River valley. Most were arrested in a series of raids on Friday, 3 January 1879. The new tactic was an almost instant failure. Six of the 'supporters' were released almost immediately, while the rest were remanded several times over the next three months before eventually being released without charge.

What was worse was that most of those arrested were their family's breadwinners, and they were locked away during the main harvest time. This alienated many that Nicolson had hoped to recruit, and for no real purpose. A month after the raids, the Kellys struck again.

* * *

The small southern Riverina town of Jerilderie was the gang's next target, chosen perhaps because one or more of the gang members was familiar with the town, and perhaps because it was a long way from where they could be expected to strike. The four crossed the Murray River into New South Wales on Friday, 7 February 1879 and made camp in the bush not too far from Jerilderie. The next day, working in pairs, they undertook a reconnaissance of the town. Slightly larger than Euroa, Jerilderie boasted five hotels, one of which – the Royal Mail – contained a branch of the Bank of New South Wales in one corner of the building. There was also a police barracks with two constables in the town.

On Sunday night the gang rode into town and made their way to the police barracks where both troopers were disarmed and locked in their own cells. When Constable Devine, the senior of the two, complained that his police career would be ruined by what had happened, Ned snapped back that he should resign anyway, and look for an honest job.

The bank was duly robbed the next day in an operation remarkably similar to Euroa. All four gang members were directly involved in the robbery, and the prisoners held in the main bar of the hotel had the opportunity to see the outlaws up close. Samuel Gill, the local printer, noted that Dan Kelly had, 'a sallow complexion, a fine pair of dark eyes and rather a pleasing look when smiling'. Dan's friend Steve Hart made a much less

THE KILLING OF AARON

favourable impression. While the two young men drank nothing stronger than lemonade and ginger beer, Steve seemed to want to act out a role. He wore two pistols in holsters on his belt, and carried another for most of the day.

He also displayed somewhat aberrant behaviour. Early in the day, Steve stole personal items from a couple of the prisoners who afterwards complained to Ned when he returned from robbing the bank. Ned ordered him to return the items, which drew a retort from Steve as he returned the items in a bad temper. Later in the day, Steve took a watch from another prisoner and again made a comment when Ned ordered him to return it. This time Ned was not prepared to brook insubordination. In front of all the others, Ned snapped back that he had given Steve a lesson once and was quite prepared to do so again.

Ned was at his mercurial best that day. He again had a captive audience so he again spoke at length about the circumstances that had forced himself, and his friends, to take the roads they had. At one moment he could speak almost tenderly about his best friend, Joe – 'true and as straight as steel' – while at the next he could issue a morbid challenge to his prisoners. Placing a pistol on the bar, he said: 'There's my revolver. Anyone here may take it and shoot me dead but, if I'm shot, Jerilderie will swim in its own blood!' No-one took up the challenge.

Apart from the robbery, there was a subsidiary purpose to the raid, the publication of a long, rambling letter that came to be known as the Jerilderie Letter. Composed by Ned and given form by Joe, its several thousand words attempted to explain and justify all that had happened in terms of a simple and simplistic Us and Them paradigm. Although the raid did not lead immediately to the publication of the letter (the printer did a runner), the gang left a copy behind for later publication, put on a series of feats of horsemanship, then rode out of town cutting down several telegraph poles as they left. They also left behind an accounting nightmare for bank personnel; the gang deliberately destroyed all the mortgage documents they could find, explaining that such documents were just another example of how the poor man was being held in thrall by big banks and big business. The Kelly Gang was again £2000 richer, and their legend continued to grow.

* * *

The Jerilderie raid had an impact on both sides of the border. The government of New South Wales had often boasted what it would do if ruffians like the Kellys ever crossed the Murray. Now they had, and a boastful government was exposed as being as impotent as its southern neighbour. The response was short and to the point; the New South Wales government posted a reward matching Victoria's: the person or persons responsible for the destruction of the Kelly Gang could expect all or part of what was now an £8000 reward.

In Victoria, the impact fell most heavily on the police force, and again the response was quick and pointed. By the time of the Jerilderie raid, Superintendent Nicolson had practically run himself into the ground. The shockwave from Jerilderie gave Commissioner Standish the opportunity to send Nicolson back to Melbourne to recuperate. His replacement was Standish's favourite, Superintendent Frank Hare. Standish decided to play a greater role in the Kelly hunt and, amid considerable fanfare, announced that he was relocating his headquarters from Melbourne to Wangaratta.

Hare already had some knowledge of the Kellys, dating back when he was involved in the successful hunt for Harry Power. His recollection of the Kelly brothers was quite precise. It was also quite useless for a man charged with the responsibility of tracking them down. The teenaged Ned, he recalled was, 'a flash, ill-looking young blackguard', while his brother Dan was, 'a cunning, low little sneak'.

Hare put his stamp on the hunt from almost the moment he took over. Ever the action man, Hare believed in doing things NOW! Convinced that the gang members remained in close contact with their family and supporters, he oversaw the establishment of observation posts overlooking the homes of those he considered their key friends and relatives. Senior Constable John Kelly, close friend of the late Sergeant Kennedy and Constable Scanlan, was leader of the group responsible for watching the Kelly home at Greta. It was the type of work John Kelly enjoyed because it suited his temperament. It was a job he could plan, monitor and oversee, and it would perhaps bring those who murdered his friends to justice. The work was not always straightforward though. When the Kellys' dogs barked at the police in their hides, the police laid poisoned baits. The Kelly girls' response was to muzzle their dogs.

Learning at least a little from the abject failure of the January roundup of Kelly sympathisers and supporters, police actions now became more sophisticated. In the middle of 1879, the *Mansfield Guardian* reported that a number of applicants had recently been refused land selections because they were known or suspected Kelly sympathisers. The police also tried to remove supporters from the network of locals who provided intelligence and succour to the Kellys by charging them whenever the opportunity arose. It was a tactic which was not always crowned with success. At one point, Mansfield police arrested the Wright brothers – Wild and Dummy – and charged them both with using threatening language. The case collapsed, as it should have, when the defence pointed out that Dummy, as everyone knew, was a deaf mute.

The police in general, and Standish and Hare in particular, came to believe that informants held the key to cracking the Kellys, and placed increasing reliance on them. One, given the codename 'Foote', was actually Pat Quinn, one of Ellen Kelly's brothers who was not too reliable at the best of times. Another, known as the 'Diseased Stock Inspector', was a good but undervalued source of information. He was a district schoolteacher and therefore well-placed to learn from the uninhibited talk of his pupils. Even in faraway Melbourne, the imprisoned Bricky Williamson was hoping to earn a remission on his sentence by passing on inside information on the Kellys and their preferred haunts in the north-east.

Up at the Woolshed, young Jack Sherrit had occasional contact with both Joe Byrne and Dan Kelly and faithfully reported all his contacts to the police. It was his big brother Aaron, though, who was emerging as the star of the show. Through the fortuitous circumstance of a forceful personality and the odd snippet of good intelligence, Aaron Sherrit became the most trusted of all the informants. Frank Hare believed that he had a special relationship with Aaron, to the point of an almost metaphysical bond. Yet, there is no evidence to suggest that Aaron reciprocated Hare's beliefs, just as there is no evidence to suggest that Ned ever felt vulnerable because of the police's use of informants.

* * *

The Euroa raid had put the Kelly Gang back on the front pages of colonial Australia's newspapers, and not always in a totally unfavourable light. The wider public wanted to know more about the gang as it seemed there may be more to them than was usually associated with groups of criminals. They had emerged from what was settled country rather than from the margins of the western frontiers. They also seemed determined to pursue a collision course with the police to highlight whatever grievances they had claimed for themselves and their families. The interest extended to all members of the Kelly family, whether they had criminal convictions or not. In January 1879, the *Benalla Standard* provided a pen picture of the seventeen-year-old Kate Kelly: 'Kate is a girl of medium height; she is good-looking with wild, dark eyes with which she seems to speak more than with her tongue . . .'

The Jerilderie raid only increased the public's fascination with the Kellys. The careful planning and execution, the distance covered, the destruction of the debt documents of poor farmers, the lack of bloodshed, and the sheer audacity of the raid titillated a public growing tired of the usual headlines of commerce and political dispute. The Kelly Gang seemed to be a whole new breed of bushrangers seeking, in part, public validation of their deeds. While Ned would always rely very much on his personal charisma, he also sought the support the underdog in a public fight always attracts. The stories published did not even have to be true so long as they sounded as if they could be. There were reports of rumours that the gang shod its horses backwards to confuse the police, while a James O'Dwyer was able to write:

> The hiding place of the gang was an old mining shaft, 25 feet deep, from which there ran a drive 30 feet long by 12 feet, 8 inches wide. It was a hundred yards from a junction of three roads – to Chilton [sic], Yackandandah and Kiewa – eleven miles from Beechworth.

But it was the family that journalists kept coming back to, and even the *Ovens and Murray Advertiser*, widely regarded as a mouthpiece of the district's squatters, succumbed to temptation.

Under the heading, 'Romance and reality – A Kelly Sketch', on 2 August the paper provided its own description of Ned's favourite sister, Maggie Skillian:

> She is nothing but a simple country girl, slight of figure and reserved in manners, with a peculiar earnest look in her dark blue eyes, which leads one to suppose that her troubles lay great upon her mind. She dresses invariably in black, and with taste; her voice is pleasant and soft; her manners gentle and quiet. She travels about in a most unostentatious manner, and is altogether one who would be the least suspected person in the world of indulging in the deeds of daring defiance of law and order commonly attributed to her.

Appearances to the contrary, Maggie was by law a criminal as she provided ongoing support for her brothers Ned and Dan, both gazetted outlaws. For much of 1879, the gang was relatively safe and comfortable. They had money and they had a wide network of loyal friends. They had hideaways no policeman would ever find, and they were able to visit family and friends more or less at will. They enjoyed their notoriety and apparently also enjoyed reading most of what was being written about them. They loved the little poems and songs that were beginning to gain currency, with the consensus favourite a ditty called 'The Bold Kelly Gang'. They even engaged in a bit of horseplay, giving each other gang names. Ned was known as 'Captain', Joe was 'Moonlight', Dan was 'Sneak' and Steve was 'Revenge'.

There were clouds on the horizon, though, and for Ned the biggest of these was the threat posed by a small band of Queenslanders who arrived in Victoria in March 1879. As well as being Queenslanders, they were Mounted Police, and Native Mounted

Police to boot. They were also widely regarded as the best man-trackers in Australia.

* * *

For a while it had seemed that the Queenslanders would not be required to travel south. The Queensland government had first offered a Native Police contingent to Victoria in December 1878, an offer which Commissioner Standish suggested the Victorian premier politely decline, fearing it might be perceived as an admission of inadequacy on the part of the force he commanded. The first Native Police unit had actually been formed in the Port Phillip District in 1837, but was disbanded for lack of work in 1852. Victoria's new governor, Lord Normanby, had previously been governor of Queensland, where he had been very impressed by the abilities of the Native Police. A little bit of pressure, plus the embarrassments of Euroa and Jerilderie, helped Standish change his mind. The Queensland offer was accepted, with thanks.

Sub-inspector Stanhope O'Connor was selected to lead the party. O'Connor was a nephew of the then-governor of New South Wales and had been an officer in charge of Native Police since joining the Queensland Police in January 1873. A man with a questioning intellect and broad interests, O'Connor was also a person who identified solutions almost as soon as he identified the problem. Sometimes, though, his enthusiasm ran ahead of his judgement and he found himself cast in the role of a champion for things he might not totally support. His second in command was another European, Senior Constable Tom King, while the Native Police contingent comprised Corporal Sambo, and Troopers Hero, Johnny, Jimmy, Barney and Jack. O'Connor had personally recruited them all; when they departed Brisbane, the oldest was 24 and the youngest just eighteen.

All had several years' police experience. They also looked the part, well-presented and well-accoutred. They were dressed in blue uniforms with red facings and were armed with both Snider carbines and revolvers. Each month while they were on detached duty, the Native Police would be paid three pounds for their service; O'Connor would receive 30.

The Queensland party sailed from Brisbane to Sydney. It seems to have been an eventful trip, as all who travelled were seasick and one – Corporal Sambo – developing badly congested lungs. From Sydney, they travelled to Albury by train, then switched to a different gauge railway for the final leg of their journey to Benalla, which was to be their base in the months ahead. They arrived on 8 March 1879. There was an unfortunate start to the involvement of the Queensland police in what was a Victoria Police operation. Anxious to commence working, O'Connor agreed to take part in an immediate expedition into the Wombat Ranges. It was not a success; the altitude and the cooler temperatures were hard on the Native Police, particularly on the already-ailing Corporal Sambo, who died of 'congestion of the lungs' (probably pneumonia) shortly after the expedition returned to Benalla at the end of March. He was buried, with due ceremony, in the local cemetery. Thereafter the Native Police always carried extra blankets on patrol, prompting some Victoria Police to claim that the trackers were slowing them down.

The real issues that soon emerged could be traced back to Standish's feeling that both he personally and the force he commanded had been slighted by the government's decision to bring in policemen from another service – and Aboriginal policemen at that – when he believed that he and his men were perfectly capable of handling the Kelly Outbreak. His fit of pique showed itself in little ways; he insisted that a Victorian policeman be attached to the unit, and had Constable Thomas Kirkham installed as the notional second-in-command. And he took to referring to O'Connor and his Native Police, unofficially of course, as 'the ornamental Queensland sub-inspector and his niggers'.

The command situation in the hunt for the Kellys was not helped by the personal animosities which soon emerged. In June 1879, John Nicolson, now physically and mentally restored from his earlier labours, resumed his position as the leader of the hunt for the Kellys, again consigning Frank Hare to a subsidiary role in that hunt. Shortly afterwards, and in Benalla, Stanhope O'Connor met and fell in love with one of Nicolson's sisters-in-law, a feeling that the young lady reciprocated. The couple had a private wedding in Benalla, intending a more public one at Flemington during Melbourne Cup week later in the year. The happy couple set up house together in Benalla, much to the chagrin of several senior police, who were not convinced that the O'Connors had ever actually married.

One of the chagrinees was Commissioner Standish, who sensed the beginnings of a challenge to his preeminent position in law enforcement. What made the situation worse for him was that O'Connor had actually married into one of Melbourne's more prominent families. His new mother-in-law had been the first white baby born in the Port Phillip District while one of his new brothers-in-law, Thomas Prout Webb, was already recognised as a rising legal talent, one whose ability would see him rise to become Master of the Victorian Supreme Court. Before they knew it, there were two mutually antagonistic camps at the top of the Kelly hunt command, with Standish and Hare on one side and the newly minted relatives, O'Connor and Nicolson, on the other. Against this backdrop, Standish announced that the hunt would now be directed by a 'Board of Officers', effective from the date of Nicolson's return to command. While Nicolson would retain some operational responsibility, he would be reporting to a new board consisting of Standish, Hare, Sadleir and O'Connor. It was a recipe for disaster.

* * *

These backroom machinations detracted from some good work being done on the ground. Ned was a good enough bushman to appreciate the capacity of the Native Police and news of their arrival in Benalla had an almost immediate impact on his plans and behaviour. From this point onwards Ned generally referred to them as 'black devils', and seems to have genuinely believed that the Queensland man-trackers possessed almost supernatural tracking powers. He now began to factor them into his long-term plans.

Mounted Constable James Dwyer, who accompanied the Native Police on one of their expeditions, was similarly impressed.

> The tracks, when we reached them, were two days old, for we had to ride some forty miles, but this made no difficulty. As the 'boys' jogged along, they could detect signs which we white police could make out only after long looking, such as sweat marks where the horsemen had laid hold of a rail, or the impression of the understrap of a spur in the damp sand where the rider had dismounted for a drink; the remains of a fire, a horse dung – the age of both of these things the 'boys' could tell after pushing their feet into them. Next they picked up a knife which had fallen from its sheath; and when at length the signs showed quite fresh we dismounted from our horses and crept along on hands and knees. It was curious to see the 'boys' as their noses seemed to flatten and their nostrils distend; sure signs of their excitement. They next led us close up to a humpy in which there was a quick rush of white police, and eight pairs of hands laid

hold of a man lying on a bunk, dressed, but asleep. He was not a Kelly. Of course, all this sort of thing got on the nerves of the bushrangers and forced them to keep so very quiet.

It certainly did get on their nerves and Ned and the others put out the story that the man-trackers' days were numbered. Knowing that Ned hated them above all others and was hoping to have the opportunity to do something about them, the Native Police were loath to expose themselves by getting too close when following fresh tracks in case they led into an ambush. This caution led to accusations of cowardice and to friction between the Queenslanders and the Victorians. The man-trackers remained, though, and Ned came to believe that sooner or later he would have to do something about them.

* * *

For sixteen months after the Jerilderie raid, the Kelly Gang stayed quiet; there were no more spectacular bank raids, no more killings, no more outrages of any kind. The lack of activity led some observers, almost exclusively those resident in Melbourne, to offer the suggestion that the gang had probably left Victoria for another colony, and indeed may even have left Australia. After all, wasn't Frank Gardiner, a bushranger from the previous generation, now resident in San Francisco where he was running a waterfront bar?

In fact, the gang had stayed very much where they were most comfortable: the hills and valleys bounded by Beechworth, Wangaratta and Benalla. There they camped or stayed overnight with one of their network of family and friends. Occasional rumours detailed more public appearances, at race meetings where they dressed as gentry and bet heavily, or in bush shanties where they stood at the bar and shouted drinks for crowds of men indistinguishable from themselves. There were even stories that Steve Hart, dressed as a woman, would ride through police patrols with a smile and a wave.

At some point, Ned and Joe made an assessment of the gang's position. The fact that no-one they trusted seemed tempted by the enormous reward and the widespread support they received throughout the north-east reinforced Ned's belief that there was a moral justification for the gang's actions and the overall 'cause' (selectors' rights, unavailability of suitable land, disenfranchisement) they represented. Nor did Ned lack self-confidence. He steadfastly believed that his native intelligence and local knowledge made him a better tactician than the police who hunted him and that, for the police to succeed he would have to make a serious mistake.

Ned did, however, harbour some concerns. While they had lifted a lot of money in their two bank raids, they had also given a lot of money away to provide support and succour to those who provided the same to them. Financially, they would make it through 1879, but sometime in 1880 they would need to replenish their funds. There was a philosophical concern as well. Despite their public and private protestations, Ellen Kelly was still in prison and the poor selectors of the north-east were still in thrall to the local squatters and their police allies. It was a situation Ned had specifically warned about in the Jerilderie Letter. And finally, there was a practical matter.

Ned's belief in the abilities of the man-trackers caused the gang to change how they operated on their home range. Instead of travelling freely, overnighting with family or friends, the gang spent more and more time in semi-fortified camps. Most nights, someone would have to perform sentry duty. It was a lifestyle that took a toll, and it was a lifestyle none wanted to countenance for the long term. To make certain that this would not be their fate, Ned formulated a plan.

The gang would create an incident, one serious enough to attract a major police response. The incident would need to be far enough away from the main police base at Benalla for the police response to require the movement of men, horses and equipment by train. That police train would be either captured or destroyed, hopefully with the Native Police aboard. If captured, those aboard would be hostages in the negotiations that followed. If destroyed, it would send a clear message to the Victorian government that would have to lead to a negotiated settlement. As a bonus, drawing the police away from Benalla would leave the town's banks without protection.

Over a period of time – weeks, perhaps months – the plan was refined. Ned knew of a spot on the main northern railway line, just beyond Glenrowan, where trains gathered speed on a downward curve for the run into Wangaratta. Tearing up the rails there would guarantee the destruction of the train. Before then, though, they would attempt to have the stationmaster signal the train to stop at Glenrowan station. If it did, those aboard would be given the alternatives of surrender or destruction. If the train failed to stop at the station, the choice would be made for them.

Through discussion and argument, the basic plan was refined and final details agreed. While proud of Ned's ability to draw people to him and to then lead those people, Ellen Kelly had always believed that the less flamboyant Dan would have made a better general. The elder brother was full of bombast and blood-curdling threats, but underneath was basically a trusting person, whereas Dan was quiet, conservative and trusted only those who had proved themselves. Dan argued that the destruction of the police was an unnecessary complication. Just draw the police away from Benalla and rob the banks there, and then decide what the best move would be. It was an argument Dan expected to lose; in this, at least, he was not disappointed. Again, the older brother – the first-born, the leader – won out with his charisma and his big-picture views of who they were and what they could achieve.

All that remained were two issues; how to equip themselves to take on a significant body of police, and how to stage an incident near Beechworth of sufficient gravity to attract those police to begin with. Ned promised to look after the first, while Joe said that he would take care of the second.

* * *

In February 1880, a number of farmers on properties between Greta and Oxley reported the theft of plough mouldboards, the metal forms that actually sliced through the soil. The Native Police were called to the scene of one of the thefts, and noted that there was clear evidence that the thief was wearing boots with larrikin heels. To Nicolson, still in charge of the hunt for the Kellys, this was clear evidence that the gang was stealing material they could use to build a stronghold. That view was soon contradicted by his best agent, the Diseased Stock Inspector. The schoolteacher reported that the mouldboards were being wrought into armour that could be used either on foot or on horseback. Once again, the police were wrong and the agent was right.

Although suspicion fell on several of the district's blacksmiths, it is likely that the gang made most of the armour themselves, improvising to get it right. The first armour they made was two centimetres thick and proved to be far too heavy to have any practical use. Halving the thickness provided adequate protection at a reasonable weight. Four suits of armour were made, each requiring four mouldboards to produce. To absorb some of the impact from bullets striking the circular helmets while also providing some comfort, the Kelly girls knitted woollen skullcaps for each of the outlaws.

With their defensive needs covered, Ned now looked to launch his offensive. In early June 1880, Maggie Skillian, Tom Lloyd and another young man from the district named Mick Nolan travelled to Melbourne by train, booking into the Robert Burns Hotel in Lonsdale Street. While in Melbourne, Maggie and Tom did some sightseeing while Mick Nolan spent a lot of time by himself. The police assigned to follow the three noted that Nolan visited Rosier's, a gunsmith in Elizabeth Street, and bought 200 Martini-Henry rifle cartridges, 200 Webley revolver cartridges and 200 Spencer revolving rifle cartridges. Nolan told the proprietor that he and his brother were going to New Zealand to do some hunting.

The purchase of the ammunition, most notably the amount and the type, was of real concern to the police, and Sadleir was instructed to have the travellers' bags searched when they hopped off the train at Glenrowan on the return trip. The search was done but without results, while the bags of a fellow traveller named Bridget O'Brien, publican of the Greta Hotel and suspected Kelly sympathiser were also searched, again without result.

Finally, on 23 June, the informant known as the Diseased Stock Inspector visited the Benalla police barracks. He asked to see Superintendent Nicolson, but was told that Nicolson had returned to Melbourne to take up a posting there. Instead the agent was shown to Sadleir's office; the two already knew each other. The informant told Sadleir that he had some vitally important intelligence about the Kelly Gang, at which point Sadleir took him straight to the office of Frank Hare, who was now responsible for the hunt. In Hare's office, the agent said that the Kellys were almost out of money and were about to stage another spectacular hold-up. They all possessed suits of bulletproof armour, capable of stopping a Martini-Henry round, and were in the process of finalising a plan that involved derailing a train and robbing all the banks in Benalla.

Hare did everything but dismiss the claims out of hand. The Diseased Stock Inspector was primarily Nicolson's agent, not his, and Hare had not had any real dealings with the man previously. The story he heard was, he believed, barely credible and there was neither proof nor substantiation offered. Besides, Hare himself had a better agent, better in all respects, and so close to the Kellys to be almost part of the gang. His codename was 'Moses', and he was a friend as well as an agent to Hare, who always called him by his given name, Aaron.

* * *

Shortly before the Jerilderie raid, Joe and Dan visited Aaron Sherrit at his home, perhaps to sound him out about a role or maybe even to pass on a little disinformation. While Joe dismounted to talk to his friend, Dan remained in the saddle, cold-eyed and aloof. He had not trusted Aaron before and nothing he had seen or heard in the last few months had convinced him to change his mind. The rest of the gang were beginning to share his suspicions.

Since Stringybark, Aaron had decided that his future lay in a different direction to that of his childhood friend. Part of the decision may have been due to his fear of Ned, and part because of the size of the reward money dangled in front of him but, whatever the reasons, Aaron Sherrit had become a well-paid police informant. There is nothing to suggest that he ever provided information of critical importance, but he was in regular contact with Joe, sometimes spoke to the others, and what he got he passed back to Sadleir and Nicolson or Hare, with Detective Ward usually acting as the intermediary.

Sherrit should have been constantly cautioned about drawing attention to himself and his role with the police. If he was warned, the vainglorious Aaron ignored what he was told and at times actively drew attention to himself. Once, Joe Byrne's mother actually found him resting in a police observation post overlooking her home, while his meetings with Ward were common knowledge. There had to be repercussions, and there were. Kate Byrne ended her 'engagement' to Aaron when she learned the full extent of his relationship with the police. An acrimonious argument over the ownership of a horse he had given her ensued. Perhaps as payback, on Boxing Day 1879, Aaron married the fifteen-year-old Mary Barry. Mary was already pregnant – malicious gossip suggested that Detective Ward was the father – and the newlyweds set up house in the two-room slab hut Aaron had built on his property to the north of Beechworth.

What had been acrimony became outright enmity. Following her unmasking of Aaron's direct involvement with the police, Mrs Byrne did not hold back in letting Aaron know what she thought of him and how she thought he would deservedly meet his end. Aaron replied in kind, telling Mrs Byrne that he expected to be there when the police shot her son dead, then allegedly detailing what he would do with the body afterwards. Returning the compliment, Joe visited Aaron's mother, and calmly informed her that he intended to kill both her son and her son's new best friend, Detective Michael Ward.

With most of their plan complete, Ned now sought to create an incident that would draw the police from Benalla to Beechworth. The murder of the most important police spy in northeastern Victoria would certainly do that, and so Aaron's fate was sealed. While part of the gang took over the railway-stop township of Glenrowan and tore up the rails beyond it, Aaron Sherrit would be executed at his home near Beechworth. Joe Byrne said he would do the job and Dan Kelly volunteered to accompany him.

By June 1880 the police were aware that Aaron's role had

been compromised and that his life may be in peril. Four armed policemen were detailed to give their star informant the protection he needed. During the day, they sat off from the Sherrit hut, paying close attention to all who looked like they were going to approach the property. In the cold nights, they had begun to take their evening meal with the Sherrits in the warmth of their hut. At around 9 o'clock on the evening of Saturday, 26 June, a voice called out at the door of that hut, speaking in heavily accented English. The man said that he was sorry for the interruption, but that he had drunk a lot of brandy and couldn't find his way home.

Aaron recognised the voice as that of Anton Wicks, a German neighbour who regularly lost his way while travelling home from a local shanty. When he opened the door, though, the light fell on Joe Byrne, a shotgun in his arms already trained on whoever was on the other side. Joe fired once, and then again. The first blast of solid shot tore into Aaron's chest, making a gaping wound and destroying most of the vital organs within. As Aaron staggered back into the hut, the second shot hit him in the side of the neck, tearing through the veins and arteries and exiting near his spine. Aaron Sherrit was dead before his body hit the earthen floor. In the split second before the screams and the cries began, Joe Byrne stepped into the doorway and looked down at the body of his oldest friend. He said: 'You'll not blow what you will do [sic] to us anymore', then turned and walked out of the hut. The Glenrowan raid had begun.

CHAPTER 4

Ann Jones's Glenrowan Inn

Ned certainly picked a quiet and picturesque backdrop for his next big outrage. In June 1880, the small township of Glenrowan comprised about a dozen homes, a general store, blacksmith's shop and two hotels clustered around a railway station and crossing. To the side of one of the hotels, the Glenrowan Inn, was a row of half a dozen canvas tents, used as permanent accommodation by contract labourers. A short distance from the geographical centre of the township, on the main road towards Benalla, was a police barracks, post office, and school.

The spread out little township lay at a gap in the low hills between Benalla and Wangaratta, at a point where the road and the railway both veered north-west for the downhill run into Wangaratta. Immediately west of Glenrowan, the Warby Ranges ended in a prominent bluff known as Morgan's Lookout, while a spur of the Great Dividing Range advanced towards the eastern margins of the township. On that side the main feature was an open-cut quarry which supplied ballast for the railways and road metal for the larger towns in the district. Known originally as The Glen, the site was settled by Europeans following the discovery of gold in the nearby Ovens River valley. Renamed Glenrowan, the settlement grew when it became a centre for the tracklayers and fettlers working on the Great Northern Railway, but declined when that section of the line was completed.

That railway line, running from Melbourne to Wodonga on the New South Wales border, was completed in 1873 and another major project, a spur line from Wangaratta to Beechworth, opened in 1876. The railways, and those who built them, stimulated the local economy; the other of the two Glenrowan hotels was known as McDonnell's Railway Tavern Hotel. The railways also brought about a minor relocation of the settlement. The original site of the Glenrowan township was around a kilometre to the south of the 1880 site, and was moved north to where the railway station was built at the crest of a slight slope. At the original site, stationary trains sometimes struggled to raise enough steam to climb that slope. The relocation meant that the little township was actually spread over a larger area than it might otherwise have been with the railway station and the two hotels clustered at one end of the settlement, some distance from the police barracks, post office and school at the other.

There were four important public officers based at Glenrowan; a policeman, a stationmaster, a postmaster and a schoolteacher. The policeman was Constable Hugh Bracken; born in Ireland in 1840, Bracken migrated to Victoria in 1861 and soon joined the Victoria Police. He had twice resigned from and then rejoined the police, most recently in November 1878 as a direct result of the Stringybark Creek killings. At the time he had been working as a guard at Beechworth Prison. A later biographer of the Kelly gang would describe Bracken as 'a courageous and intelligent man. He had been stationed at Glenrowan at his own wish as he knew the Kellys and their allies'.

The Glenrowan barracks commanded by Bracken was almost brand new. It was located in a large building next door to the post office (and owned by the postmaster) several hundred metres from the railway station on the main road to Benalla. Bracken lived at the barracks with his pregnant wife and young son, but coming into the weekend of 26/27 June, he was not a well man. Because of the danger to those posted there, the police had closed their Greta barracks some time earlier. Reports of Kelly supporters gathering at McDonnell's Hotel began to emerge in the early months of 1880, and the Glenrowan barracks was opened in response. Unfortunately, Bracken inherited some of the Greta barracks' duties. Earlier in the week he had spent several nights watching Maggie Skillian's home. As a result, he had suffered a 'bilious attack' – gastric flu – and on Saturday morning was very ill and bed-ridden.

The postmaster at Glenrowan was the elegantly named Hillmorton Reynolds who lived in the residence at the rear of the post office with his wife and seven-year-old son, Alexander. Hillmorton's brother, Edward, was a local farmer who spent a lot of time at the Reynolds' home, visiting his brother and catching up with his friend, another farmer named Robert Gibbons who boarded with the Reynolds at the post office. The stationmaster was John Stanistreet, married with three small children. The Stanistreets lived in a railway house alongside the railway gates, about 100 metres from the station on the western side of the tracks and facing the township's second hotel, the Glenrowan Inn.

Thomas Curnow was the schoolteacher at the Glenrowan State School. Born in Cornwall in 1855, he moved to Australia with his family two years later. The year 1880 was his fourth teaching at a school that most years enrolled about twenty students. Since his arrival in the township, Tom Curnow had married Jean Isobel Mortimer (commonly called Isobel), the daughter of a prominent local landowner. The couple lived in a house alongside the school, about 200 metres past the post office and police barracks on the road to Benalla. The popular young teacher was a distinctive figure; a congenital hip deformity gave him a peculiar shuffling walk. Recently, Isobel Curnow had not been well – she was three months' pregnant and already had a small child – and one of Tom's sisters had been staying with them to lend a hand.

The newest building in the township was probably the Glenrowan Inn, and among the newest residents were the hotel's owner, Ann Jones, and her children. It had taken a lot of time and effort for them to get there, and there had been setbacks on the way. Ann Jones had been born Ann Kennedy in Tipperary in 1833. She migrated to Victoria in 1854 and later that year married a Welsh labourer named Owen Jones at St Francis' Church in Elizabeth Street, almost exactly four years after Red and Ellen Kelly had married at the same church. After moving around the goldfields for several years, the Joneses settled in Wangaratta around 1870, opening tearooms there. By then, the couple had produced eleven children, three of whom did not survive infancy.

When their tearooms went bankrupt, Owen Jones sought work on the railway line then pushing into Gippsland, while Ann borrowed money to firstly purchase land and subsequently build a hotel on that land. Owen would live in Gippsland throughout the years that Ann was building and running her hotel, the Glenrowan Inn, but regularly sent home part of his wages to support his wife's enterprise. In 1880 their eldest son, the 25-year-old Thomas, also moved away from the district seeking work, and he too would regularly send money back to his mother. Thomas had moved away to start a shearing job in March 1880, leaving his mother with her six remaining children.

Even as her dream of owning a successful business looked like being realised, another tragedy struck. In 1878, just as the final fittings of the hotel were in place, one of the girls, a sixteen-year-old daughter also named Ann, was killed when she was crushed by a tree that she and her fourteen-year-old sister, Jane, were felling. Ann Jones – plump and hearty, buxom and talkative – grieved a while and then got on with her life.

The business had really started in 1873 when Ann bought a cleared town lot in Glenrowan. The block had stables and a slab hut on it, and sometime in the mid-1870s, Ann and her children moved from Wangaratta to Glenrowan and took up residence in the three-room hut. It is likely that Ann sold sly grog from the hut, and the small profits she made from that trade plus the money her husband and oldest son remitted home were enough to allow her to make a start on the new hotel in 1878. The Glenrowan Inn was constructed by two Wangaratta builders named Emery and Jarvis at a cost of £200. Ann did not have this much and had to borrow £71 from Jarvis. Some costs were saved through Tom and the other children helping with the construction when they could.

When completed, the new building had a frontage of nine metres and was eight metres deep. The builders used what was then known as a weatherboard shell construction with white painted stringybark weatherboards attached to a joisted wooden floor and frame. The interior walls were of a hessian and paper mix, while the ceilings were of simple calico. This main building had two gabled roofs, both of which were covered with corrugated iron. A veranda was attached to the front of the building, and was protected by the eaves of the roof.

The building was aligned fairly closely with the compass; the front looked directly east over a paddock known as the Railway Reserve to the stationmaster's house and railway gates some 200 metres away. Looking at the hotel from the front, a dining room was on the right. The largest room in the building, it had a fireplace and two doors, one opening onto the veranda and the other onto a central passageway that ran from a front to a rear door. It also had a window looking out onto the Railway Reserve. Across the passage was the main bar area, complete with bar counter and shelves.

A small parlour was to the side at the southern end. Behind these front rooms were two bedrooms, one larger than the other. The original slab hut, a few metres to the rear, was kept in use. Its main room became the hotel's kitchen while the two smaller rooms remained bedrooms for the Jones's younger children. The two buildings were connected by a covered walkway, known as a bull run or breezeway, about a metre wide and partially protected on the southern side by a small paling fence. The hotel was complete when a hitching rail and horse trough carved out of a tree trunk were placed in front of the veranda.

The rear paddock, containing stables and outhouses, had been cleared and sloped gently upwards into lightly timbered country, with thicker patches of scrub and regrowth. The slope gradually increased as it led upwards to Morgan's Lookout and the Warby Ranges beyond. The entire property was bordered by a split-rail fence. Also fenced was the Railway Reserve, and its fence – flat rail topped with three of four strands of wire – ran parallel to the railway line and around 30 metres in front of the hotel. Criss-crossed by a number of rivulets, there was also an old creek bed which had been extended to form a drainage ditch around 1.6 metres deep. Around 50 metres from the front of the hotel, this ditch also ran parallel to the railway line. A clearly defined path led diagonally across the reserve from the railway station to the wicket gate in front of the hotel. This was a small revolving gate made of wrought iron that allowed just a single person at a time to pass through.

Directly opposite the railway station, and also beyond the Railway Reserve fence, was a cluster of half a dozen canvas tents set up in a glade in the light timber. Attached to frames and with doors and windows, the tents provided permanent accommodation to labourers working at the Glenrowan quarry on the other side of the railway line. Those living in the tents had come to an arrangement with Ann Jones, and were allowed to use the hotel kitchen to cook their evening meal.

* * *

Right from the beginning, Ann Jones's intention was to attract a more respectable clientele than that which she believed drank across the tracks at McDonnell's. She was especially interested in passengers from the trains that stopped regularly at Glenrowan station. To this end she spent more money on furniture and fittings than might otherwise have been the case. By the end of 1878, the Inn was operating at a profit and Ann could see that she had made the right decision.

Her hotel was attracting a regular clientele of townspeople, quarrymen and those associated with the railway, while McDonnell's remained the hotel of choice for the selectors, small farmers and farm labourers. When the Joneses had run the tearooms in Wangaratta, they had been neighbours of, and friends with, the Hart family. In 1879 and again in 1880, Ettie and Julia Hart stayed for several weeks at the hotel, renewing their friendship with the Jones girls. Their brother Steve also called in on occasion.

GLENROWAN

The familiarity of the Kelly Gang with Glenrowan was well known to the police; the establishment of a police barracks there was partly a response to reports of them visiting the township. Another response was that, between October 1878 and June 1879, Detective Michael Ward attempted to set up a network of informants in and around Glenrowan. While doing so – and he does not appear to have been particularly successful – Ward several times visited Ann Jones at her hotel seeking information on the movements of the gang. While no evidence exists to suggest that Ann assisted the police, Ned let it be known that he did not trust her, while neither Maggie nor Kate Kelly would speak to her.

For two weeks in mid-June, Ann Jones was very ill, bed-ridden with neuralgia. During that time, her eldest daughter Jane, just sixteen, had been responsible for cooking and cleaning and serving in the bar as well as caring for her four younger brothers John, Owen, Jeremiah, and Headington. By Saturday, 26 June, Ann was feeling much better and thought she soon might be up and about.

CHAPTER 5

Saturday Night and Sunday, 26/27 June 1880

At approximately 10 o'clock on the night of Saturday, 26 June 1880, Ned Kelly led a small band of men and horses into Glenrowan from the direction of Greta. The men included his fellow outlaw, Steve Hart, and a group of supporters who, while never formally identified, were widely known in the district. The men were riding their own horses and leading a number of pack-horses, several of which were heavily laden. Distributed among them was a twenty-kilogram drum of blasting powder, fuses, rockets and a large supply of ammunition of various calibres. Plus, four sets of heavy armour fashioned from the mouldboards of ploughs. There was little to note about Glenrowan that evening. The two hotels had closed earlier and, while the occasional glow of a lamplight shining through a window was visible in one or other of the buildings that lined the main road, there was no-one visible outside their homes on what was a crisp and clear winter's night.

That was good, thought Ned, because this was not a social visit to one of his family's many friends in the township or its surrounds. Tonight was business for Ned. Business that began when he and his friends were hounded into outlawry by the police and the powers of the state who directed what the police should do. By placing four young men beyond the boundaries of the law, the Victorian government had issued a challenge that Ned had accepted. The unfinished business that had started at the Kelly hut all those months ago would be finished at Glenrowan. It might be tonight, it might be tomorrow, but it would end here.

The horses were tied up or hobbled at the rear of McDonnell's Hotel, the supporters melted into the night, and Ned and Steve set about putting their part of the grand plan into action.

The two outlaws knew where they were going; all the gang members had visited the township at least once in the preceding months and were familiar with its layout. They also knew there was no telegraph station in the town and that the last train had passed through earlier in the evening and that the next scheduled service would be a passenger train on Monday morning. And so they set off along the railway tracks, walking north in the direction of Wangaratta. They were looking for a suitable spot to ambush and derail a train. When they found what would be the ideal place – a downward curve above a gully – they discovered that they would be unable to lift a single rail without tools and by themselves. That part of the plan had fallen over at the first hurdle.

* * *

SATURDAY NIGHT AND SUNDAY, 26/27 JUNE 1880

Realising now that they would need specialised assistance, the two returned to the township, Ned leading Steve to the cluster of tents that Ned assumed, from their proximity to the Railway Reserve and station, would be occupied by railway workers. The first tent they came to was occupied by John Lowe, a nineteen year old from Benalla who was in business with his father carting crushed rock from the Glenrowan quarry to Benalla for use as road metal. Lowe was sound asleep but was roused by a male voice outside his tent door telling him to get up. Thinking it was one of the other labourers having a joke, Lowe said go to hell.

After a brief silence, a different voice from somewhere to the rear of the tent said, 'Put a bullet through him Strahan', (Strahan being the name of a well-known local policeman, one whose temper was a byword in the district) followed by, 'We are police. You had better get up.' Lowe complied with the direction. In answer to some sharp questioning, Lowe explained just who occupied the tents, and Ned made the decision to rouse them all. By then, Lowe was aware that the two were not actually policemen but were the notorious outlaws Ned Kelly and Steve Hart; he had previously seen both of them several times in Benalla. The three went from tent to tent and soon had a group that included James Simson, John Delaney, William Sandercook, George Metcalf, John Maitland and Jock McHugh, all labourers employed at the quarry. Things went relatively well until Ned came to the furthest tent, one occupied by the works foreman, Alphonse 'Louis' Piazzi.

When Lowe called on Piazzi to come out of his tent, the foreman refused and furthermore threatened to shoot anyone who tried to enter his tent. This response infuriated Ned who kicked the door open and stepped inside. As he did so, Piazzi raised a pistol towards him. In an instant, Ned spat at Piazzi, 'You bastard. You lift a gun to me', bringing up his own rifle and firing as he did so. Piazzi knocked the barrel to one side as Ned fired, and the bullet passed harmlessly through bunk bed and floorboards and into the dirt below.

The *whipcrack* of the rifle shot was followed instantly by a female scream, and a woman emerged from the tangle of bedclothes at the other end of the bed. Covering Piazzi with his rifle, Ned turned on Lowe, abusing him for not saying that there was more than one person in the tent. Lowe responded apologetically, saying that the woman was not a regular visitor. Ned then turned to Piazzi and the woman, asking both if they knew who he was. The woman, apparently intoxicated, said, 'I know you, Ned Kelly', put her arms around his neck and attempted to kiss him. Ned pushed the woman away.

From their new prisoners, Ned learned that laying and lifting rails was a specialised task, but that there were two platelayers – the name given to those who performed this work – living in Glenrowan, in houses that were not too far away. Before visiting those two, though, Ned wanted to check out the building clearly visible through the trees to see if his rifle shot had prompted any response. The building was Ann Jones's Glenrowan Inn.

* * *

Ned and Steve led their prisoners the short distance through the bush to the hotel, where Ned strode up to the front door and called out: 'Jump up and open the door!' Ann Jones, sharing the larger rear bedroom with her daughter Jane, called back telling Ned to wait. Ned left Steve with the prisoners and walked around to the back door where he again demanded entry. After a sharp exchange of words, Ned was admitted, immediately informing Ann that she and her family were now his prisoners. Ned waited outside in the passageway while the women dressed, and with them checked that the Jones boys were all asleep in their bedrooms in the rear building. Ned then led Ann and Jane

SATURDAY NIGHT AND SUNDAY, 26/27 JUNE 1880

Jones back to the group standing and waiting in front of the hotel. From there, they were all led across the Railway Reserve to the stationmaster's house. It was a few minutes after one o'clock on Sunday morning.

* * *

Stationmaster John Stanistreet was wakened from a deep sleep by the knocking on his front door. Suspecting that it was probably someone who needed to get through the closed railway gates in a hurry, he pulled half his clothes on, and was halfway to the front door when it burst open. A tall figure in a coat stood in the doorway and Stanistreet asked, 'Who are you?' 'I am Ned Kelly,' was the reply. Ned then told the stationmaster to get dressed and follow him, adding that he would suffer no harm if he followed instructions. Stanistreet completed dressing and followed Ned outside where he was surprised to see a group of men standing quietly and looking across at Jones's hotel.

When asked by Ned if he would help to destroy the railway lines, Stanistreet replied, 'I know nothing about lifting rails off the line. The only persons that understand it are the repairers and they live outside and on the line.' It was an answer that Ned had already heard and, after a pause for thought, he issued instructions. Ann and Jane Jones were to stay inside the Stanistreet house with the stationmaster's wife and children, while Steve would guard Stanistreet and the labourers, and looked for any rail-laying tools they could use. Ned knew the names of the platelayers and where they lived. He would go and round them up.

Ned, who'd ridden his horse across to Stanistreet's, remounted and trotted off down the Benalla road. The first house he stopped at was occupied by Dennis Sullivan, a platelayer who had originally lived in Euroa but who had followed the railway as it pushed north to Wodonga. Sullivan was quickly bailed up, allowed to dress, then instructed to follow Ned to the next house, occupied by the railway's senior platelayer, James Reardon, and his family.

The Reardon house was about 500 metres from the railway station and on that Saturday night contained James Reardon, his wife Margaret, their eighteen-year-old son, Michael, a seven-year-old daughter, three-year-old son and their baby girl, Bridget, then just a few months old. There was also a labourer named John Larkins boarding at the house. Sometime in the early hours of Sunday morning, James Reardon was awoken by the barking of the family dog. He wondered aloud how it had got out of the stable where it usually slept. Margaret, also awake by now, said that she thought she had also heard the sound of a horseman jumping their fence. Reardon decided to investigate, and got dressed. He went to the front door and opened it; standing on the other side were his workmate Dennis Sullivan and a man who introduced himself as Ned Kelly.

Again, the family was given time to wake up and dress before they and John Larkins were escorted back to the Stanistreets's which, by now, was becoming quite crowded.

* * *

While waiting for Ned to return with the platelayers, Steve Hart organised the tools they would need to tear up the tracks. Those tools were held in a locked chest in a storage shed located about halfway between the Stanistreet house and the railway station. Steve escorted his little group to the shed and, when Stanistreet said he did not have the key to the locked chest, ordered one of the other men to snap the lock off. All the tools were removed and taken back to the stationmaster's house. Ned and the platelayer's party arrived shortly afterwards.

SATURDAY NIGHT AND SUNDAY, 26/27 JUNE 1880

After collecting the appropriate tools, Ned and the platelayers followed the tracks to the point he had selected for the ambush. There, he directed Reardon and Sullivan to start tearing up the rails. James Reardon believed that if he and Sullivan only pulled up one length of rail from each track, a train travelling at near full speed might just be able to clear the gap; tearing up more than one length would guarantee a disaster. He was able to convince Ned that one length would certainly be enough to cause a crash, and the two platelayers set to work.

Each rail was around seven metres in length and every metre or so was attached to a wooden sleeper by a plate and spike arrangement. Working alongside each other on the parallel rails, Reardon and Sullivan laboriously removed each spike and every plate and threw them aside. As they started, Ned explained why they were doing this: 'I expect a train from Benalla with a lot of police and blackfellows,' he said. 'I am going to kill them all.' Later, when it seemed to Ned that the work was not progressing as rapidly as it could have, he walked up to James Reardon, saying, 'Old man, you are a long time breaking up this road. If you don't look sharp, I'll tickle you with this revolver.' But then it was done, with two lengths of rail, several sleepers and a dozen spikes and plates torn up and thrown into the gully. It had taken them 90 minutes; Reardon later estimated that, on a good day, he and Sullivan could have done it in five.

Ned and the platelayers were away for two hours, during which time Steve Hart had little to do beyond stamp his feet in the cold and keep an eye on his equally cold prisoners. When they did return though, Ned grabbed John Stanistreet and took him into the house. Stanistreet offered Ned and the platelayers a nip of brandy against the cold, while his wife produced a platter of bacon, pig's cheek, and bread. Then Ned started to question Stanistreet about the various railway signals, especially how the trains were signalled to stop. Stanistreet quoted a little railway-man's ditty:

> White is right and red is wrong,
> And green is generally 'Come Along'.

Stanistreet also told Ned that, while his signals would certainly stop a regular passenger train, he could not guarantee that they would stop a police special. Fortified by food, brandy and information, Ned rejoined Steve outside with their prisoners. The sky was beginning to lighten in the east; the world continued to turn.

* * *

With the coming of dawn, Ned was forced to re-evaluate his plan. He had originally thought the police train could be passing through Glenrowan before dawn. His discussions with Stanistreet made him reconsider his timetable, as he now understood that both rail and police authorisations would need to come from Melbourne. He knew the train would be coming, but expected it may not be until around the middle of the day.

What Ned did not know was that the four policemen who had been guarding Aaron Sherrit had been traumatised. They had convinced themselves that the gang was lurking outside in the dark, just waiting for a chance to kill them all. So they cowered in the house throughout Saturday night and well into Sunday morning. Eventually one of them, Constable Harry Armstrong, agreed to return to Beechworth to report the death of Aaron and seek reinforcements. Nor did Ned know that Frank Hare would only learn of his best agent's death much later in the day and while consuming a late lunch at the Commercial Hotel in Benalla. Further south, in Melbourne,

SATURDAY NIGHT AND SUNDAY, 26/27 JUNE 1880

Commissioner Standish would not even be found until 4.30 in the afternoon.

* * *

While Ned had been speaking with Stanistreet, Ann Jones had been fluttering around the edges of the conversation. She took the opportunity the end of that conversation presented to suggest that Ned go across to her hotel for a meal and a wash, saying it would be good for him. Ned declined the offer, partly because his brother Dan and Joe Byrne were now riding towards where the group stood outside the stationmaster's house. When they had dismounted, Ned questioned them about the previous evening. Joe told how Aaron had died and how he and Dan had stayed outside the hut for an hour or so, taunting the police inside and challenging them to come outside and fight like men. In return, Ned brought them up to date on what he and Steve had achieved in Glenrowan.

Ned now believed the police special would not arrive until late morning at the earliest, and so continued to make adjustments to the master plan. By this stage – it was probably around 8 o'clock on Sunday morning – there were more than twenty adults and half that number of children gathered in and around the Stanistreet house. The fact that there were a large number of prisoners was not an issue in itself as the gang had controlled similar numbers at Euroa and Jerilderie. The problem was that they were responsible for a large number of prisoners when they no longer held the initiative. At both Euroa and Jerilderie, prisoners were held to facilitate bank robberies. Here they were held while the outlaws waited to execute an ambush. Unlike the robberies though, the outlaws would only be able to determine the where. The when had been taken out of their hands.

Faced with this uncertainty, Ned reverted to type and exercised control over those things that he could. He was nothing if not a man of action, and he now began to take actions on the basis of what he thought needed to be done. Their horses would be vital, one way or another, and so he asked Ann Jones if she had any horse feed at her hotel. When she replied that she had both chaff and oats, Ned asked Joe to get three of their horses and take them across to Jones's for a feed. They agreed to leave four other horses at McDonnell's and not worry about those that had been hobbled and turned loose.

There were other concerns as well. All the prisoners were hungry, and the children were certainly letting everyone know. Although she would later claim that she was under duress at the time, Ann Jones apparently offered to host breakfast at her hotel. There was no reason to reject the offer, so Ned promptly accepted. When he said that he doubted whether the hotel would be big enough for all of them, Ann assured him that it was. She also complained of not feeling well.

Both issues were addressed at once. Jane Jones would return to the hotel and light the kitchen fires. While there, she would also find a bottle of brandy. Joe would accompany her there and back. They were away a bit longer than the others expected – Jane had to look after her younger brothers while there – and when they returned Ann poured herself a nip of brandy before offering the bottle to Joe. After she had drunk, so did he.

Ned called the crowd together and told them that he would be taking all the men present across to Jones's hotel for breakfast, and all who wished to join them would be welcome. Dan even said that the outlaws would be paying. Those who chose to remain at the Stanistreets's could organise themselves, he said, adding that he would be leaving Steve Hart behind to keep an eye on them.

Before the group split in two, Ned called the three others to

SATURDAY NIGHT AND SUNDAY, 26/27 JUNE 1880

join him. Many would later recall that the four made quite a striking sight in the early morning sun. Two were of average height, while Ned and Joe were well above that. All were well-dressed in colourful shirts, serge pants, and jackets that appeared to have been tailored for them. All were wearing long fawn oilskin dustcoats and flat-crowned hats with the straps worn under the nose. They also wore custom-made riding boots, thin-soled and high-heeled, the uniform of the Greta Mob. Ned's boots were especially noticeable; their heels were higher than the others and they had patent leather tips.

The get-together was not to show off their apparel or weaponry but to hold a brief planning session. Ned outlined his thoughts on what might happen with the police special train, suggesting it might arrive around midday. Before he left, he nodded to John Stanistreet, standing nearby and watching, and said loudly to Steve: 'Watch his countenance, and if he gives any signal, shoot him.' Otherwise, Stanistreet may signal the train to stop, which was no longer part of the plan. Ned believed they would see and hear the train some distance off, allowing he and the others time to set up the ambush.

Ned, Dan, and Joe then led the group of men across the Railway Reserve and into the Glenrowan Inn. Ann and Jane Jones and the younger boys worked in the detached kitchen, preparing meals of ham and eggs and pannikins of hot, sweet tea. The outlaws also ate, making certain that one of their prisoners always sampled the food first. They also worked. Most of the time the Kelly brothers left Joe in charge of the prisoners, at that stage confined to the dining room.

Ned also helped Dan unload the packhorses that had been led across to the Jones's hotel. They each carried several heavy bags which contained pieces of armour or ammunition. Ned then led the horses to the hotel stables where he unharnessed, fed and watered them. While he was doing so, Dan carried the bags, one at a time, into the hotel. There he placed them in the smaller of the two bedrooms, locking the door and pocketing the key when he was not in the room. By the time the brothers had finished these tasks, it was after 9 o'clock. Meeting together again, Dan spoke up in front of Ned and Joe, suggesting that it seemed unlikely that the police train would be coming at all, so their best course of action may well be to pack up and leave. Ned vetoed the idea immediately. He was sick of running, he said, and wanted to end it. Whatever was going to happen, he added, would happen here, in Glenrowan. Again, Ned would brook no opposition to this plan, least of all from someone whose support he expected as a matter of family duty.

* * *

One of the reasons a police barracks had been established at Glenrowan earlier in the year was the regularity and frequency of reports suggesting that supporters of the gang were occasionally meeting at McDonnell's Hotel. There were even reports of gang members visiting the hotel and, when they first arrived in the township, Ned and Steve did leave their spare horses and pack animals at McDonnell's. Perhaps to divert attention away from the support they had received there, Ned and Joe only rode across to McDonnell's after they had stowed their equipment and supplies and eaten at the Jones's hotel.

Ned knocked on the front door and called on the McDonnells to dress and come outside. They were quickly out front where Ned said it would be best if they came with him to the stationmaster's house. Ned joked with Hanorah McDonnell, the publican's wife, that although they knew one another, in front of the others at Stanistreet's house she should call him 'Jack Doyle' instead of Ned. Joe Byrne also joined in the banter, apologising

SATURDAY NIGHT AND SUNDAY, 26/27 JUNE 1880

to Hanorah. He said that he had visited her hotel several times in recent months but, not wanting to attract any attention, he too had always used another name. Thus a pleasant few minutes passed in the short walk from McDonnell's to Stanistreet's.

The inclusion of the McDonnells was also part of a larger plan. The outlaws had agreed that anyone who came into the township would be taken prisoner and held at either the stationmaster's house or Jones's hotel. While the gang had many supporters in and around Glenrowan, there were also many residents they either did not know, or knew and didn't trust. For all they knew, police mounted patrols may be heading their way, patrols that could include the dreaded Queensland mantrackers. The gang could simply not afford to let anyone report their presence and activities to the police, or the ambushers might find themselves being ambushed. All who entered the township while they were in control, friend and foe alike, would therefore be held. Ned ordered Ann Jones to make certain that food and drink would remain available for all who were there for as long as they remained, and then told his prisoners that all drinks were free and there were no limits.

The number of those prisoners steadily increased as Sunday went on, sometimes by just one and sometimes by several. One of the solo parties was Martin Cherry, a 60-year-old railway navvy who lived a kilometre down the Benalla road from Jones's hotel. Unmarried, Cherry was one of the area's original settlers. Well-liked by all who knew him, Cherry was also regarded as very old and very harmless. The first group to be made prisoners came from the opposite end of the age spectrum to Cherry.

There were two separate Delaney families living in the Glenrowan area. One, a family with a small property on the outskirts of Wangaratta, included several known Kelly sympathisers. The second Delaney family were selectors from Greta, with three sons: John, aged eighteen; William, fifteen, and Patrick, thirteen. Ned bailed up the three Delaney boys and their greyhound as they walked through the railway gates heading towards Morgan's Lookout and the Warby Ranges beyond. They had walked in from their Greta home and called in at the Reardon's to see if Michael wanted to hunt kangaroos with them. Finding no-one home, they had continued on into the township where Ned intercepted them.

Ned's family and the bush telegraph had always kept the gang up to date with what was happening in and around the district. Ned knew, for example, that the Delaneys' father had recently sold a horse to the police to be used as a remount, and that young John Delaney had enquired about joining the Victoria Police. Ned knew these things, and chose to make an example of young John Delaney in front of the others.

Ned knew the young Delaneys by sight, and they certainly knew him. He was on his horse when he ordered them to stop and remained on it through all that followed. Speaking loud enough for all those still held at the stationmaster's house to hear, Ned declared that he would take the life of anyone who aided the police in any way or even expressed sympathy for them. He could and would find such things out. Ned said that the government had made it a crime for anyone to aid the Kellys; he would now make it a crime for anyone to aid the police. In John Delaney, he had caught his first criminal. 'But I'm a fair man,' he said, and taking a pistol from his belt, offered it to Delaney, saying he could take the first shot. The terrified eighteen-year-old, shaking and with tears streaming down his cheeks, could do little beyond say no to the offer. By then, a number of the women held at Stanistreet's were calling out to Ned to let young Delaney go, fully convinced that Ned was about to shoot him dead. Ned did not respond to the women, but told Delaney to stay where he

SATURDAY NIGHT AND SUNDAY, 26/27 JUNE 1880

was and not move. A horse and buggy had just halted near the railway gates, and Ned wanted to see who it was.

* * *

On Sunday morning, schoolteacher Thomas Curnow decided to take his family for a drive to Greta for a picnic. Curnow, his wife and sister would travel in their buggy and would be accompanied by Dave Mortimer, his brother-in-law, on horseback. The group left the Curnow house at mid-morning and a few minutes later, as they approached Glenrowan township, Tom Curnow noticed that a crowd had gathered at Jones's hotel. His first thought was that Ann Jones, who he knew had been ill, may have passed away. He also noticed a man run from the hotel to the stables at the rear.

Curnow drove past the hotel towards the railway gates, stopping short of them when hailed by John Stanistreet. Curnow asked the stationmaster what was happening and in reply heard that he and his family could not go through the gates because the Kellys were here. Glancing towards the gates, Curnow saw a man on horseback leaning over and talking with some animation to a young man he knew to be John Delaney.

Tom Curnow had assumed that Stanistreet was making a joke about the Kellys, and made to move off. As he did so, the horseman ahead swivelled around and, looking directly at Curnow, asked, 'Who are you?' It was only at this point that Curnow noticed that the horseman had two revolvers tucked into his belt and the realisation set in; this was not a joke. He answered the horseman's question by identifying himself as the Glenrowan schoolteacher. The horseman then pointed to the others accompanying Curnow and asked who they were. Curnow identified his wife and sister and then Dave Mortimer before saying they were on a Sunday drive to Greta.

Looking down at the group, the horseman said, 'I'm sorry, but

I must detain you.' He ordered the Curnows from their buggy and Mortimer from his horse, directed the women to the Stanistreet house and the men to Jones's hotel, and then trotted back to where John Delaney waited. Curnow and Mortimer tied up their horses and, accompanied by John Stanistreet, walked down the road towards the hotel. As they walked Stanistreet explained that Glenrowan had been taken over by the Kellys in the early hours of Sunday morning. He told Curnow that James Reardon and others had torn up the railway track beyond the township and said that the gang planned to wreck a special train containing police and the Queensland trackers that would be passing through sometime that day. When they arrived at the hotel, one of the prisoners already there added that the Kellys had been in Beechworth the night before and had shot several police there.

* * *

When Ned returned to where John Delaney stood waiting, he made the young man promise that he would never again seek to join the police force. He then paused and said, 'I forgive you this time, but mind you be careful in the future.' He then sent Delaney to join the others at Jones's hotel.

* * *

Tom Curnow estimated that, between the stationmaster's house and Ann Jones's hotel, he was one of around 50 prisoners held in Glenrowan. They had been roughly divided between the two locations, with women and children being held at the Stanistreets's and the boys and men across the reserve at the hotel. There were no hard and fast rules in place though. One of those who remained at the Stanistreets's was Tom Cameron, the fifteen-year-old son of a railway gatekeeper from a little further down the track. Young Cameron had gone to school with sixteen-year-old Jane Jones, who was now across at the hotel helping her mother and younger brothers serve food and drink to the growing number of prisoners being held there. Most were unhappy with their situation but all – even those who sympathised with the Kellys – knew of Ned's mercurial temper, and none dared provoke it.

Around the middle of the day, Ned and Joe called all the male prisoners together in front of the hotel. After reminding those present that he, Joe, and the others were outlaws and that their instructions must be obeyed, Ned laid down a few ground rules. The prisoners, he explained, were allowed inside the hotel, and moreover could move around freely in it with the exception of the small bedroom at the rear of the main building. It would be kept locked at all times, and only the outlaws would have a key. The prisoners were also allowed to go outside but could not leave the vicinity of the hotel. Finally, the quarry labourers would be allowed to return to their tents for lunch; all others would be provided meals at the hotel by Ann Jones and her family.

Shortly after Ned's little speech, Tom Curnow entered the hotel. Just inside the front door he was approached by a jovial Dan Kelly who invited him to have a drink at the bar. Anxious to know more about what had happened and what might happen, Curnow agreed. Dan asked for brandies for both of them and as the two were drinking, Joe Byrne walked in. Noticing Dan's glass, he said, 'Be careful, old man.' Dan replied, 'All right,' and topped up his glass with water.

Curnow saw his chance. He took the opportunity to speak to both Dan and Joe, expressing obvious interest in the direction their lives had taken. He began by expressing surprise that the gang had chosen to take over Glenrowan. The reply was that Glenrowan was chosen specifically in order to wreck the train they knew would come, a train that would carry, 'inspectors, police and blacktrackers' heading to Beechworth to pick up their trail. Dan added that they had been in Beechworth the night before and that they had 'done some shooting' there. Finally, in answer to one of Curnow's questions, Joe said that while the gang had lived and eaten well, all had found the occasional lack of sleep trying. It was a conversation which started to prey on Tom Curnow's mind almost before it was over. He was now privy to the plans of an outlaw gang, plans that included the cold-blooded slaughter of men who, like him, were simply trying to do a job to the best of their ability.

After finishing his drink, Tom Curnow went outside to where most of the prisoners had formed themselves into small groups. There were a few more there now. A local farmer named Matthew Ryan and his wife and children had been detained when they ventured into Glenrowan. Curnow also noted James Kershaw and Con Maloney, farm labourers who were both thought to be Kelly sympathisers. It was now around one o'clock in the afternoon, and just as Curnow was looking for Dave Mortimer, Dan came out of the hotel with Ned a short distance behind. Dan told Curnow that Ned had decided they would have a dance. Knowing that Curnow was reputed to be a good dancer, Dan wanted to invite him to be his partner in the first dance.

Tom Curnow thought the invitation to dance might be the opportunity he had started to look for. He said he would be happy to dance with Dan, but pointed out that he was wearing heavy hob-nailed worker's boots, and suggested that he be allowed home to change into his dancing shoes. If necessary, Ned or one of the others could accompany him. Curnow's home was on the far side of the police barracks from where they now stood, and the teacher knew that Constable Bracken – whose judgement he trusted – would recognise whichever gang member went with him. Dan suggested that Ned stay and that either he or

SATURDAY NIGHT AND SUNDAY, 26/27 JUNE 1880

Joe accompany Curnow. Before a decision was made, however, one of the prisoners called out that they would have to pass the police barracks to reach the schoolteacher's house. When Ned asked him if that were true, Tom Curnow admitted that it was, and said that he had simply forgotten about it. Sparking up, he said he probably wouldn't need his dancing shoes anyway, and led the others inside.

* * *

The dance was a success. Ann, ever the survivor, looked for a way to turn the situation to her advantage. She organised for some of the men to help her clear out the dining room. The large dining table was taken outside onto the veranda, with the dining chairs stacked alongside it. Jane Jones found a fiddle and a concertina left outside where her younger brothers had been playing with them. Dave Mortimer was quite an accomplished dance caller and concertina player, while one of the other prisoners could play the fiddle. Tom Curnow and Dan Kelly led off the first dance.

It was good fun for an hour or so, the men jigging and dancing away with Dave Mortimer playing and singing and calling the dances. They would break every fifteen minutes or so to catch their breath and have a drink. While Ned, Dan and Joe all joined in at times, they stayed alert and armed and, when they drank, it was in little sips from their own glasses. When it seemed interest was flagging, Ned suggested they all go outside and he led his prisoners out the back door and into the enclosed yard.

There Ned announced that he would challenge all comers in a couple of sporting events. One was a hop, step and jump competition. Ned competed with a revolver in either hand and a third tucked into his belt. He lost, but didn't seem perturbed by this. Next was a standing long-jump, with competitors leaping from a line Ned had drawn in the dirt. Again he challenged all comers and this time his loss was a narrow one. He took the defeat in good grace, pointing out that he had been handicapped by the three pistols which conspired to weigh him down.

The sports afternoon finished with an exhibition of horse-riding and show-jumping by the three outlaws. When they finished, it was around four o'clock and the sun was beginning to drop towards Morgan's Lookout.

* * *

When the show-jumping finished and most of the men drifted back inside the hotel, Tom Curnow walked across the Railway Reserve to Stanistreet's to see how his wife and sister were faring. Both women came outside to meet him, and Tom was particularly taken by a scarf his sister was wearing. It was made of fine llama wool and it had been dyed a brilliant red. As soon as he saw it, Curnow realised that the scarf would make an excellent danger signal. Still musing about this, he followed the women back into the stationmaster's house where the first thing he saw was Steve Hart lying full length on a sofa, nursing three loaded guns.

Steve's day had so far been a long way removed from what he had hoped it would be when it started. When the others had all departed for breakfast at Jones's hotel, he had been left in charge of the women, children and sundry young people, most of who seemed to him to be either Reardons or Stanistreets. While Ned and the others were bailing up the Delaneys, the Curnows, and the Ryans, he supervised the arrival and disposition of the little members of the various families. And while the singing, dancing and games were taking place at the hotel opposite, he had to listen to the complaints and problems that young Tom Cameron, the crossing guard's son, seemed to thrive on.

To make the best of a bad situation, Steve turned to the bottle. When Ann Jones returned to her hotel to start cooking breakfast for the outlaws and their prisoners, she left behind the bottle of brandy that Jane had brought across to help Ann deaden the neuralgic pain she was suffering. Steve commandeered the bottle and its contents and used them to assuage whatever hurt feelings he may have harboured at being some distance away from where the real action seemed to be. He was a good drinker, a happy drinker, confiding to Hanorah McDonnell at one stage that he had already drunk six nobblers of brandy that morning, that it was 'bad', and that he would 'lose his head' if he did not stop.

Yet, Steve stopped drinking by noon and made certain that he had most of his wits about him. By lunchtime on Sunday there were around twenty persons, child and adult, confined in his care at the Stanistreets's. The children in particular grew restless at times, so Steve would occasionally escort small groups outside to stretch their legs. When inside, he would take up his favoured position on the sofa. At times he seemed to drift off, but then would come awake at the slightest noise, and he was never without a revolver in his hand. Ned, Joe, and Dan all paid visits during the day, laughing and joking with everyone at the Stanistreets's when they did.

Around 4.30 in the afternoon, Ned again visited the stationmaster's and announced that all adult males were to now return to Jones's hotel with him. Women and children who wanted to join their husbands and fathers were also welcome to do so. He did, however, make a couple of exceptions; Hanorah McDonnell was free to return to her hotel with her children and the Stanistreets were to stay in their home. Steve Hart would remain with them. Before he departed, John Stanistreet asked Ned if he would allow the torn-up rails to be repaired before the Monday morning passenger train came through and was wrecked; Ned refused the request. Ned's announcements had also been preceded by a couple of little incidents.

Just before Ned arrived, Tom Curnow and John Stanistreet were able to have a brief and private conversation at the rear of the stationmaster's house. The main point Stanistreet wanted Tom to understand was that someone must warn the train they were all awaiting, as otherwise there would be a massacre. Ned arrived as the two were talking, and was immediately confronted by Mrs Stanistreet who told him that Mrs Curnow should be allowed to go home because of her 'delicate state'. Ned did not agree to that, but shortly afterwards did release Hanorah McDonnell.

Tom Curnow had fragments of ideas and plans floating around in his head but none were complete and he suspected that several were either foolhardy or suicidal. Tom knew he could not afford to attract suspicion or appear to be anything but sympathetic towards the gang. He also knew he needed the gang to trust him more than they trusted the other prisoners, as this would give him more freedom to act. Tom therefore decided to ingratiate himself with Ned and the other outlaws.

The first opportunity came almost immediately when Steve Hart complained loudly about his swollen feet. Hart explained to anyone interested that he had been wearing his boots for three days and three nights and was now in some pain. Curnow took charge, quickly organising a basin of hot water for Steve to bathe his feet in. As this was happening, another incident occurred. Dan Kelly suddenly arrived and announced that he was looking for a small bag he had apparently lost. Dan was anxious, searching the whole house thoroughly but without success. Shortly after he left, Ned led his group back across to Jones's hotel.

* * *

Soon after he arrived back at Jones's, Tom Curnow approached James Reardon and asked the railwayman if he would care to share a pipe. Reardon, whose own pipe had remained on the mantelpiece at home since his rude awakening hours earlier, said he would. The two men went outside to where a group of prisoners was lighting a fire around a log. Standing a little apart from the others as they shared Curnow's pipe, the two spoke quietly about how to avert a disaster. Like Stanistreet, Reardon believed the police train must be stopped, before it entered Glenrowan if possible, but Reardon also believed that both he and the stationmaster would be too closely watched for them to do anything.

Still thinking the problem through, Tom returned to the hotel and went inside. Looking down the passageway he saw Ned talking to Ann Jones in the breezeway as the two stood close together. Curnow moved down the passage until he was near enough to overhear what they were saying. He heard Ned tell Jones that later in the evening he would go to the police barracks to capture Constable Bracken, and thought he might take Jane Jones with him to call the policeman out. Fearing he would be spotted, Curnow backed into the hotel proper and heard no more.

Postmaster Hillmorton Reynolds also saw Ann and Ned talking in the breezeway. He had noted how Jones always addressed the outlaws by their first names, and was not at all surprised that Jones appeared to be resting her arm on Ned's shoulder. He was surprised though, when Jones spotted him standing quietly near the stables, turned to Ned and said, 'Look out, Ned, he is going to escape.' He did not believe the words were spoken in jest, but rather were typical of Jones's ongoing attempts to be everything to everybody and rather than risk any unpleasantness, he too decided to join the others inside the hotel.

Ann then asked Ned what he and the others wanted for tea, and he jokingly replied that 'there are plenty of fat dogs about'.

It was not the answer Jones wanted to hear. She probably had enough fresh and preserved meat to feed the prisoners, but she was running short of everything else. Ned simply asked that the available food be brought to the dining room and then he went back into the main building. There he learned that the quarry labourers had a good supply of bread, so he sent a couple of them to their tents to bring back as much food as possible.

By now, the sun had set and it was getting dark. Later, a full moon in a cloudless sky would illuminate the scene, but for now it was becoming increasingly difficult to recognise friend from foe any distance away from the hotel. Ned crossed the reserve to the Stanistreets's and asked all left there to return to the hotel with him. The Stanistreets and Steve Hart would remain. At Jones's, he directed the remaining women and children inside. He then went across to the group standing around the fire they had made in the front yard, and spoke to them: 'Boys, you had better come in now as I cannot mind you out here, and I believe half of you are gone already.'

When all were inside, Ned ordered that the doors be locked and all keys given to the outlaws. The long day was over.

CHAPTER 6

The Dark Hours: 27/28 June 1880

Shortly before he joined the others inside, James Reardon practised his mental arithmetic, trying to add up the total number of people being held in and around Jones's hotel and the stationmaster's house. He thought of the quarry labourers and the railwaymen in their various capacities, the township dwellers and the farmers, and the wives and friends and families. The number he came up with was 62. He suspected that it might be fewer now, as the outlaws had apparently let some prisoners go home, but he also suspected he may have to add a few more before the night was over. He also knew that most of those present were, at the very least, growing apprehensive. They believed that crossing the Kellys or thwarting their plans was a death sentence. By now, they all knew what had happened to Aaron Sherrit on Saturday night.

Ann Jones locked the bar room door onto the veranda and gave the key to Dan who in turn gave her the key to a locked drinks cabinet. In a loud voice Ned then addressed those inside, telling them they were in for the evening but would soon be fed, and that there would be some entertainment afterwards. Before he organised the food, though, Ned needed to know exactly how many prisoners were being held. He told them all to stay still while Dan moved among them, counting the numbers; as he needed both hands free, Dan asked Jane Jones to hold one of his pistols. When this was finally done (although the outlaws could not agree on the final figure), Ann, Jane, and John Jones took plates of food into the dining room, parlour and bar as the prisoners all tried to find comfortable places to sit and eat. As they did so, Ned moved from room to room, speaking to some of the prisoners, nodding to others. Dan and Joe found a small table and sat down to play cards. Little things started to assume a greater significance than before, perhaps because all the prisoners were now held in relatively close confinement. Someone overheard Dan tell Ned that he thought their plan was finished and they should now leave Glenrowan. He was overruled by Ned, who said, 'I'm tired of running. We'll stand and fight.' The looks on the faces of the brothers suggested that the relationship between the two was becoming strained. The story soon circulated among the prisoners, with Tom Curnow in particular taking note of Ned's comments.

After allowing time for people to finish their evening meal, Ned announced another dance and again he oversaw the clearing of the dining room. Dave Mortimer took up his accordion, one of the labourers the fiddle, and the dance began. This time, Ned, Dan, and Joe all joined in the dancing, as did Ann and Jane Jones, and three or four others. The involvement of the Jones females was not well-received by all present. The ever-suspicious

THE DARK HOURS: 27/28 JUNE 1880

James Reardon watched closely and believed he heard Ann telling someone that Ned was a 'fine fellow'. Young Tom Cameron was even more acerbic, and would later state that Jane 'was making very free with them, getting on their knees and dancing with them and kissing them. I think six months in gaol would do her no harm'.

As the dancing continued in the dining room, outside Edward Reynolds, Hillmorton's brother, and Robert Gibbons – who boarded with the Reynolds – left their home, and walked past the hotel and up to the stationmaster's house. Young Alexander Reynolds had headed off to Sunday school earlier in the day and his non-return had become a cause for concern. The eight year old would often remain in the township on Sundays, playing with children at someone's house, but he would always return by dark, in time for dinner. The Stanistreets's was one house he liked to visit as he could pretend to be a train driver or stationmaster, and this was the first house Reynolds and Gibbons approached. Mrs Stanistreet answered their knock, telling them that the outlaw Steve Hart was inside and that the township had been held up since 3 o'clock that morning. Hart then appeared behind the stationmaster's wife, showed two revolvers, and invited them inside.

* * *

Tom Curnow made his decision. He and the other 'responsible' prisoners simply could not let the outlaws' plan succeed. Neither Stanistreet nor Reardon were in a position to be of any real assistance because they were being too closely watched, and Tom doubted whether many of the other prisoners had either the inclination or the courage to try to interfere with the outlaws' plan. He doubted that he would have the opportunity to sound out any other prisoners and recruit one or more to his cause and, besides, he was not certain who among them he could trust. If anyone was going to act, Tom decided it would have to be him.

Curnow reckoned that Ned viewed him as being neutral or perhaps slightly favourable towards the outlaws. His clumsy attempt to warn Constable Bracken earlier in the day had been dismissed as a simple mistake by a lame schoolteacher, and he knew they had all been impressed by his willingness to join in the afternoon dancing and his concern for his 'delicate' wife. Dan Kelly in particular seemed to like the little schoolteacher. All this was not enough, though, and Curnow knew that he had to win more trust, as more trust meant more freedom and he would need that freedom to carry out the plan that he had formulated.

As the evening wore on, the dancing slowed and by 9 o'clock had ceased as the prisoners started wondering how much longer they would be there and what would happen next. Seeing Ned standing alone, Tom Curnow took the chance to ask Ned if they could have a few quiet words. When Ned said yes, Curnow told him that stationmaster Stanistreet kept a loaded revolver in his office at the station in case of robberies. He said that only a few people knew of the gun, but added that while Stanistreet himself was unlikely to use the weapon, Tom could not vouch for any others who might know it was there. Ned looked closely at Curnow for a few minutes, and then thanked him for the information.

A few minutes later, Ned announced to all in the dining room that he would shortly be going out to collect Constable Bracken but that he wanted them all to continue dancing while he did so. As he walked past Tom, the young teacher joked that he would give £100 to see Ned arrest Bracken, and asked if he could go with him. Ned indicated that Curnow should just wait. Leaving the hotel, Ned walked across to the Stanistreets's where he met Edward Reynolds and Robert Gibbons and then told them to return with him at once to Jones's. Gibbons estimated the time to be 10 o'clock.

THE DARK HOURS: 27/28 JUNE 1880

Once back at the hotel, Ned and Joe disappeared into the small back room, leaving Dan to keep an eye on the prisoners who were now sitting and talking in pairs and small family groups; none were dancing. When the two outlaws came out of the bedroom about ten minutes later, Ned was wearing armour. Although the prisoners all knew that the outlaws possessed armour, and a privileged few had been given a showing of it, this was the first time the majority of those present had actually seen what it looked like. The effect was impressive; already a tall man, Ned appeared to be a giant when wearing his armour, an effect accentuated when he also donned his heavy helmet. If the intent had been to either impress or intimidate the prisoners, Ned succeeded on both counts.

Tom Curnow again approached Ned, this time asking if he could take his family home when Ned went out to collect Bracken. He reiterated his point about supporting the Kellys 'heart and soul'. Ned replied that he could see that, and Tom said his family could also offer some practical support. If his brother-in-law, Dave Mortimer, came with them, Mortimer would be able to call Bracken out from his house because the two men were friends and knew each other's voices. Ned finally agreed with all this, and directed Curnow to leave through the back door – unlocked for him by Dan – hitch up his buggy, and meet them at the front of the hotel.

After Curnow left, Ned called over Edward Reynolds and Robert Gibbons and told them that they would be accompanying him to the police barracks, as would young Alexander Reynolds, who could ride in the buggy with the Curnows. While he appreciated the assistance that Dave Mortimer offered, Ned was also aware that Reynolds and Gibbons were Bracken's immediate neighbours and, as they had seen at the Sherrit's, neighbour's calls could be more compelling than others'. Young Alexander

103

Reynolds also provided some kind of guarantee that everyone would cooperate.

When all was ready, Ned led the little group, including the Curnow women, out to the front of the hotel. When Tom arrived, Ned directed the two ladies and Alexander Reynolds into the buggy; he, Joe and Dave Mortimer mounted and rode, while Edward Reynolds and Robert Gibbons walked in front. It was only a few hundred metres to the police barracks; they would be there in five minutes. As they moved off, Ned said coldly that if there was any resistance, the rats of Glenrowan would feast on the carcases of fat policemen that night.

* * *

Ned ordered a halt just twenty metres short of the police barracks, then dismounted and told Dave Mortimer to do the same. Leaving Joe to keep an eye on the rest of the party, Ned led Mortimer to the front of the barracks. While he took up a position that allowed him to cover both Mortimer and the front door with his rifle, he told Mortimer to knock on that door and to call for Bracken. This Dave Mortimer did for a full two minutes, but without result. Puzzled, Ned led Mortimer back to the buggy, and called on Edward Reynolds to come with him to the barracks.

Inside the barracks, Constable Hugh Bracken was struggling to wake up. He had been bed-ridden with gastric flu for several days and was drifting in and out of sleep, unsure whether Mortimer's knocking and calling had been a dream or not. He was certainly awake, though, when he heard and recognised Edward Reynolds asking him to open the front door. As he pulled on his clothes, he was certain that he heard a second voice joining in. Arming himself with his service revolver and a shotgun, Bracken cautiously opened the front door.

THE DARK HOURS: 27/28 JUNE 1880

As he did so, a large man in an iron helmet held a revolver to his head, ordering him to 'Bail Up!' The man then identified himself as Ned Kelly. It didn't seem real to Bracken, who asked the helmeted figure if he were another policeman having a bit of a lark. This brought an instant response: 'Throw up your arms or you are a dead man', spoken in a tone that was flat but deadly serious. Bracken put his shotgun against the wall, his revolver on the floor, and did as he was told.

Ned took off his helmet, and gave it to Reynolds, telling him to take it back to the others and wait for him there. He then followed Bracken into the barracks, to the bedroom where an anxious Mrs Bracken was sitting up in bed with their young son. Ned introduced himself, shaking hands with the boy and quipping, 'I may yet be worth £2000 to you, my child.' He asked Bracken for handcuffs but accepted with equanimity the policeman's claim that they were locked away elsewhere in the building.

Ned told Bracken to dress fully as he would be coming with him, but moved to reassure Mrs Bracken that as long as her husband followed orders no harm would come to anyone. Ned and Bracken chatted quite amiably as the policemen finished dressing. Ned allowed Bracken to farewell his wife, and then led the horse and rider back to where the others waited.

The moon had risen and visibility was good but it was becoming very cold back at the buggy where a nervous Tom Curnow rubbed his hands and stamped his feet to stay warm. When Ned arrived leading the mounted policeman, Tom was calculating how close to midnight it actually was. Without any real preamble, Ned told Tom that he and his family were free to go, suggesting that they go directly home and then straight to bed, warning Tom, 'Don't dream too loud.' He then casually suggested that if they did otherwise they would probably be shot. He added that he would be sending a man down later to check on them.

105

With that, Ned and Joe mounted their horses, the Curnows climbed back into their buggy, and the two groups went their separate ways.

* * *

Ned's party headed north towards Jones's hotel, Robert Gibbons and Edward and Alexander Reynolds on foot, followed by Dave Mortimer, Hugh Bracken, Joe, and Ned all on horseback. Joe held the reins of Bracken's horse, as Ned said that he was not ready to trust him. As they walked their horses slowly down the road, Ned and Hugh Bracken continued the conversation they had started in the policeman's bedroom. Bracken told Ned that he believed in all sincerity that the only reason he was captured so easily was that he had been ill in bed all day. He added that had his horse been in its prime, it would have taken more than Ned Kelly to have kept him prisoner. Ned listened and brooded. They were soon back at the hotel. Ned led the prisoners inside while Joe tied up the horses. When he came back inside, he locked the door behind him.

Heading in the other direction, Tom Curnow waited until he was certain they were well clear of the outlaws before he began to tell his wife and sister about his plan. He would go to Benalla, he told them, and warn the authorities that the Kellys had taken over Glenrowan and planned to destroy the police train sent to capture them. If Tom had expected support for his plan, he was sorely disappointed. Both women argued vigorously with him. Did he really think, they asked, that the Kellys would let them leave the hotel if someone wasn't keeping an eye on them? And how could he think that the Kellys wouldn't have spies watching every road and track out of Glenrowan? And even if by some miracle he did succeed, would not the entire family be hunted down and killed afterwards? At this point they arrived home.

THE DARK HOURS: 27/28 JUNE 1880

Tom would not and could not let the carnage he foresaw in the Kelly's plan take place, and so he changed tactics. Tom sent the ladies inside, saying he would tidy up outside. He unhitched the horse from the buggy, and led it into the stable, saying he was going to feed it there.

* * *

After he closed and locked the front door, Joe Byrne placed the key on the mantelpiece above the fire in the dining room, then turned to look at the crowd. There were more here now than there had been when he and Ned had left almost two hours earlier, and the reason was soon obvious. In their absence, Steve Hart had brought all the prisoners across from the Stanistreets's. Hart and Dan were currently in the bar, talking to Ned, asking him whether it was time to recognise that the plan had been overtaken by events and that they should leave Glenrowan. With a flash of anger, Ned said that the time for running was over, and the issue would be decided here, in Glenrowan. He instructed Steve to collect John Stanistreet and return to the stationmaster's house.

Ned then crossed the passageway and entered the dining room, calling for quiet as he entered. Perhaps he was angry at his brother and Steve Hart or there may have been something building since Bracken suggested that, if fit, he was more than a match for Ned. He was tired and he was frustrated and nothing seemed to be happening in the way he had hoped it would. Whatever the reason, a reservoir of anger and frustration came boiling out of Ned and, addressing those in the dining room, he launched into a tirade initially against the Victorian government. He was especially critical of a parliamentarian named Graves who had suggested that a scorched earth policy be implemented in the north-east to force the gang to surrender. He also attacked

Premier Graham Berry for giving the police far too much money when funding the hunt for the Kellys.

Turning to stare at Bracken, he asked him to describe the policeman's oath. Bracken replied that, 'policemen were sworn to do their duty, without malice or favour, and to deal even-handed justice all around'. Ned scoffed and responded that one of the Greta constables had once told him, 'the oath was that a policeman had to lag any person, no matter whether it was father, mother, brother or daughter, if they were but arrested'.

Ned then suggested that there were probably twenty men in the Victoria Police who were greater rogues than he, a point Bracken conceded. Warming to the topic, Ned said, 'We have just shot one bloody traitor, and now we want that bloody Detective Ward, but he is not game to show up. The next I want are those six little demons [the trackers], then O'Connor and Hare. If I killed them, I would feel easy and contented.' He added, for emphasis, that he doubted the ability of the Queensland natives to operate successfully in Victoria, whereas he could track an emu all across Queensland.

Turning to the prisoners, Ned said, 'If any of you ever see or hear any of us crossing the railway, or at any other place, and if the police should come and ask you if you had seen any such party, you must say, "No, we saw nobody." If I ever hear of any of you giving the police any information I will shoot you down like dogs. I do not mind a policeman doing his duty as long as he does not overdo it.' Bracken could not let this pass, calling back that the police were only earning an honest living. He asked Ned how, if he were an honest man, he could get on with life without the police.

Ned: Am I not an honest man?

Bracken: I'm damned if you are!

Most laughed at this exchange.

THE DARK HOURS: 27/28 JUNE 1880

Ned then called up a man named Sullivan, probably not the Dennis Sullivan who had helped tear up the rails earlier. He said to this man, 'I have seen you somewhere else. Have you been in Wangaratta lately?' Sullivan replied that he had. Ned then asked if he was the Sullivan who had informed on his mates in New Zealand. For Ned, as low as he believed most policemen were, there was always a rank below them, men who lagged on their mates and who were prepared to put their own skins ahead of all else. In the same rank, Ned included those who killed from ambush, who shot from behind, like the man who killed Dan Morgan. Ned again turned to Bracken and the wider audience: 'Eight thousand pounds has been offered for our capture. I promise to give you a similar amount if you tell me where that Sullivan is to be found and the same amount for information as to where I can find Quinlan, the man who shot Morgan.' And then, his passion spent, Ned stopped talking.

* * *

The back and forth argument between Ned and Bracken was being matched as it occurred, and not too far away, in the kitchen of Tom Curnow's house. The argument that had started in the buggy continued after the Curnows arrived home. When he came inside from stabling the horse, Tom suggested they all have a light supper before retiring, and said he was going to tidy himself up before eating. When he could see the two women immersed in food preparation, he collected his sister's red scarf, a candle and some matches.

As the three sat in the kitchen to eat, Tom explained that his plan was a good one, a safe one. He would not travel by road, he now said, as that would be too dangerous. Instead, he would travel on or alongside the railway line. If the police special train left before he arrived at Benalla, he would be able to flag it down.

The slight variation made the plan acceptable to his sister but not his wife, who was becoming hysterical. She turned on Tom and screamed at him that if he left then she, their unborn child, and his sister would all stay in the house where they would all be murdered.

Seeking some way to calm his wife, Tom suggested they all go to see her parents, whose farmhouse was just a few minutes' walk away. Eventually Isobel Curnow agreed to the proposal and the three rugged-up and set off. Tom was very cognisant of Ned's earlier warning that someone would be around to check up on them. He therefore left the doors unlocked and put a note on the kitchen table saying that they had all gone to the Mortimers to get medicine for Curnow's sister, as she was very ill. As they set off, Tom guessed it was around one o'clock in the morning on Monday, 28 June.

* * *

Ned's speech had been confronting, as he probably intended, and when he finished the mood in the hotel was sombre. He recognised this, and it was not the mood he wanted. What he wanted was support, a feeling of camaraderie and, most of all, he wanted people to both understand and appreciate the forces that had brought him to this place. A number of small children were growing increasingly restive, and Ned made the snap decision that he would release those who could do him no harm. Thus, he announced that Mrs Stanistreet and her children were free to return home. There was no real risk in the decision as Steve Hart was still at the stationmaster's house, and his wife and children would remain hostage to John Stanistreet's continued cooperation.

When the Stanistreets had departed, Ned said they would now have a Sunday night concert and dance. He directed the

THE DARK HOURS: 27/28 JUNE 1880

labourers to clear all the furniture out of the parlour and invited young John Jones to open the entertainment. The boy did so, singing his version of 'The Kelly Song'.

> Farewell to my home in Greta, my sister fare thee well,
> It grieves my heart to leave you, but here I must not dwell,
> They placed a price upon my head, my hands are stained with gore,
> And I must roam the forest wild within the Australian shore,
> But if they cross my cherished path, by all I hold on earth,
> I'll give them cause to rue the day their mothers gave them birth.
> See, yonder ride four troopers, one kiss before we part,
> Now haste and join your comrades, Dan, Joe Byrne and Stevie Hart.

His singing earned John both the appreciation of the outlaws and sixpence from his mother. Dave Mortimer and his concertina were next put to good use, and the dancing commenced with a series of quadrilles; Ned dancing with Jane Jones, Dan with her mother, and Joe with one of the other prisoners. The dancing ended around half past one in the morning, many of those present by now close to collapse, and again John Jones was asked to sing. He sang a popular favourite, 'The Wild Colonial Boy', and finished with a traditional Irish ballad, 'The Pretty Girl Milking the Cow'. When he finished it was quiet as most in the room looked inwards at the end of a long and trying day.

* * *

As the Curnows finished their preparations to visit Isobel's parents, Tom produced his sister's red scarf and asked her to wear it. The walk to the senior Mortimer's house was less than a kilometre and normally took around ten minutes. This evening, though, the journey seemed to take forever. As they walked, Isobel grew increasingly agitated and was again nearing hysteria as they approached her parents' home. She only began to calm down when Tom agreed that they would turn back home. There, Tom and his sister told Isobel that he would now abandon his plan, and they convinced the distraught woman that it was now safe for her to go to bed. As his sister was helping Isobel do just that, Tom slipped out the back door, made his way to the stable, and began to harness his horse.

Curnow estimated that the time must have now been around two o'clock in the morning and, as he prepared to lift a saddle onto his horse, he heard the sound of a train in the distance, towards Benalla, building up speed for the long straight run to Glenrowan.

At that sound, Tom Curnow made a snap decision, something the careful young schoolteacher had rarely done. He grabbed his matches, candle, and scarf, and set off on foot for the railway line. There he stepped between the rails and walked, in his peculiar shuffling gait, down the track towards Benalla. When he came to the long straight stretch, Tom lit the candle and held his sister's scarf in front of the flame. He hoped that whoever was looking ahead from the train coming down the tracks would see his little signal and, moreover, see it for what it was: a warning to stop.

The shape ahead gradually resolved itself into a railway engine, one that slowed to a stop well short of Tom Curnow, who walked towards it. As he did so, a guard stuck his head from the engine's cabin and hailed Curnow. A voice said, 'What's the matter?' Tom Curnow called back, 'The Kellys'.

*   *   *

In the brief silence that followed John Jones's singing, Ned thought about letting all the prisoners go home, knowing that in doing so he would be abandoning his Glenrowan plan. He

THE DARK HOURS: 27/28 JUNE 1880

told Dave Mortimer that he doubted whether a police train had even been despatched. When Mortimer asked him if that meant the prisoners would now be released, Ned said yes, it did, and they would probably be released in a very short time. New rumour that they were about to be released swept through the hotel, gaining some additional detail as it went. Some prisoners were told that the police knew they were there, and the Kellys were simply withdrawing in order to attack the police from a different angle. Most of the prisoners didn't really care anymore. They did not feel as though they were under any direct threat and simply wanted to go home for a good meal and a sleep.

* * *

When the engine came to a complete stop, the guard jumped down and approached Tom Curnow, by then standing at the side of the rails. Curnow explained that the line beyond Glenrowan had been torn up while the township itself had been taken over by the Kelly Gang. The Kellys were still there, waiting to ambush the police aboard the special train. Unfortunately, Tom didn't specify where 'there' was, leaving the impression that the gang could have been anywhere amongst the cluster of buildings that made up the township.

The guard explained to Tom that his was a pilot engine, and he believed they should take it into Glenrowan to await the arrival of the police special travelling a short distance behind. Curnow was appalled, and called out, 'No! No! Don't do that or you will all get shot.' At this, the guard said that he would have to go back to warn the police special, and he asked Tom who he was. Curnow replied that he was the Glenrowan schoolteacher, but he also asked the guard to keep his identity a secret or his life would be put at risk.

As the two were speaking, the driver of the pilot engine noticed the police special approaching. It seemed to be slowing but to make sure the pilot engine sounded its steam whistle. It sounded one continuous blast at first, the railwayman's signal for 'Caution – danger ahead'.

* * *

Ned called all the prisoners into the dining room and stood on a chair at the back. Old Martin Cherry, about to leave with one of the Ryan children, was directed away from the door by Joe and stood in the passageway to listen to what Ned had to say. Ned opened with a familiar theme, warning those present against cooperating in any way with the police. 'If I hear of anyone doing so,' he said, 'I will shoot him!'

Ned then again expressed his fear of the Queensland trackers, saying that a white man stood no chance with them. He said the main reason he had torn up the rails was to kill them all. He said that he was also surprised that a police train had not yet arrived, and surmised that it was either taking another route or else the police suspected that the gang were waiting for them somewhere, and were seeking further information before they travelled. He then went into an explanation of the Euroa and Jerilderie raids, suggesting the latter was simply a by-product of his ongoing search for the New Zealand informer, Sullivan, whom the gang had tracked to the Riverina. Ned said that he would personally promise £500 to the man who told him where Sullivan could be found.

Ned told his audience how he had organised travel to Melbourne to purchase revolvers, rifles and ammunition, and he was detailing those purchases when a sound in the distance made him pause. Some thought it might have been a rooster crowing but when it was repeated Ned recognised it as a train whistle. He jumped from the chair, looked across at the other outlaws, and said, 'By God, that bastard Curnow has deceived us.'

* * *

Back at the railway line, the guard promised to keep Curnow's identity a secret, and invited the schoolteacher to climb aboard and travel with himself and the driver. Tom declined, saying that he had to return home to his wife and sister. It was just as well that he did. Isobel Curnow had not gone to sleep and in the absence of her husband had worked herself into a nervous collapse. Their house was close to the railway engine and every noise from that engine and the following train could be heard quite clearly. Isobel Curnow flinched every time a train whistle blew.

As far as Tom was aware, he and his family were the only prisoners the Kellys had released who were not long-time sympathisers. They were therefore the only ones who would have been likely to stop the train. Any retribution would probably be directed at them. When he arrived home, Tom spent several minutes calming and reassuring his wife, telling her they had certainly done the right thing and that everyone would be safe because of what they did. Tom wasn't going to take any unnecessary risks, though; he and his sister extinguished all the lights in the house and hid the red scarf and wet clothes that he had worn. The three agreed that should one of the gang call in at their house, they would deny Tom had stopped the train.

* * *

At the hotel, the gang sprang into action. Dan was despatched to confirm what they all suspected, and was shortly heard galloping away. He was back within five minutes, bursting through the front door and saying, 'Ned, here comes the bloody train.' Ned told all within earshot that Curnow had betrayed them, and that there would now be shooting. As the outlaws spoke to one another, the prisoners too started moving and talking among themselves. Tom Cameron spoke to James Reardon, saying he believed they could now all go home, a comment which was overheard by Jane Jones. She warned both against leaving without permission.

Ned went very briefly into the small bedroom at the rear which the outlaws had turned into a combined armoury and storeroom, then went outside and rode off. Joe locked the front door after his departure, again returning the key to its place on the mantelpiece. When Joe then left the room for the rear bedroom, Hugh Bracken quickly snatched the key and dropped it into the cuff of his trousers.

Ned had ridden across to the Stanistreet house where he told Steve that he and the stationmaster should now return to the hotel. Ned rode back and tied his horse to a rail in the hotel's rear yard as Steve and John Stanistreet walked across the Railway Reserve. All three entered the hotel through the back door, although Stanistreet quickly left the main building and joined Ann and Jane Jones, two younger children and Jock McHugh in the rear kitchen. Ned and Joe walked out front to where they could see the now-moving trains, and then returned to the hotel.

Time now seemed to compress as events piled one upon the other. Ned and Joe had been wearing their armour for some time, although without helmets, and as they kept an eye on the prisoners, Dan and Steve went into the small bedroom to don theirs. The prisoners again heard grunting and thumping, plus the occasional swear word, and then Dan and Steve appeared in full armour. The four made an impressive sight. One of the prisoners, probably Dave Mortimer, was struck by what he saw:

> This was the first time that I had seen the men in their full dress and the thought inwardly struck me that the police would stand

a very poor show indeed when opposed to these desperate men, clad as they were in what seemed complete armour.

By now, the prisoners and outlaws could clearly hear the train's whistle and the sound of the engines and carriages slowly clanking up the rise and into the station. They then heard the train stop, John Lowe recalling, 'We heard the dropping of truck doors, unloading of horses, men talking, and things were all of a bustle for a short time.' As the train slowed, Ned had called out, 'You will see some play now boys. We will shoot them all.' He told them there was likely to be heavy firing and – if so – they should all get as close to the floor as possible. He then ordered that all lights and fires inside the hotel be extinguished and all curtains drawn. Dan pulled the curtains together and tipped water on the fire in the dining room. Ann Jones, who had come inside to hear any instructions issued, doused the lights and emptied a bucket of water on the parlour fire.

The four outlaws then went down the passageway and out the back door, where they stood talking quietly in the breezeway. Not far behind them, Hugh Bracken, too, moved quietly along the passageway and made his way to the larger bedroom, where many of the women and children had now taken shelter. He told those inside that, no matter what happened, they should stay where they were and try to stay calm. And, he added, 'Lie down as flat as you possibly can on the floor, it is the only chance you have got.' He returned to the dining room, still not noticed by the outlaws at the back door, and thought that he would never have a better chance to escape. He took the key from his trouser cuff and unlocked the front door. He paused briefly before telling those inside to stay down. Then he stepped out, crossed the veranda and ran down the path towards the train that he could see being unloaded at the station.

Dan returned to the dining room shortly after Bracken had left and loudly told those present that anyone who attempted to leave would now be shot. He then rejoined the others, and the four men in armour walked down the side of the hotel to the front veranda where Steve, Dan and Joe took up positions looking across the Railway Reserve to the station. Ned walked some little distance further, before turning back to the hotel where he took up a position in front and to the side of the others. With no outlaws present in the hotel, a small group of prisoners went to the back door and ventured outside for a look. They could see the train and the station quite clearly and watched as two small groups of men left the platform and proceeded, by different routes, through the open countryside towards the hotel. They could see, too, that the men were heavily armed and that they were moving quickly, as if eager to get something over and done with.

CHAPTER 7

The Police Special

On Monday morning, the Melbourne *Argus* would publish a front page report on the origins of the incident still unfolding at Glenrowan. The report would begin:

> The first intimation of the affair received by the police in Melbourne was the following telegram: 'Watch party stuck up by the Kelly gang at 6 o'clock Saturday night. Aaron Sherrit shot dead . . . Joe Byrne shot him through the eye, next through the body . . . It was only at half-past 11 one of the constables was able to get to Beechworth. M. E. Ward, Detective.

The timings were wrong and the facts either mismatched or imagined. It was the beginning of a cover-up of police incompetence from one angle, and of sheer cowardice from another. But in many ways it was symptomatic of what was becoming characteristic of the events unfolding at Glenrowan – confusion. Confusion, with an early dash of spin thrown in.

* * *

At 10 o'clock on Sunday morning, Superintendent Frank Hare had walked from the Benalla police barracks to the Benalla Post Office where the telegraphed reports from the various police barracks across north-east Victoria indicated that all was quiet in the region. Hare spoke to the postmaster and arranged to return at 9 o'clock that evening to receive updates. Yet a railway messenger interrupted Hare's lunch at the Commercial Hotel with a message from the Benalla stationmaster directing him to the post office, where he met John Sadleir and with him read and digested the news from Beechworth.

Sergeant Steele had been the first recipient of Detective Ward's news about the death of Aaron Sherrit, news delayed by the seventeen hours it had taken Constable Harry Armstrong to travel to Beechworth from Sherrit's hut. When he did receive the news, Steele had sprung into action. He first ordered a subordinate to pass Armstrong's news on to Benalla and Melbourne, and then set about securing his own part of the north-east. He organised a mobile patrol and static watch-posts at all the local bridges and crossing places on the Ovens River, posting his best trooper – Mounted Constable James Dwyer – at the most crucial of these, the railway bridge near the station. Then he sat back to wait for either further orders or further developments, whichever came first.

Hare and Sadleir also spent most of Sunday afternoon sitting down. In their case, both were working, sending and receiving telegrams and trying to get a feel for what was happening at both ends of a line stretching 250 kilometres from Beechworth to Melbourne. From the Beechworth end, there were a few additional details about the Sherrit murder, but nothing concrete on the whereabouts of those responsible. The responses, or lack thereof from the Melbourne end, were also puzzling. Hare's first telegrams had been sent to his boss and patron, Commissioner Standish, but several hours later he had still not received a reply. Instead, Hare was communicating directly with Victoria's Chief Secretary, Robert Ramsay, and these communications were somewhat terse at times. One of Hare's early requests was for Inspector O'Connor and his Queensland Native Police. Ramsay responded by saying that they could not possibly be sent before Monday morning. Suspecting that the Kellys would be long gone by then, Hare shot back: 'If they are not sent up by special train tonight, they need not come.'

Feeling increasingly alone and exposed in Benalla as the day wore on, Hare wondered what was actually happening in Melbourne.

* * *

Inspector Stanhope O'Connor and his Native Police were doing nothing more than relaxing on that Sunday afternoon. They had returned to Melbourne from Benalla just two days previously, and now had a few free days in Melbourne before returning to Queensland. The Victorian and Queensland governments had agreed that O'Connor's troopers would be replaced by another team of Native Police specifically recruited for service in Victoria; O'Connor and his men would depart for Brisbane as soon as the replacements arrived. In the meantime, O'Connor and his wife were staying at the Prout Webb's residence, The Ferns, in Flemington; his troopers were quartered at Essendon police barracks.

Because all government offices were closed on Sundays, Robert Ramsay set up a temporary headquarters at the Melbourne Club in Collins Street, and it was here that Commissioner Standish found him in the early evening. Quickly apprised of the circumstances of Sherrit's murder, and of what had and hadn't been done since, Standish also took decisive action. Recognising that the Native Police would be central to any response Frank Hare proposed, he sent an immediate message to O'Connor and another to the Railways Commissioner, asking that a special train for police use be prepared at Spencer Street station.

At 7.30 pm, relaxing in Flemington, O'Connor received a note from Commissioner Standish:

> Melbourne Club, 27 June 1880. My Dear Sir, I have just received telegraphic information that the outlaws stuck up the police party that was watching Mrs Byrne's house [sic] ... Could you return to Beechworth with your trackers by the early train tomorrow, or by a special train if that can be arranged ...?

The note was brought by hansom cab and O'Connor immediately took the cab back to the Melbourne Club where he agreed to assist the Victoria Police if the Victorian government sought and gained approval from the Queensland government for him and his troopers to offer further assistance. Standish agreed to this condition, which was met within the hour.

O'Connor returned to Flemington to prepare himself and then travelled to Essendon to prepare his men. All were ready to depart by 9.45 pm.

* * *

Like their colleagues elsewhere in the Victorian public service, Sunday was also a day of rest for the staff of the Victorian railways, and people had to be called in to crew the police special train. Eventually a driver named Henry Alder, a fireman named

THE POLICE SPECIAL

Hugh Burch and a guard named Archibald McPhee arrived at Spencer Street station. While Alder and McPhee had been easily located, a railway messenger had to wait at Burch's home until he had returned from evening services at his local church. All three were told that they were required for a 'fast' special train that had been requested by the police commissioner himself. The only problem was that all the railway engines were cold, and it would take until after 10 pm to build up a large enough head of steam to depart.

While no-one would ever take personal credit (or responsibility) for issuing the invitations, when the police special pulled into the platform at Spencer Street prior to its departure, there was a small party of journalists waiting to board. Thomas Carrington of the *Australasian Sketcher* joined the *Age*'s John McWhirter, George Allen from the *Daily Telegraph* and Joe Melvin of the *Argus*. All were rugged up against the cold while Melvin was carrying a little extra something, a small pistol he sometimes took on assignment, 'for protection'.

What stopped in front of the reporters, though, were an engine, a guard's van, and a first-class carriage containing several luxurious compartments. What it did not contain and would not pick up at Benalla was a first aid kit or anyone with medical or nursing training.

The police special pulled out of Spencer Street station at almost exactly 10 pm. Gradually picking up speed as it headed north, the train passed through several darkened inner-suburban railway stations before stopping at Essendon. There, waiting patiently on the platform, were Stanhope O'Connor, his five Native Police and two ladies. Mrs O'Connor and her sister, Mrs Prout Webb, would be travelling to Beechworth with the police contingent, although, as they assured the reporters, they would only be doing so as 'observers'.

The introductions over, the various passengers settled down in the carriage, O'Connor and the two ladies in one compartment, the reporters in another and the Native Police in a third. They had been told they were aboard a 'fast' train; most wondered just what exactly that meant.

* * *

Superintendent Francis Hare loved movement and action. As Sunday afternoon moved towards Sunday evening he found himself sitting in a room in the Benalla post office, reading and composing telegrams while fighting off the after-effects of a heavy cold. His body might have been confined to a room but his imagination was free to wander and he soon came up with what he thought was a workable plan. He was still uncertain whether or not a police special would be despatched from Melbourne, so his plan had to be flexible. Hare's plan was that, at or around midnight, a train carrying policemen, their horses, supplies and equipment would depart Benalla and travel to Wangaratta where it would be attached to an engine sent from Beechworth with the specific purpose of taking the police party as close as possible to the site of the Sherrit atrocity. The Victorian police, with or without the Queensland trackers, would detrain at Beechworth and ride to Sherrit's hut where their real work would begin.

Planning completed, Hare sent for Senior Constable John Kelly, instructing his subordinate to meet him at the post office. When Kelly arrived, Hare gave him a full briefing on what had happened in both Beechworth and Melbourne and on what he now planned to do about the circumstances that had arisen. He then gave Kelly his orders. Firstly, he was to go to Benalla railway station and there see Stationmaster Stevens and ask him to have a special train made ready for later that evening. By Hare's estimation, even if they left Benalla by midnight, they would not

THE POLICE SPECIAL

be in Beechworth much before 4 o'clock in the morning and at Sherrit's hut before dawn.

Kelly should then return to the police barracks and set about organising horses, provisions and equipment for a police party of up to a dozen troopers and officers who may be in the mountains for several days. He should also put Constables Barry, Canny, Gascoigne, Kirkham, Arthur, and Phillips on notice for probable travel later that evening. After Kelly had departed, Hare sent off a runner with an invitation for a civilian to join the police party. The civilian was Charles Rawlins, a well-connected local grazier, stock and station agent who was also an excellent bushman with an encyclopaedic knowledge of the north-east and its inhabitants. Stationmaster Stevens soon assembled his team for the Benalla police special, summoning a driver named Coleman, a fireman named Bowman and a guard named Bell. He also put on notice another guard, a slight young man named Jesse Dowsett, telling him not to go too far from Benalla station as he too might be needed later that evening. Hare's last instruction was that everyone would meet on the platform at Benalla station at midnight. He suggested that those who were able to grab some sleep should do just that as they all had a long night ahead.

* * *

His men and the civilians were all waiting on the platform when Hare arrived promptly at midnight. All were rugged up against the cold – overcoats, hats, scarves and the like – and they stood in a little group that clearly had two components. The first was the civilians. Jesse Dowsett and his gun had been sent home to get as much sleep as he could, but guard Bell and Charles Rawlins stood apart from the others. Rawlins was at least as nervous as the others, and tried to laugh things off with a joke about bringing back the remains of the Kellys for interment in Benalla cemetery.

The larger group was the police party, standing and stamping their feet as they tried to keep warm. They stood under the watchful eye of John Kelly, who was perhaps thinking of his two friends, Michael Kennedy and Michael Scanlan; dead at the hands of the Kellys and buried these eighteen months or more. John Kelly had assembled a good team to take to Beechworth, a mix of youth and experience, with a variety of backgrounds and skills but, more importantly, with steadiness of character and strength of will. His team included Mounted Constables Daniel Barry and William Canny, the latter an especially valuable policeman as he was widely regarded as one of the best trackers in the Victoria Police. Canny may not have been as good as the Queensland Native Police but if they did not arrive, he would be the best tracker available in the north-east. While the other police carried Martini-Henry carbines as well as Colt revolvers, Canny was armed with a double-barrelled shotgun. If he was called into action, he suspected it would be at close range.

For direct support, John Kelly would be relying on the experience and judgement of Mounted Constable James Arthur. A native-born Australian from Victoria's Western District, for several years Arthur had been a model of what a Victorian country policeman should be. He had all the necessary skills; as a trainee at the police depot, his drill instructor had written that 'he is the grandest shot in the depot', but his judgement and tact were most valued by John Kelly. Arthur was one of those rare policemen who was both respected and liked by his local community for his honesty and for the way he handled sometimes difficult arrests. Arthur also had the advantage of knowing Ned Kelly, having first met him when he escorted the then sixteen-year-old Ned to court on a charge of horse theft.

THE POLICE SPECIAL

Kelly had also included two of the younger policemen, firm friends who did not have a depth of police experience like Arthur, but who had personal qualities that he believed would be important in whatever lay ahead. The two were Mounted Constables William Phillips and Charles Gascoigne. Prior to being posted to Benalla, Phillips had been an orderly to Commissioner Standish, giving rise to a rumour that Phillips had never fired a gun. In fairness to the young policeman though, it should also be pointed out that in the eighteen months he had so far spent in Benalla, Phillips believed that the furthest he had travelled from the police barracks was around four kilometres. He also had a somewhat caustic sense of humour. When Hare first met Phillips in Benalla, he jokingly asked the younger man why he had not yet caught the Kellys. 'Because they haven't visited our camp yet,' was the reply. Since that exchange, Phillips had spent all his time guarding banks in Benalla's main street.

Phillips' contemporary and best friend was Patrick Charles Gascoigne, known to all as Charles. All except Phillips, that is, who called him Paddy. Like Phillips, Charles Gascoigne was a recent recruit, having joined the Victoria Police in March 1879. Gascoigne was also one of the few Australian-born policemen, and had grown up in the north-east where both his parents had been born into pioneering families; he knew the area and its people well. He had already accompanied several patrols into the mountains, and had acquitted himself well.

The final member of the team was the young and fair-haired Mounted Constable Thomas Kirkham. Like several of the others, Benalla was Kirkham's first posting and he had been there since early 1879. Kirkham was chosen because he had been working closely with O'Connor and the Native Police. If they arrived, he would again be a valuable go-between because both groups of police knew and trusted him. If they did not arrive, he was another body who could aim a gun and pull a trigger.

And so the little groups waited on the platform at Benalla. They had loaded their horses aboard a stock carriage, and then stacked their arms, ammunition, and provisions on the platform. The police special from Melbourne was a fast train, and they had all been informed that it had left Melbourne at 10 o'clock on Sunday evening. Melbourne was 200 kilometres away. They wondered how long the train would take to cover that distance.

* * *

After pulling out of Essendon station, the police special quickly reached top speed on the long, gentle, downhill run through Broadmeadows and beyond. It was not a particularly gentle ride for those aboard, however, with their carriage swaying from side to side quite alarmingly at times. It was definitely a fast ride, at least until the small township of Craigieburn. A minute or so after they sped through the station, those aboard felt a bump and heard a sharp sound, almost like a rifle firing, before the train gradually lost speed and came to a halt. Just over a kilometre past Craigieburn station they had hit a pair of heavy iron railway gates that should have been open for them, and Henry Alder stopped the train to see what damage had been done.

The carriage doors were unlocked and passengers mingled with crew to examine the train. The engine had two distinct braking systems, a hand brake and an automatic brake, and both were destroyed in the collision. As well, the footbridge on the guard's van had been torn off and the lamp smashed to pieces. The piece of iron that had caused this damage had narrowly missed guard McPhee, who had been looking out of the van at the time of the collision. The damage, although serious, was not fatal to the mission. The guard's van had its own braking system

THE POLICE SPECIAL

and it would be strong enough to slow the entire train. Twenty minutes after they had stopped, they were again on their way.

There was one more brief stop at Seymour where the engine, carriage and guard's van were again checked while the passengers and crew enjoyed cups of coffee on what was a very cold night. Then the bone-rattling journey continued until they pulled into Benalla station at 1.30 on Monday morning. Taking off the time they had spent stationary at Essendon, Craigieburn and Seymour, they had completed the 200-kilometre journey in around two and a quarter hours. Given the circumstances of that journey, it was a remarkable achievement.

* * *

By the time the police special pulled in, there was a crowd on the platform at Benalla, as those who would be joining the police special were in turn joined by other police, railwaymen, relatives, and one or two onlookers just there to see what was going on. For Frank Hare, the first order of business was a council of war with the senior police and railway officers present. Hare was aware of rumours that the Kellys possessed explosives and suspected that they may use those in an attempt to destroy the railway line. John Kelly concurred, saying that the gang's knowledge of police movements was such that they would probably be well aware that a police train was on the way.

The railway officials, too, had heard rumours of either the Kellys or their sympathisers interfering with the line, but were somewhat taken aback by Hare's proposed solution. He would, he said, have Constable Daniel Barry tied to a bar at the front of the engine. It was a very clear night, Barry was young and possessed excellent eyesight, and he would be able to sound a warning well in advance of them encountering any trouble on the railway lines. Fortunately for Barry, who would have frozen to death long before they reached Wangaratta, the idea was vetoed immediately by Stationmaster Stevens and both engine drivers. Instead, a more practical solution was offered.

The Benalla engine already had steam up and was ready to go; the Melbourne engine had already sustained damage and no longer had the braking control of the Benalla engine. The Melbourne engine would therefore be used as a pilot, travelling relatively slowly along the line to Wangaratta. Its carriage and guard's van would be attached to the Benalla engine, which would precede about 200 metres behind the pilot engine. Additionally, guard Archibald McPhee would travel on the pilot engine to provide an extra pair of eyes.

All were in agreement with the plan, which was put into effect immediately. The seventeen police horses that would accompany the party had already been placed in their own transport and this was now attached to the rear of the first-class carriage, which in turn was attached to the rear of the guard's van. That van was connected directly to the Benalla engine in a reversal of the usual configuration, as Hare and John Kelly wanted their men as close as possible to any potential trouble. Everyone now boarded. Hare and Charles Rawlins joined O'Connor and the ladies in their compartment while Thomas Kirkham joined his friends, the Native Police, in theirs. The rest of the Benalla police travelled in the guard's van.

As the reporters settled into their compartment, they compared notes. Two of them had been told by strangers on the platform that the lines had already been torn up somewhere between Benalla and Wangaratta.

* * *

Twenty three passengers and crew were aboard the two trains that pulled out of Benalla within a minute of each other shortly after 2 o'clock on Monday morning. Most of those aboard, while apprehensive, hoped for a trouble-free trip to Wangaratta and then on to Beechworth. As the pilot engine pulled out first, Henry Alder, Hugh Burch and Archibald McPhee all shook hands and wished each other good luck; while the three all hoped for the best, they were preparing themselves for the worst. In the guard's van in the following train, John Kelly was also feeling uncomfortable. He stood, opened one of the small side windows and looked out, past his engine and the pilot engine ahead, into the distance where he suspected trouble lay in wait.

From Benalla, the journey was a lot more cautious than it had been on the run up from Melbourne. The train reached only about 40 kilometres an hour, less than half the speed it had earlier in the evening. The first station they would pass through was Glenrowan, 22 kilometres beyond Benalla and at the top of a long incline; both engines increased speed to cope with this. As he felt this slight increase in velocity, Frank Hare put his rifle in the luggage rack above his head, stretched out on the bench seat, and closed his eyes. As he did so, he felt the engine slacken off and he heard several blasts of the pilot engine's whistle from somewhere ahead.

Henry Alder had slowed and then stopped the pilot engine two kilometres short of the Glenrowan station, between properties owned by the Playford and De Soir families. As he slowed the engine he gave several short blasts on the steam whistle to let the train behind know what he was doing. When his engine had come to a halt, he displayed the red danger lamp and sounded a long continuous whistle. It was the agreed railway signal for 'Danger Ahead.'

A short distance behind the pilot engine, the Benalla train had also stopped, but there was a moment of confusion. Hare was the senior officer present, but he was locked in the first-class carriage as regulations required passenger carriages to be locked from the outside during travel between stations. Quick-thinking Joe Melvin climbed through a window, got the key from a guard and had the carriage doors open within a minute of the train stopping. Hare grabbed his rifle before exiting his compartment, directed O'Connor and John Kelly to mount a guard, and then strode off between the rails towards the stationary pilot engine. Behind him, nervous police and civilians looked around. 'It was a splendid night,' John McWhirter wrote, 'the moon shining with unusual brightness, while the sharp frosty air caused the slightest noise in the forest beyond to be distinctly heard.'

Halfway towards the pilot engine, Hare met guard Archibald McPhee coming back the other way. McPhee quickly explained to the superintendent that his engine had been stopped by a man waving a red danger signal. That man, 'who was in a state of great excitement', explained to those aboard the engine that Glenrowan had been stuck up by the Kelly gang. The Kellys had also torn up the train lines two kilometres beyond Glenrowan to destroy the police train they knew would be sent after them. The man had identified himself as the Glenrowan schoolteacher, but had also asked the railwaymen that his identity be kept a secret. He had refused an invitation to board the engine, saying that his wife needed him, and had then disappeared into the darkness.

John Kelly had arrived at where Hare and McPhee stood in time to hear the end of the guard's story, and McPhee gave him the other details as the three walked back to the Benalla train. There, Hare called O'Connor over, apprised him of what he had learned and outlined what he thought they should do next. Hare said he was not certain about the bona fides of the man who had flagged down the pilot engine, and feared he may have been part of some kind of trap. However, they could see where Glenrowan

THE POLICE SPECIAL

station was situated a short distance ahead, and he proposed that they proceed slowly and carefully to that station. O'Connor also expressed reservations about the 'schoolteacher', but agreed with Hare's proposal, as did John Kelly, who pointed out that they would be unable to unload their horses where they were currently stopped.

Hare's plan was now to proceed to Glenrowan station and stop there. The troopers, horses and supplies would be unloaded and Hare would then lead his men to where the outlaws had torn up the rails. The pursuit would start from there. He was still concerned about the possibility of an ambush however, and decided to place men on both sides of the engines. Hare outlined this to the others and called for Daniel Barry, Charles Gascoigne, and William Phillips to join him. The three walked with him back to the pilot engine where he explained to Henry Alder what he wanted done. The driver listened, then suggested that the two engines be coupled together for the short run into Glenrowan. He pointed out that the damage his engine had sustained at Craigieburn meant that it would not be able to stop and reverse quickly if such actions were called for.

Hare agreed with Alder's suggestion, and the police walked alongside the pilot engine as it was shunted slowly back to the Benalla train. When the two engines had been shackled together, Hare directed Barry, Gascoigne, and Phillips to arm themselves and take up positions on the left side of the pilot engine where they were to keep a sharp lookout for trouble coming from that side of the tracks. He then directed John Kelly, William Canny and James Arthur to take up positions on the right side of the Benalla engine. Finally, he ordered that all carriage doors be left unlocked and that all lights aboard the train be extinguished. The train would then proceed into Glenrowan at a pace just above walking speed.

In their compartment, the reporters were excited, understanding that they might become eyewitnesses to one of the nation's biggest ever stories. They were also realistic about the possibility of danger, and wedged the seats and furnishings against the windows for protection. The policemen were also excited, but theirs was the nervous excitement that arises before big sporting events – or entering into danger.

It took just a few minutes to reach the platform at Glenrowan. From his position, perched on the side of the pilot engine, Daniel Barry glanced at his watch to note the exact time the engine came to a halt. It was 2.40 am on Monday, 28 June 1880.

* * *

Frank Hare was one of the first onto the platform, with Charles Rawlins a couple of paces behind him. Apart from those now disembarking from the train, there was not a soul to be seen. Looking back down the tracks towards Benalla, Rawlins noticed a light in the stationmaster's house. He knew John Stanistreet and his family, and suggested to Hare that they visit the stationmaster to seek further information on the Kellys. When asked by Hare whether he was armed, Rawlins said that he wasn't; Hare handed him a Webley revolver. Hare also told John Kelly to organise the men, ordered Phillips to accompany him, and set off towards Stanistreet's.

The others had now all disembarked. For artist Thomas Carrington the most striking thing was 'a dim, uncertain kind of light'. The police did not have the opportunity to make such observations, they were too busy organising themselves and their horses for the chase. Charles Gascoigne was helping Canny to detrain the horses. As he led one of them down from the platform he thought he saw a figure on horseback some distance off – perhaps 100 metres or more – just in front of Jones's hotel.

He walked over to where John Kelly stood directing the efforts of the men and told him about the horseman. Kelly immediately sent two Native Police to stand guard on that side of the platform, with Daniel Barry performing guard duty on the other side.

The light that Rawlins had seen at the stationmaster's came from a bedroom window and, when he and Hare arrived at the house, they looked in to see Mrs Stanistreet sitting weeping on a bed, surrounded by children and clothes. She was startled by Hare's knock on the window and only moved towards the front door when Hare identified himself as a policeman and when she recognised his companion as Charles Rawlins. When she opened the door, the men saw that she was near hysteria. They spoke calmly and soothingly, and when she had settled Hare introduced himself and asked where her husband was. Although the question provoked more weeping, she was able to reply that her husband had been taken away by the Kellys not ten minutes earlier. When asked by Hare where he had been taken, Mrs Stanistreet pointed towards Jones's hotel; Hare assumed she was indicating the Warby Ranges beyond.

Both men thanked Mrs Stanistreet, assured her that she and the children were now safe, and headed off back to the platform. As they half-walked, half-trotted, Rawlins told Hare that he knew the Warby Ranges well and could act as a guide for the police. When they arrived at the station Hare asked Phillips to find Inspector O'Connor and John Kelly to ensure that all the horses were saddled and ready to go. He also noticed that there was some kind of commotion further down the platform.

* * *

Just as he finished helping unload the horse carriage, Charles Gascoigne also became aware of a disturbance on the platform. He saw a small group of policemen moving towards Superintendent

Hare, who he knew was just back from the stationmaster's house. Two of the Native Police were talking loudly to another man who Gascoigne now recognised as the Glenrowan constable, Hugh Bracken. Bracken was in a state of high excitement, calling out, 'They are here! They are here!' He composed himself and told Hare that he had just escaped from the Kelly Gang. They were at Jones's hotel, he blurted out, and unless the police went there immediately, they would escape.

Hare seemed galvanised by the news. He called his men to order first. Thomas Kirkham, who had been helping unload the horses, was standing by himself and holding the leads of six horses when he heard Hare call out, 'Let the horses go and come on.' He did just that. Also still helping with the horses, Charles Gascoigne heard Hare's order to let the horses go, but he also heard someone else, probably Hugh Bracken, call out, 'They are at Mother Jones.' Both men returned to the platform where Frank Hare climbed onto the running board of one of the engines and spoke to the men gathered. He told them that they were not to fire unless fired upon, that they were to all do their best and, he added, they were to leave any wounded to those who would be following. Their priority would be the destruction of the Kelly Gang.

As Hare jumped down onto the platform, he was again acting upon his assumptions and his instincts, this time assuming that Ann Jones's hotel was occupied only by Ann Jones and her family, the outlaws and those who supported them. He left the platform in a hurry, eager to come to grips with the men he had chased for so long, and convinced that he had them on the run. As he crossed the grass into the Railway Reserve, he called for the others to close up and follow him. Proceeding at a fast trot along the path between the station and the hotel, he crossed to the wicket gate at the edge of the reserve, looking intently ahead at the hotel. Charles Gascoigne had been the first to follow Hare, with others in close, singly and in pairs. In the rush to leave the platform, a stack of rifles had been knocked over, and two of the troopers were delayed as they tried to sort out the mess. O'Connor and his Queenslanders followed a little bit later as well, but moved as a group and hurried to catch up. Caught up in the moment, journalist Joe Melvin drew his pistol and set off to follow Hare. Within twenty metres, he realised that he was actually there to watch and write, so he turned back to the platform and his fellow reporters.

John Kelly did not like the way the first police who set off across the reserve had bunched up. When he left the platform, he turned to the left, towards the stationmaster's house, the railway gates and the road that went through them and past Jones's hotel. This would allow him to approach the hotel from a different angle. Rawlins and one or two of the others followed him. Kelly estimated that he and his group would probably arrive at the hotel at the same time as Hare.

As he led his men across the reserve and through the gate, Hare urged the police to be swift but silent. The advice was well-intentioned yet superfluous. Their rush from the platform had been watched every step of the way. As they passed through that gate, four men standing in the shadows of the hotel cocked their weapons, raised them, and took careful aim.

CHAPTER 8

First Blood

Those who had remained on the station's platform – the reporters, the ladies, and one or two policemen recovering weapons or horses – had a grandstand view of the action as it unfolded on the other side of the reserve. There was a bright full moon which provided clear illumination, but which also cast everything into monotones; blacks and greys and silvers. The position of the moon also provided both police and spectators with a complication. The moon was shining down from almost directly above Morgan's Lookout. While Glenrowan station, the Railway Reserve, and the yard in front of Jones's were clearly visible, the face of the hotel was in deep shadow. The men standing there could see clearly all that was happening before them; they, however, were invisible to police and spectators alike.

Ned, standing in front and to the left of the others, watched Frank Hare negotiate the wicket gate and stride rapidly towards the front of the hotel with several other policemen trailing in his wake. Some distance short of the veranda they were joined by a smaller group who had come from the direction of the railway gates. Ned's armour may have provided exceptional protection, but it also made it difficult to aim a weapon. Ned was forced to hold his revolving rifle out from his body before taking what he thought was careful aim.

Frank Hare slowed a bit as he came to within twenty metres of the hotel veranda. As he slowed, he practised the words he would use when he called on the outlaws to surrender. And as he rolled those words around inside his head, he thought he saw – there, at the edge of the shadow – a large man holding a rifle away from his body. As this registered, Hare saw a flash, heard a noise, and felt a hammer blow to his left wrist. Hare called out to no-one in particular, 'Good gracious, I'm shot.' As these words left his mouth, the figure standing on the ground fired again and was joined in doing so by three figures back in the darkness of the veranda.

There was a moment of clarity as the firefight began, a small moment of relative intellectual calm before those involved forgot about everything but survival. Years later, Frank Hare could recall quite clearly:

> When I was within sixteen yards of the verandah I saw a flash and heard a report from a rifle fired about a yard in front of the verandah and my left hand dropped beside me . . . Three flashes came from under the verandah . . . The man who fired the first shot stepped back under the verandah and began firing upon us.

James Arthur was just a short distance behind Hare, and concentrated on simply keeping up:

A shot was fired as Hare and one or two others just cleared the wicket gate ... there was a pause and then a volley was fired from the front of the hotel. After a brief pause, a second volley was fired.

Arthur heard Hare call out that he was shot, but for some reason believed that the superintendent was joking. John Kelly, coming from the left and slightly behind Hare recalled that, 'When we were about twenty yards from the hotel a tall man appeared upon the verandah and fired at us; his shot was quickly followed by three shots'.

Charles Rawlins, by now almost alongside Hare, heard a noise on the veranda. Just as he called, 'Look out!' the firing began. Finally, and on the Wangaratta side of Hare, Charles Gascoigne's angle of approach enabled him to see one figure standing clear of the veranda. As he watched, that figure fired a rifle at the approaching group and immediately afterwards a row of flashes lit up the veranda. The response to the outlaws' firing was immediate and identical from all those who had been converging on the front of the hotel. They returned fire and looked for somewhere to take cover.

* * *

Soon after the main body of police had been led away from the station by Hare, the reporters were told that someone had heard a gunshot and that the Kellys were somewhere out there in the darkness. The police remaining at the station responded immediately, letting go of the horses, grabbing their weapons and heading off across the reserve towards the hotel. They were only part-way there when the firing erupted. The police horses, left to their own devices, trotted away and bunched up at a fence in the corner of the paddock at the Wangaratta end of the station.

FIRST BLOOD

Even before the first police had departed, the reporters began to stack the saddles into a combined viewing platform and protective wall at the Benalla end of the station. They looked and listened as they built, hearing first the single shot and then the volley. To one reporter, 'the whole front of the house seemed a blaze of light'. By contrast, he noted that all the police fire seemed to originate from one spot. The reporters winced and ducked when the occasional bullet zipped overhead.

Joe Melvin was probably the most focused of the reporters at this stage. Putting his pistol away, he concentrated on recording the sights and sounds around him. He noted that, 'the two ladies . . . behaved with admirable courage, never betraying a symptom of fear, although bullets were whistling about the station and striking the building and train'. He was unable to report much more about the fighting at the hotel because after just two minutes, gun smoke obscured the entire front of the building. As they peered over the saddles towards where the gunfire crackled and snapped, the little group of reporters was again startled by the sudden appearance of Hugh Bracken. He was 'extremely animated' and told them again that he had just escaped death. He then disappeared from the platform and a couple of minutes later they saw him riding a police horse along the railway lines towards Wangaratta.

* * *

Many months later, Charles Rawlins would recall the confusion of those first few minutes: 'the smoke was so thick, and the yells, you could not see one another, the firing was so rapid . . . You could not see anything at all, you could only hear people yelling and talking'. Apart from Ned, armed with the Spencer revolving rifle, most of those involved were firing single shot weapons – rifles and shotguns – with smokeless powder yet to be developed. There were two immediate results. The first was that the whole scene was enveloped in a thick cloud of smoke which, as there was no breeze, hung still in the air, dissipated only very slowly. The second was that the early firing came in volleys. The police were trained to reload in a particular sequence, so most of them fired and reloaded at around the same time; at the station, the reporters said they heard two or three distinct volleys.

The yells that Rawlins heard came from both sides and also from inside the hotel. The outlaws took the opportunity to vent their anger at the police, screaming taunts and abuse. One of them called out, 'Surrender you bloody dogs! You can't hurt us. Fire away!' while another called, 'Come on you dogs!' Ned himself called out a challenge, identifying just who he was and saying that he was made of iron. In a break between volleys, his voice rang out clearly: 'Come on you cocktails! You can't hurt me. I'm in iron.'

The noise ebbed and flowed during that first clash. Hare guessed that in the opening exchange, a period that lasted just a few minutes, the police fired around 60 shots and the outlaws another 40. Others present put the figure even higher. The volume of fire from the front of the hotel was so heavy that several of the police believed that all the outlaws must have been armed with repeating rifles. And, despite the outlaws' claims that they couldn't be hurt, they were. In that initial exchange, Joe Byrne was shot clean through the right calf, while Ned was shot in both the right hand and right foot. After those first two or three volleys, there was a short break in firing, as both sides sought cover and time to regroup and plan their next moves. That short silence was soon followed by shouts and scream from inside the hotel.

* * *

To those inside, that initial exchange of gunfire seemed to last a lot longer than the three or four minutes that it actually took. The prisoners were spread throughout the hotel; most of the men were in either the dining room or the parlour, with the women and small children in the larger bedroom at the rear or in the small bedrooms and kitchen in the second building. All had followed the advice proffered by both Ned and Hugh Bracken, and were lying on the floor, seeking whatever shelter they could. Nothing, though, could prepare them for the firestorm that erupted.

The police fired at the muzzle flashes the outlaws' weapons made when they discharged, with most of their shots missing the outlaws and striking the building behind. That building, though relatively new and structurally sound, was not built to resist sustained rifle fire, especially from the large calibre weapons with which the police were equipped. The weatherboard walls provided little protection and the internal walls absolutely none. The two chimneys were of solid brick construction and could stop a bullet, but they could only partially shield one or two people. The solidly constructed bar helped to stop bullets penetrating into the bedroom behind it, but the fact was that most of the bullets fired by the police passed more or less directly through the main building and finished either in the rear building or in the bush beyond. In those first few minutes, there were up to 60 bullets fired into the hotel, and there they did some damage.

In the largest room, the dining room, small groups of terrified prisoners lay huddled on the floor. As the bullets started crashing through the windows and walls, a labourer named George Metcalf called out in pain as a ricochet, its force almost spent, struck him in the eye. An alarm clock on the mantelpiece above the fireplace started to chime when struck by another bullet. It rang and rang and rang until another bullet smashed it beyond repair.

Those in the front rooms – in particular the dining room and bar – felt very exposed because most of the furniture had been removed to create more space for the prisoners. In the doorway into the parlour, Dave Mortimer and Martin Cherry lay as flat as they could, trying to hide behind a lounge, looking across at Michael Reardon and John Jones who were doing the same in the bar. In the rear building, generally referred to as the skillion kitchen, John Larkins found a number of bags of oats and stacked them, one on top of the other, to make a barrier of sorts which would provide cover for himself and one or two others. Other prisoners were lying on the kitchen floor or were in one of the two small bedrooms which opened off it.

There was some protection within the two buildings, but the unpredictable nature of direct and ricocheting bullets illustrated just how illusory this could be. John Stanistreet had taken cover in the kitchen in the rear building with Ann Jones and several of her children, sitting down on the floor next to the stove and trying to make themselves as small as possible. Shortly after the firing started, Jane Jones let out a cry, put a hand to her temple and called out that she had been shot. A ricochet, badly flattened and almost spent, had struck her just back from her eye and above her ear, and had lodged below the skin. Her mother and Stanistreet were able to remove the bullet without too much difficulty, but both mother and daughter were badly shaken and weeping.

Just as Ann and Stanistreet finished dealing with Jane's wound, one of the male prisoners crawled to the back door of the hotel and called across the breezeway to Ann that her son John had just been shot. Ann screamed and caring nothing for her own welfare, rushed from the kitchen, down the passageway, and into the bar. Young John Jones had suffered a terrible wound. A bullet had entered his body just above his left hip, traversed his trunk and exited through the ribs just below his right armpit. Ann was crying loudly when she reached her son, who was screaming in pain. When she arrived, John stopped crying, looked up at her, saying, 'Oh, Mother, I am shot', as he tried to pull himself upright on her leg.

There was a moment of almost awkward silence, interrupted by old Martin Cherry saying to Dave Mortimer, 'Come on lad, we'll carry him in'. Both men rose and walked into the bar where they lifted John as gently as they could. They carried him back down the passage and across the breezeway, and carefully placed the boy in a corner near the stove. Jane, recovering quickly from her own trauma, went into a bedroom and returned with a pillow which she placed under her brother's head. She brought him a drink of water and tried to make him comfortable. Dave Mortimer returned to his cubby hole in the parlour, while Martin Cherry chose to stay in the rear building with the Joneses.

By then, the firing had died down to an occasional shot, with a flurry of bullets every few minutes. It was pandemonium inside the hotel; most of the children were crying, many of their mothers were weeping, and several people were praying at the top of their voices.

* * *

The police did not emerge unscathed from the firefight either. Frank Hare's injury was serious; he seemed to be in great pain but was not yet prepared to relinquish the field. The shock of being wounded impacted his judgement, and he seemed to be confused as to his role. He had swapped his rifle for a shotgun before leaving the station and, with the barrel resting across his injured left arm, he fired two shots at the outlaws before retreating back through the wicket gate into the Railway Reserve. There, he tried to reload the shotgun, breaking it open and holding it between his knees. Unable to complete the task, he gave the weapon and his ammunition pouch to Charles Rawlins, who had stayed close when Hare retreated to the reserve. Hare sat on a tree stump and began to call out orders.

After the first volley from the outlaws, Stanhope O'Connor supervised a return volley from his Native Police, and then led them back through the gate and into the reserve. There he found an excellent firing position in a half-moon shaped excavation in the deepest of the drainage ditches traversing the paddock. Originally shallow creeks, these ditches had been deepened and extended to cope with the run-off from the rains after the forest had been cleared. The position was about 40 metres in front of the hotel, and deep enough for O'Connor and his men to be completely protected unless they stood upright. This is precisely what Trooper Jimmy did almost as soon as O'Connor had placed him in position. He must have also been turning his head, as an outlaw bullet sliced open both his eyebrows. Jimmy dropped down, fired five shots into the hotel, and then called out, 'Take that, Ned Kelly.'

John Kelly and his Victorian troopers had also returned fire before Kelly called on his men to separate, find cover, and wait for orders. Most of the police moved back and sought protection behind trees, fence posts, or in depressions in the ground. All this repositioning and redeployment meant a considerable slackening of the police fire, and this was matched by a falling off in the outlaws' fire as they, too, took time to adjust to the new circumstances. In this relative quiet, the screams, yells, and prayers from inside the hotel could be heard, as could Frank Hare issuing orders from the tree stump. The first was to cease firing, as Hare now understood that there were civilians inside the hotel. The Victorians stopped immediately, but the Queenslanders continued. Both John Kelly and Charles Gascoigne called out to them to stop shooting, but it took a direct order from Stanhope O'Connor for them to take heed. O'Connor would later testify that, in Queensland, the Native Police were trained to obey only their officer in charge.

It was to that officer that Hare directed his next, shouted commands. 'Come on, O'Connor,' he said, 'the beggars have shot me. Bring your boys with you, surround the house.' He followed up by calling out to John Kelly: 'Kelly, surround the house, for God's sake, do not let them escape.' He then attempted to rise from where he had been sitting, but felt faint and sat back heavily on the stump. He again called out to O'Connor: 'O'Connor, I'm wounded. I'm shot in the arm. I must go back.' And, calling on Rawlins to assist him, Frank Hare staggered back along the track to the station.

Behind him, Sub-Inspector Stanhope O'Connor of the Queensland Police and Senior Constable John Kelly of the Victoria Police struggled to understand what Hare had actually meant with his final orders. O'Connor realised that his men's blood was up and decided they needed some time to settle. They were in a good place to do just that. John Kelly decided that he could not afford to let the outlaws escape and that the hotel would have to have a cordon thrown around it. Calling out for James Arthur, he set out to find his men and then place them where they could be put to best use. Anyone planning an escape from the hotel would now have to shoot their way out through his men.

* * *

The four outlaws also sought a place of relative safety. Although their armour had kept them alive, it had not kept them physically or mentally unscathed. All were shaken by the intensity of the police fire, and both Ned and Joe had suffered nasty wounds. The four made their way through the smoke and along the

Wangaratta side of the hotel to the breezeway and the back door. Ned and Joe spoke of surviving the storm, but they then had a sharp exchange over the value of the armour. At first, though, Ned asked Joe to help him reload his rifle as he was 'cooked'; Joe responded that he, too, was 'gone' and said he thought he may have broken his leg.

The two friends had a significant disagreement. Joe said that he and the other two had spoken earlier, and he was now of the opinion that it would probably be best if they ditched their armour, as it was becoming a hindrance, collected their horses, and headed off through the unguarded bush at the rear of the hotel before the police surrounded them. As if he had expected this, Ned had his counterargument already prepared. He repeated that he was sick of running and hiding, and he said that they were in a position to counterattack. He agreed that the armour was cumbersome, but it had kept them alive so far and would continue to do so.

What Ned now proposed was that he and Joe go into the bush behind the hotel and work their way around through the heavier timber until they were in position to attack the police, now clustered in front of the hotel, from the flank and rear. When they did so, Steve and Dan would attack from the front; between them, they would slaughter the police in the crossfire. With that, he sent Steve inside to try to exercise control over their prisoners, who sounded close to panic. Ned himself had no intention of going inside and showing that he had been wounded.

Ned and Joe then spoke for perhaps two minutes but what they discussed is not known. It is probable that Ned told Joe that he was badly wounded and that he needed him and that together they could see this thing through. Dan interrupted by calling out that he thought Bracken had escaped, while Joe stood in silence and pain. Ned and Joe then agreed to go their own ways, for a short time at least. Ned limped towards the stables while Joe limped inside the hotel.

* * *

Sitting on or lying behind their improvised breastworks, the reporters continued to watch the action taking place just over 100 metres away in front of Jones's hotel. Every now and then one of them would jot down a description of what they saw; the exception was Tom Carrington, the artist, who would draw outlines for future sketches. As the firing died down, they heard the sound of footsteps coming along the track through the reserve and soon afterwards the tall figure of Frank Hare came into view, with Charles Rawlins trailing along behind. They could see that Hare was in difficulty; he was staggering and the left leg of his trousers was drenched in blood.

When Rawlins assisted Hare onto the platform, the reporters and ladies saw that he was pale and troubled, and that he was cradling his shattered left wrist, blood from which had flowed down the left side of his body. Tom Carrington, who claimed some knowledge of first aid, took charge of Hare's treatment. He sat the superintendent on the saddles and examined the wound. He plugged both the entry and exit points with cotton from a clean cotton handkerchief. Finally, he bound the wound with strips of cloth cut from a silk handkerchief. That handkerchief, and the scissors Carrington used to cut it into strips, were both supplied by the ladies.

Hare thanked Carrington, stood up a little unsteadily, and said that he had to return to his men. He stepped down from the platform and set off along the track leading to the hotel. He had not gone far, however, when he began to stagger and sink to his knees. Before he collapsed completely, Rawlins and the reporters had rushed down from the platform and helping Hare to his feet.

He seemed to recover a little when he was back on the platform, but he soon collapsed onto stacked bags of horse feed. The reporters again lifted the ungainly policeman and carried him into a compartment in the first-class carriage, laying him on one of the bench seats.

Frank Hare revived very quickly when one of the ladies gave him a healthy dose of sherry and, while his body may have been sinking, his mind was racing. He had led his men from the front and he had been brave. But in doing so he had been gravely wounded in a vicious gun fight and was now in real danger of dying. He needed professional medical care which meant he had to get back to Benalla as soon as possible. His part in the battle may have been over, but there were people who needed to know exactly what he had achieved. The most dangerous gang of criminals in the country had been brought to heel and could now be destroyed at will. He himself had been honourably wounded in combat with that gang. Those two coincident facts could now be leveraged into something important in the career of Superintendent Frank Hare.

* * *

Ned's last words to his outlaws were snapped-out instructions to barricade the hotel's windows and walls. He then moved slowly and deliberately towards the hotel's rear holding paddock where several of the gang's horses, including Ned's favourite mare, Mirth, had been tethered at dusk. These movements took Ned away from the shadows cast by the hotel and away from the cover the gunsmoke had provided. His movements were in the open, illuminated by the bright moonlight, and he was spotted by at least two of the police, Charles Gascoigne and James Arthur.

Gascoigne had taken cover behind a corner post of the reserve fence and had a clear view of the figure shuffling away from the hotel. He took careful aim with his carbine, and fired. The bullet struck and severed the leather strap which held Ned's shoulder plate to the main part of his armour. That shoulder plate fell to the ground and – at almost the same instant – two rockets exploded in the sky above Glenrowan in a display that has never been completely explained. Gascoigne noticed the rockets but did not allow them to distract him, reloading as fast as he could.

A short distance to Gascoigne's left, James Arthur had also seen the figure of one of the outlaws emerge from the shadows and the smoke. He did not have a clear shot, and as he was waiting for the opportunity to fire, he heard the sound of the rockets rising from somewhere behind him, and turned to look. Arthur estimated that they had been let off from somewhere between the railway station and McDonnell's Hotel. He also thought that the first rocket was very faint, but that the second was very bright. As he watched them rise then fade, Arthur surmised that they had probably been fired off by a Kelly sympathiser to let others know that the fighting had begun.

Turning back towards the hotel, Arthur witnessed the last of the exchange between Ned and Gascoigne. His heavy helmet prevented Ned from watching the rockets as they arced into the sky, but he felt and heard the bullet that nicked his armour and spotted the smoke that gave away Gascoigne's firing position. Cradling his rifle in his left hand, Ned fired a shot in the general direction of that smoke. Before he could fire a second shot, Gascoigne returned fire and his bullet struck home. Ned's exposed left arm had been bent to support and help aim the rifle, and Gascoigne's bullet smashed through it. It left entry and exit wounds above and below the elbow.

The impact staggered Ned and the pain washed over him. Yet, he kept moving and within a few paces was swallowed up by shadows of the trees. He found Mirth still tethered to a fence rail, untied her and led her up into the bush towards Morgan's Lookout. Gascoigne thought he saw movement in the distance, but the shadows and smoke would not allow a clear shot. He squatted, reloaded, and waited for orders. For the next few hours he would tell all those he spoke to that he believed the outlaw he had fired at – he had no way of knowing it was actually Ned – was clad in iron because none of his shots seemed to have any effect.

* * *

When Joe staggered back into the hotel he was swearing loudly, cursing the police. He and Dan moved from room to room, searching for Hugh Bracken and leaving no-one in any doubt about what they would do to the policeman if they found him; Joe was heard to say, 'Let me just find him and I'll make bracken of him.' But, without Ned, some of Joe's spirit seemed to desert him. As he moved through the hotel, Joe struck many of the prisoners as not really caring whether he lived or died. To Dave Mortimer, Joe 'was perfectly reckless of his life'. To Joe himself, life had been turned on its head in the twenty-four hours since he had killed his childhood friend, Aaron Sherrit, and he was no longer certain where events were leading.

Shortly after the initial exchange of fire, one of the prisoners went to a front window and waved a white handkerchief which was immediately shot through. For most of those inside the hotel, this one act drove home the realisation that their survival would come down to luck and what they themselves could make of the situation. Several started making plans, and when the three remaining outlaws went out the back door to talk without being overheard by their captives, a number of the prisoners prepared to make a dash for freedom.

Ann Jones, returning to the main building from the kitchen

where she was tending her wounded son, saw the three outlaws standing near the breezeway, discussing something in low voices. It was too much for her, and nearing breaking point she turned on them saying, 'You cowards. Why don't you go out to fight them hand to hand?' She yelled more abuse at them, then walked into the open and screamed similar abuse at the police she knew were out there.

When the three outlaws returned inside after their short conference, Dave Mortimer said to Joe that now might be the time to let the prisoners go. Joe grunted back that they could try but anyone who left the building would probably be shot down by the police. Mortimer and several others thought this could be their last opportunity to escape and were prepared to take that chance. Ann Jones went back to the kitchen and started organising her children. John Stanistreet, who had remained in the rear building, simply walked out:

> I left the kitchen into the back yard and passed the gang there. They were standing together at the kitchen chimney . . . One of them said, 'If you go out, you will be shot.' I walked straight to my house. Firing was going on, but I was uninjured. Of course, I was challenged as I passed through.

All the way back to his house, he called out loudly to the police not to fire.

In the kitchen, Ann Jones brought her family together to escape the fate overtaking them. Neil Jock McHugh, a quarry labourer, lifted young John up and draped him across his shoulders in the fireman's carry-grip. Ann and Jane had organised the smaller children and then shepherded the group down the side of the hotel, across the front yard and into the Railway Reserve, calling out to the police to hold their fire the whole way. McHugh did not stop once he passed through the wicket gate and the police lines, carrying the badly wounded boy all the way across to the stationmaster's house, arriving there shortly after Stanistreet had made it home.

Stanhope O'Connor would later claim that he stood up out of the drain and twice loudly called: 'Let the women out', and that shortly afterwards a group of women and children emerged from the front door. In the main bedroom, the women there noted an easing of the firing at the departure of the Joneses and made their own preparations. Just before they had made their escape, Ann and Jane had briefly visited the large bedroom, telling the women sheltering there with their children, just what they were going to do and urging them to do the same. All those in the bedroom chose to follow the Joneses. Matthew Ryan, his wife and their three children led the way, followed by a person James Reardon would always remember as 'a strange woman from Benalla', and then the Reardons themselves. There was a temporary delay as thirteen-year-old Mary Reardon, who had been sheltering under the bed, suffered a cramp in her leg.

Thus it was that two groups made their escape, two groups with three children in between. Those three were all Reardons: Thomas, aged sixteen; Mary, aged thirteen, Ann, who was just ten. A short distance behind them was another group, also composed entirely of Reardons. Margaret led the way carrying the baby, Bridget, with James behind leading two small children. Michael brought up the rear. Then the situation suddenly changed. At first while the prisoners were escaping, none of the outlaws fired a shot and there was only an occasional round fired by the police who were now spreading into a cordon. Now, however, the volume of fire increased substantially with no apparent reason. It may have been that a ricochet set off a chain reaction or that the gap between the senior Reardons and the others led some police to think that the three adult Reardons were actually the Kelly Gang using human shields to escape. Whatever the reason, the firing increased and the senior Reardons scurried back into the hotel with their small children and baby to seek shelter.

Inside, the outlaws went to the windows and gazed out. Outside, O'Connor and Tom Kirkham called and waved to those prisoners who did make it out, checking them as they passed to ensure that there were no gang members among them. O'Connor and John Kelly then set about positioning their men in the best firing positions, while, on the platform, Frank Hare fretted about his wound.

* * *

A minor problem emerged in the Railway Reserve. The withdrawal of Superintendent Hare from the field had left behind a power vacuum. While Stanhope O'Connor was a commissioned officer of police, it was with another service and neither he nor the Victorian police were certain about the legality of their accepting orders from him. Similarly, recent experience had shown that the Queensland Native Police would only accept orders from O'Connor. Fortunately, both O'Connor and John Kelly were reasonable men and common sense prevailed. O'Connor and his Queenslanders remained in their firing positions in the ditch. From there, they could cover the front of the hotel and all the cleared area on the hotel's northern, or Wangaratta, side.

Kelly called Charles Gascoigne back from that side, and the pair set off to the southern, Benalla, side where Kelly and O'Connor had agreed the Victorians would be placed. Kelly led the way to the light scrub on the side, and began assigning firing positions. He placed Gascoigne first, in a position which allowed him to cover both the front and the southern side of the main building. A further twenty metres along, he placed William Phillips and, a short distance further around, found Daniel Barry a spot with a clear view of the skillion kitchen and rear yard. He kept James Arthur with him as he completed a partial circumnavigation of the hotel, sealing off all possible escape routes as he did.

A second problem which had emerged was ammunition, which was in short supply. John Kelly guessed that he had already fired between ten and fifteen shots, and Daniel Barry had fired a similar number. As he placed the men, Kelly assured them that they would soon be resupplied with ammunition. O'Connor faced the same problem with his Native Police, who had probably fired off even more shots than the Victorians. Tom Kirkham, renewing acquaintances with his friends among the Queenslanders, was asked by O'Connor to return to the station to check on ammunition supplies there. He should also, O'Connor added, check on the welfare of the ladies while reassuring them of his own.

Kirkham, weighed down by a carbine and two revolvers, had fired some twenty rounds and was also happy to spend some time away from the excitable Queenslanders who seemed to attract more of the outlaws' return fire than anyone else. He made his way back to find Hare in his carriage and reported to him. Hare directed Rawlins to assist in the collection and distribution of ammunition, then thanked and dismissed Kirkham. Kirkham found the ladies, gave them O'Connor's regards and then wandered off to where the reporters had set up their little post on the platform. Charles Rawlins had already set off with ammunition for the police and Joe Melvin was about to do the same. Kirkham thought his efforts might therefore be superfluous, so he hunted down a loaf of bread (brought across by Mrs Stanistreet) grabbed some ammunition for himself, and returned to the firing line, finding a cosy little spot at the Benalla end of the hotel.

Not all that far away from Kirkham's cubby, Frank Hare was becoming increasingly irrational. By now, he had convinced himself that his wrist wound was even more serious than it actually was, and now believed that without treatment he faced amputation at best, with death a distinct possibility. He was also unsure of the size of the gang he was expected to subdue. He knew there were only supposed to be four members, but the volume of fire he had faced during the initial clash suggested that there might be more involved, while the firing of rockets may have been a signal for other brigands join the fray. He needed medical assistance and he needed reinforcements, and Benalla was the only place where both were available.

Within a few minutes, the idea became a fixation. At one stage, he called out to his companion, 'For God's sake, Rawlins, send me back to Benalla', and followed this up with a request that Rawlins saddle him a horse so that he could ride back. The ladies were also becoming increasingly concerned about Hare's welfare, believing him to be in great pain and in shock. A consensus formed; the Benalla train – engine and carriages – would be sent back to Benalla to collect Superintendent John Sadleir and reinforcements. Frank Hare would return on that train.

It is not known if he looked back at the little township that was to have been the scene of his greatest triumph, the place where he destroyed the Kelly Gang and staked a claim for the future advancement that such a feat should have guaranteed.

CHAPTER 9

Reinforcements

If Frank Hare was obsessed with getting to Benalla, Hugh Bracken also had a single fixed idea and his took him in the opposite direction, north to Wangaratta. While Hare was driven primarily by concern for his own health – both physical and professional – Hugh Bracken was driven primarily by concern for his fellow man; specifically, by concern for the police and railwaymen he believed were coming to Glenrowan from the police barracks at Wangaratta. Bracken knew that the failure of the police special from Melbourne to arrive in Wangaratta would prompt a response, which he believed would most likely be the despatch of another police train down the tracks towards Melbourne to identify the problem. That train would be travelling at or near top speed when it hit the torn-up tracks. Hugh Bracken was trying to prevent a disaster.

Bracken's assessment of the situation was fairly accurate.

REINFORCEMENTS

When Sergeant Arthur Steele, officer in charge of the Wangaratta police barracks, learned that the police special had left Benalla shortly after 2 o'clock in the morning, he alerted several of his officers, expecting that Superintendent Hare would require some form of assistance or support when he arrived. When Hare's train had not arrived by 3 am, Steele was worried. Always a restless man, he decided to walk off his anxieties and set off between the railway lines towards Benalla. When he had walked several hundred metres, he was well clear of the hustle and bustle of the barracks and the station, and could hear clearly in the still night air. What he heard made him pause. From the direction of Glenrowan came the sound of gunfire. Steele recognised volleys being fired and thought he could even hear individual shots.

As he stood and listened, Steele became aware of another sound, that of a horse galloping towards him. Bracken and Steele probably saw each other at around the same time. The men knew one another and Bracken burst out immediately with his story about what was happening down the tracks at Glenrowan. In describing the Kellys, Bracken outlined the armour they were wearing, a fact Steele filed away for future use. He asked Bracken to dismount and walk the rest of the way into Wangaratta, while he rode ahead to alert the police and begin preparing a response.

Steele first rode back to the railway station where he asked the stationmaster to immediately ready an engine for despatch to Glenrowan. He then rode the short distance to the police barracks where he instructed Constable William Moore to ride to the railway bridge to tell James Dwyer, stationed there, what had happened and to bring him back immediately to the police barracks. Moore checked the time when he and Dwyer returned to the barracks; it was 3.40 am.

The barracks was now a hive of activity, with horses being saddled and led about, and arms and ammunition issued and stacked. In Moore's absence, Steele had issued a series of instructions and sent a stream of telegrams. The telegrams were to John Sadleir in Benalla, and through them he informed Sadleir of what he had learned from Bracken and what he now intended to do. He would later recall that the first response he received from Sadleir simply said, 'Mr. Hare just arrived, not seriously injured.'

Satisfied that everything he had asked for had been done, Steele chose five troopers to ride with him to Glenrowan. He ordered Constables Montford, Causey, Patrick Healey, and William Moore to mount up and he asked James Dwyer to give his horse to Hugh Bracken as he wanted the Glenrowan policeman with him when they entered the township. Dwyer was instructed to travel with the Wangaratta pilot engine, which would be driven by a local railwayman named Morgan. Dwyer would be accompanied by a young constable named Welch. With that, Steele led his party off into the night.

It took Steele and his men around 35 minutes to ride to Glenrowan. As they approached the township, Steele thought that everything seemed calm and he could see no lights showing at Jones's hotel. He had his men dismount around 300 metres short of Jones's, tie up or hobble their horses, and then walk single file through the scrub towards the hotel. As they approached the police cordon, a voice called out a challenge, to which Steele replied, 'Wangaratta police.'

Steele and his men were then directed to where John Kelly and James Arthur had established a position in the light scrub at the rear of the hotel. Steele told Kelly to dispose of the Wangaratta troopers as he thought appropriate, and then scurried off to find his own firing position. The spot he chose was behind a tree on the Wangaratta side of the hotel, overlooking the back door and just over ten metres from the breezeway. John Kelly directed Healey fifteen metres uphill from Steele and a short distance

REINFORCEMENTS

from James Arthur, and then directed Moore further around towards the Benalla side. He told the remaining police to move beyond Moore and select positions that would not interfere with those already established.

Elsewhere, Driver Morgan had eased the pilot engine out of Wangaratta station some fifteen minutes after Steele had galloped off with his troopers. They soon reached top speed and were almost halfway to Glenrowan when Morgan noticed a light on the tracks ahead, and slowly brought the engine back to a walking pace. The engine was soon approached by a man who introduced himself as Charles Rawlins, from Benalla, but more recently of Glenrowan. He had signalled them with lit matches, he said, to stop the train before it crashed where the rails were torn up a short distance ahead. Morgan was shocked, as he believed he was still some distance from the danger point, but agreed to stay with the engine while Rawlins, Dwyer and Welch walked the rest of the way into Glenrowan. A few minutes later, the reporters on the station were bringing the Wangaratta reinforcements up to date on what had occurred since Rawlins left. As they were doing so, a train from Benalla eased into the station.

* * *

In Benalla several hours earlier, John Sadleir had farewelled Frank Hare and Stanhope O'Connor and their men before heading back to his hotel and going to bed. It seemed that he had only just closed his eyes when he heard his name called, and he opened the door to find a young constable with a telegram in his hand. That telegram informed Sadleir that the police special had not yet arrived in Wangaratta; soon afterwards, a second telegram said it had arrived, a third then cancelled the second while a fourth said shooting had been heard in the direction of Glenrowan. A final telegram, the only one dictated by Steele, said that Hare had been wounded and that the Kellys were holed up in Glenrowan.

Telegrams arrived in a steady stream as Sadleir dressed and hurried to the police barracks. He knew there was an engine waiting at Benalla station, steamed up and ready to go, so he went straight to the barracks and issued orders for men and equipment to assemble at the railway station as soon as possible. He understood that there had been a clash at Glenrowan and suspected that there had been casualties; he also suspected that there could be more before the affair ended. He therefore sent constables to the homes of Drs Hutchison and Nicholson to see if either or both were available.

Sadleir had to pass the telegraph office on the way to the station and when he saw the office brightly lit, he went inside. Much to Sadleir's surprise, among the post and telegraph clerks sat Frank Hare, arm wrapped in a bloody bandage. He was dictating a series of telegrams to Standish in Melbourne, most of them variations on the theme of the opening clash between bushrangers and police, and Hare's heroic role in that clash. Since arriving back in Benalla, Hare had gone straight to the telegraph office and, after sending a young clerk off to fetch Dr Nicholson, sat down and started dictating telegrams to Commissioner Standish in Melbourne, where the chief of all police was waiting anxiously at the Melbourne Club. In the first of his telegrams, Hare described how, 'I went up towards Jones's and when I got within fifty or eighty yards, a shot was fired from the house and struck me in the arm (not seriously).' Hare was determined that his Commissioner, friend and patron would be the first to know what was happening in Glenrowan, and of his part in the events.

Spotting Sadleir, Hare called him over, gave him a potted version of the events at Glenrowan and asked Sadleir to hurry off and make certain that he finished the job. He then asked for a drink of water, took a sip, and fainted. Sadleir took the opportunity to send a response to Steele at Wangaratta before continuing to the station.

When the engine carrying Hare had arrived back in Benalla, the driver had offered his belief to those already at the station that up to nine policemen had already been wounded in the fighting. No-one bothered to ask him the basis for that assessment. That story, and several variations of it, hung over those assembling on the platform like a dark fog.

As with Hare and O'Connor's earlier party, Sadleir's group included both police and civilians. Altogether, there were eleven policemen, led by Sadleir and Sergeant James Whelan, The lawmen included two Victorian Native Police; one impact of the Kelly Outbreak was to have that unit re-established. Sadleir's departure meant that there were now no police reserves left in Benalla, so at least that part of Ned's grand plan was successful. The three civilians who joined included the two doctors, Hutchison and Nicholson, and the little railway detective/guard, Jesse Dowsett. Dowsett was carrying his work-issue Colt revolver and was determined to give a good account of himself whatever the circumstances. He, too, was responsible for public order and he took this responsibility very seriously indeed.

A new driver, Richard Coleman, opened the throttle on the train around 5 o'clock and applied the brakes to stop the train at Glenrowan just over 30 minutes later. There was intermittent firing as the train stopped, and as the passengers disembarked a couple of bullets fired from the hotel thudded into the dirt behind the platform. Shortly after he strode towards the Railway Reserve, Superintendent Sadleir was stopped by John Kelly who said he could now give the senior policeman at the scene an update on what had occurred since Frank Hare's departure.

* * *

Senior Constable Kelly first told Sadleir of his own actions in the immediate aftermath of Hare leaving the field. He described sending a number of Victorian troopers to take up specified firing positions in a perimeter around the hotel, and then outlined a curious little incident in which he had been involved. Both Sadleir and John Kelly had always regarded James Arthur as one of the best troopers in their command, and Kelly explained how he had asked Arthur to accompany him as he made a tour of the cordon he was setting up. They found Daniel Barry, with Trooper Hero, to be closest to the rear of the hotel buildings, an area Kelly considered to be both virtually unprotected and a likely escape route for the outlaws. Kelly and Arthur both decided that Arthur, a crack shot, should establish a firing position somewhere in the light scrub, to the rear and on the Wangaratta side of the hotel, and stay there at least until reinforcements arrived and the cordon could be strengthened. At times crawling on hands and knees, the two policemen continued around the rear of the hotel until they came to a fallen log alongside a small copse of trees almost 100 metres to the north-east of the hotel, with a clear view over the rear paddock and the hotel buildings. As Arthur knelt down near the base of one of the trees, his hand first brushed a rifle and then a knitted skullcap; it came away sticky with blood.

It was now approaching 4 am, almost an hour since their train had pulled into the station and the gunfight began. While Kelly did not realise the rifle he and Arthur had found was the one he had given his friend, Michael Kennedy, at Mansfield all those months ago, what he did know – and Arthur agreed with his assessment – was that one of the outlaws had been wounded, possibly quite badly, and seemed to have escaped this way through the bush. Kelly proposed that Arthur stay where he was as it seemed an excellent firing position, while he returned to

REINFORCEMENTS

the station with what he had found. Before he left, though, both men fired two rounds into the hotel to show the outlaws inside that they were now surrounded. His last instruction to Arthur was to shoot anyone he thought was an outlaw trying to escape.

James Arthur wasn't convinced his firing position was as good as it had first appeared and, spotting another fallen log 30 metres closer to the hotel, crawled to it. A near miss from an outlaw's bullet then convinced him to crawl to the fat end of the log. The new position was not as good as the old for viewing and firing, but it offered considerably more protection and he could now also clearly see four horses tied to the rails in the hotel's rear paddock. Still not satisfied, he made a third move, again closer to the hotel and again behind a fallen log; now, though, he had a clear and unobstructed view of the hotel's rear door and breezeway.

John Kelly, meanwhile, made his way back to the railway station, firstly moving slowly and cautiously through the bush and then darting across to the drain in the reserve where he showed O'Connor what he and Arthur had found at the rear of the hotel, and telling him what he thought it meant. From there, Kelly scurried back to the station and onto the platform, where he was almost instantaneously surrounded by reporters. He showed them the rifle and the blood-soaked skullcap and again offered his opinion on the find. Mrs O'Connor was more concerned about the welfare of her husband, and Kelly was able to reply that he had left the inspector safe and sound and in good spirits.

In return, Kelly asked the reporters and ladies what had happened at the station while he was away. Kelly was aware of the prisoners' escape – he had seen most of it – but the reporters were able to tell him what they had learned from those escapees, and it was this information which Kelly would later pass on to Sadleir. Jock McHugh had been the most voluble of those who had fled and, after dropping the wounded John Jones at the Stanistreet house, he returned to share his observations with anyone who would listen.

McHugh told his audiences that there were 'about 30' in the hotel, meaning prisoners. He also said that the outlaws were wearing armour. These two separate pieces of information somehow became conflated, giving the police in particular an exaggerated idea of the outlaws' strength. McHugh further stated that he thought the outlaws would attempt to break free at dawn, and stated his belief that at least one of the gang had been wounded. Finally, he said he was convinced that a man with red whiskers had helped the outlaws put their armour on.

* * *

John Kelly also briefed Sadleir on the placement of police in the cordon, explaining that this would only be an approximation as the individual police could move if they saw a better position or if they thought they were too exposed. He began by outlining how, when Hare departed, he and O'Connor had made a rough division of the area around the hotel, with O'Connor and his men taking responsibility for the front of the hotel and the Railway Reserve. The position they had occupied in the drainage ditch also gave the Queenslanders line of sight along the Wangaratta side of the hotel and because of this, Kelly had chosen to place his Victorians primarily on the Benalla side and in the bush behind the hotel.

Moving to the left from O'Connor's position, the first of the Victorian policemen was Charles Gascoigne, whose firing position was behind a small tree just a few metres from the south-eastern corner of the hotel. Tom Kirkham had originally been just a bit further around, but he was off visiting friends and the next policeman was William Phillips, further up the slope and near the position where Ned's rifle and skullcap had been

REINFORCEMENTS

found. Daniel Barry was a little further back and slightly more elevated. Further around the cordon were James Arthur and William Canny, the latter not all that far from the extreme right of O'Connor's position.

When he had finished the briefing, Kelly was thanked by Sadleir who then asked him if he would see to the placement of the men he had brought from Benalla while he in turn sought out O'Connor for an update. Kelly led Sergeant Whelan and most of his men away from the platform and past Stanistreet's before placing them in positions along the Benalla side of the hotel, as he knew the Wangaratta reinforcements had taken positions on the opposite side. As they moved away from the stationmaster's house, Kelly told them to be as quiet as they could and proceed in single file. Even though they did so, their movement still drew fire from the hotel.

Kelly led Whelan to a position beyond William Phillips, further up the gradual rise in the north-west with the hotel and railway station some distance below him. Most of the Benalla reinforcements – Smyth, Hewitt, Walsh, Reilly, Patrick Kelly and the two Victorian Native Police – were placed in the light brush in front and on both sides of him. The closest to him was Reilly, although he was well back from the hotel as the bush had been cleared in his general area. As well, Reilly was armed with a double-barrelled shotgun and a revolver, both useless at his distance from the hotel. Consequently, Reilly would not fire a single shot during the siege. Even further back was Patrick Kelly, usually referred to as 'that big fat constable from Benalla'. An enormous man, Patrick Kelly was placed where he was to keep an eye on the hotel, the station, and, more importantly, the road and rail lines in from Benalla.

After he had completed placing the Benalla reinforcements, John Kelly left Whelan in charge of that side of the hotel and continued around through the scrub. He spoke briefly to James Arthur then stopped and spoke to Arthur Steele, outlining what had happened and where he had placed the Benalla men. He also told Steele that his position was now the closest to the hotel before continuing around towards the Railway Reserve and the station beyond. After he left, Steele inched his way a little closer to the back door.

* * *

Back at the station, Constables Kenny and Wilson had escorted Sadleir to O'Connor's position in the drain before finding their own places in the firing line. As they left the platform the little group was joined by James Dwyer, and the four men scurried down the track and into the Railway Reserve. Their movement was spotted by the outlaws who fired two volleys – one of four shots and one of three – at the policemen. Apart from encouraging the men to move faster and lower, the shots had no effect.

Arriving unscathed at the drain, Sadleir immediately sought out Stanhope O'Connor and asked the Queenslander for his take on the situation. O'Connor told Sadleir that they were up against a well-organised and well-armed opponent. O'Connor and his men believed the four outlaws remained inside the hotel, where he also believed there were up to 30 Kelly sympathisers. He also said that he suspected the hotel had been fortified. He had reason to believe that furniture had been used to make barricades while bags of horse feed had been used to build a barrier. In summary, O'Connor stated his conviction that any attempt to storm the building would inevitably lead to heavy casualties among the police.

Curiously, and perhaps because he was caught up in the moment, O'Connor does not seem to have mentioned something he had noted down just a couple of hours earlier as being

REINFORCEMENTS

important. When he was screening the prisoners who escaped after the first clash, one of the female escapees, probably Mrs Ryan, told O'Connor that there was still a considerable number of civilians held prisoner inside the hotel, including women and children. O'Connor had thanked her and said that he would take note of her information.

Sadleir now said he appreciated O'Connor's views and stated that he was inclined to agree. The volume of firing, especially in the recent volleys, did indeed suggest that there were more than four gunmen inside the hotel. If, as O'Connor suggested, the hotel had also been reinforced and fortified, any police assault would be suicidal and was therefore something he would not contemplate. Instead, he proposed to take his time and, accompanied by Constable Dwyer, inspect the police cordon around the hotel. Where necessary, he would make adjustments to that cordon. When that was done, he would return to the platform to supervise what had evolved into a siege.

As Sadleir and Dwyer prepared to move off, they heard an unusual sound; it was the ringing of metal on metal as the outlaws tapped the barrels of their revolvers on their armoured breastplates. They also heard a voice call out, 'Come out, you dogs, and we'll put daylight through you!' Sadleir looked over the edge of the drain and saw muzzle flashes at two of the hotel's front windows. He turned to O'Connor and suggested they give the outlaws a volley of their own. With that, he rested a borrowed rifle on the parapet, took careful aim at a window and fired.

Sadleir's single shot was immediately followed by a ragged volley from those alongside him in the drain. This in turn was followed by single shots and clusters of shots from police around the hotel. Even before the echo of the last shot faded away, other sounds could be heard from inside the hotel. Alongside the baritone calls of men pleading for both safety and survival could be heard the higher shrill of a woman's voice and the still-higher trills of children in mortal fear for their lives.

'Cease fire,' shouted Sadleir. 'Cease fire.'

CHAPTER 10

The Siege

i. 03:00–05:00 Monday

Glenrowan became a siege the moment the leaders of the opposing forces, Ned Kelly and Frank Hare, staggered away, wounded, from the first contact. Like all sieges, it became a battle of tactics and wills and, again like all sieges, those on the outside were never certain what those on the inside were doing, and vice versa. Because of this, no-one ever really saw the big picture; instead, those present saw a series of little pictures, snapshots almost, that reflected time and space and perspective. It is by putting these little pictures together, like a mosaic, that the reality of Glenrowan – the big picture – becomes visible.

After the initial exchange of fire which they all recorded so graphically, the reporters realised that yes indeed, they were now part of the biggest story that any of them would probably ever witness, let alone write about. They were also ideally placed to do that writing, being far enough back to see most of the arena in which the action was occurring but not so far away that the finer elements – the individual players and what they were doing – were lost. Early on, however, their main focus was on ensuring they lived long enough to write the story.

Before that initial exchange they had used the discarded police saddles to construct a sort of combination viewing platform and protective breastwork, although it wasn't really needed for the latter purpose as the shooting was concentrated in a small area more than 100 metres away. It was when the incident became a siege that they realised that they would be left pretty much on their own.

Nevertheless, an exciting little element of danger added spice to their situation. The sporadic fire which continued during the first hour after Frank Hare had left and the escaped prisoners passed through caused an occasional concern. A stray bullet clipped the outer wall of the stationmaster's office and another hit the railway fence, while a third zipped right by where the reporters were standing and struck McDonnell's Hotel, a hundred metres behind them. While Thomas Carrington would later recall the bullets 'whistling and pinging' among them, the reality was that the bullets that came their way were rare stray shots rather than aimed rounds, and they were never really in the firing line.

After the first shots, the reporters had also decided that the best contribution they could make would be assisting the police with logistics as there were no spare policemen for that task. The reporters proceeded to empty the guard's van of luggage, spare saddles, ammunition, and anything they thought might be of use to either themselves or the police in the coming hours. After the excitement of Frank Hare's departure and the release of prisoners, things grew quiet on the platform. An occasional policeman would appear out of the gloom seeking food or ammunition or both.

This prompted two of the reporters, Joe Melvin and John McWhirter, to sort through the boxes and loose rounds of ammunition that had been carelessly strewn across the platform and in the guard's van. The two journalists created separate piles of carbine, shotgun, and pistol ammunition. When a policeman subsequently came to collect more ammunition, he would be directed to the appropriate pile.

Otherwise, there was not a lot for the reporters to do or write about. They talked among themselves or to the two ladies, walked up and down the platform, stamping their feet to stay warm, and quizzed the occasional policeman or civilian visitor about what was happening on the front line. When it was very quiet and still, they would listen to the police horses snorting and restlessly moving about in the railway paddock, almost as if there was something to fear in the dark bush beyond the hotel.

* * *

Most of the police in the original cordon moved during the first hour of the siege, primarily to find better positions. They would not move too far from where they had been placed, but would seek out somewhere nearby that offered a little bit more protection or a slightly better view. And then they would sit and wait for something to happen.

Shooting broke out roughly every fifteen minutes, and it often followed a pattern. The police in front of the hotel would see – or imagine they saw – movement at a door or window and then fire off a ragged volley. Police elsewhere in the cordon, alternating between fear and boredom, would hear something happening on the other side of the building, and shoot a round or two of their own. At times, bullets fired by police at the rear of the building would pass through the hotel and narrowly miss officers at the front. Those police, thinking they were under fire, would shoot back, and there would be sustained shooting for up to a minute.

After such shooting, those at the front would sometimes call out for any women or children inside to make their escape. But they did so without conviction for, from the early stages of the siege, most of those on the outside operated on a number of assumptions about most of those on the inside; assumptions that were invariably wrong. The first was that, after the initial escape of prisoners early in the stand-off, there were no more civilians inside. A second assumption, perhaps built on the first, was that if there were any civilians still inside the hotel, they were now there by choice and had obviously thrown their lot in with the outlaws. Either way, everyone inside was a combatant. This was openly discussed among the police.

Other police were under the impression that any civilians still being held by the outlaws were all in the skillion kitchen at the rear. Shooting into the main building would therefore pose no risk to civilians who had been unable to escape.

Finally, there was a real belief that the outlaws would attempt a break-out, probably around dawn. Some believed they would sally out as a group, shooting at police, and then either ride or run into the bush and the Warby Ranges beyond. This would pose the problem of recognising just who was an outlaw and who was not; only a few of the police in the cordon had ever set eyes on the gang.

For most of the police and for most of the time, there was little to see and even less to do. Those in the cordon would fire at muzzle flashes in the hotel and contribute to the regular general volleys. Between times, they would call out challenges to the outlaws, partly out of bravado and partly to reinforce the impression that the hotel was surrounded and those within were held in an iron grip. They would also call out to each other, exchanging observations, news, and rumours. While most stayed where they had been placed, others took the opportunity to move around.

Shortly after Frank Hare's train departed for Benalla, Stanhope O'Connor, wearing a large, colourful scarf, wandered across the Railway Reserve to the station where he greeted the reporters and spoke to his wife and sister-in-law, reassuring both of his wellbeing before returning to his men in the drain. John Kelly also moved around the site, and he twice returned to the station to update the reporters and civilians on what was happening. During the first of those visits, he also called in to the stationmaster's house to see how Mrs Stanistreet and her children were coping. He told her that the house was not completely safe as it was within firing range of the hotel, and suggested she and the children go further back into the bush or across the paddocks to McDonnell's Hotel. Mrs Stanistreet thanked him and stayed where she was.

On both visits, Kelly also collected ammunition for his men. He would then make his way around the cordon, stopping at each firing position to drop off ammunition if it was needed, and to exchange a few words with the occupant of the post. While dropping ammunition to Daniel Barry, he told the policeman that his position was a good one and that he should remain there. With Charles Gascoigne he shared both news and views. 'You should see O'Connor down in the drain,' he said. 'If you gave him £1000, he wouldn't stick his head up!' And then he moved quietly on to the next post. Kelly felt, perhaps rightfully, that he and his men were taking more than their fair share of the risks.

The most active of all though, was Mounted Constable Tom Kirkham. Barely fifteen minutes after taking up his original firing position, Kirkham called out that he was going back to the station for more ammunition. He left, but did not return. He didn't quite make it to the station either, instead joining his friends, the

Native Police, in their drain in front of the hotel. There, he chatted amiably about the situation and fired the occasional shot at the hotel. John Kelly found him there and publicly berated him for leaving his position. Tom took this with good grace and said he would collect ammunition for distribution and then return to his spot.

Tom did collect the ammunition, but somehow managed to spend 30 minutes at the station while doing so. He also distributed that ammunition, but only to those who were reasonably close to the station. Then he returned to his friends in the drain to continue the conversation that had been rudely interrupted an hour before.

* * *

Talking was about the only thing those inside the hotel could do safely. Any movement within the building that could be seen from outside instantly attracted police fire, even if there was nothing threatening about the movement. Early in the siege, a prisoner had waved a white handkerchief out of a broken window; three shots were immediately fired at it. At regular intervals the police would fire a volley of shots into the hotel and, when they did, all the prisoners would throw themselves flat on the floor. They noted that, when those volleys were fired, the heaviest shooting always came from the drain at the front.

While lying flat on the floor, some of the prisoners chose to analyse various aspects of the extremely perilous position in which they now found themselves. Some listened carefully to the bullets ripping through the outside and inside walls and thudding into the chimneys. They were soon able to distinguish between bullets smacking through walls, roof, doors, or window frames by the different sound each impact made. One of the prisoners early on realised that the police bullets could not penetrate brick. He crawled to one of the fireplaces and squeezed into the base of the chimney. A large calibre Martini-Henry bullet partially dislodged one of the bricks he was leaning against, so he carefully crawled back to his original position.

Some of the prisoners took advantage of lulls in the firing to move around the hotel, staying low and slow to avoid drawing police fire. They called the small bedroom 'The Kelly Room' and no-one entered it after the fighting started. Instead, many made their way to the parlour which soon became crowded; it probably appeared safer because it did not have a window. The close-packed prisoners also held little discussions among themselves. The idea of rushing out in a group with hands in the air was put forward, but no-one was prepared to take the lead. There was even a suggestion that they borrow weapons from the Kellys to give the police back some of their own medicine. This too was rejected, and the man who had suggested it was afterwards watched with suspicion.

The three remaining outlaws were in markedly better circumstances. They were able to move around in relative safety because of their armour; James Reardon would later recall hearing bullets ricocheting off the outlaws several times. All three were quite solicitous of Margaret Reardon – now the only woman left in the hotel – and her children, but they were also happy to shoot at the police from doors and windows. They sometimes communicated using whistles, and occasionally called each other by the assumed names they had chosen. But mostly they waited for Ned, who had promised to do something spectacular. No-one, outlaws or prisoners, had seen him since he disappeared into the bush after the first clash with the police, and at intervals during the night various gang members would go to the back door and call out his name. And then, just after 5 o'clock in the morning, he was there.

* * *

If Tom Kirkham was busy catching up with friends, Charles Rawlins was just busy. After escorting the wounded Frank Hare back to the station, Rawlins filled Hare's ammunition pouch with rifle cartridges and took them back to the drain where John Kelly and Stanhope O'Connor were deep in conversation. When Rawlins told them what he was carrying, Kelly asked him if he would do them a further favour and distribute the ammunition to police in the cordon. Rawlins headed off and made a complete circuit of the hotel.

He arrived back at the station at around the same time as the escaped prisoners and immediately set about doing what he could to assist. He heard Ann Jones's screams before he saw her, but soon spotted Ann and Jane Jones on the road near the railway gates. He hurried over and found Jane bleeding from her head wound, and Ann very close to hysteria. He escorted the women back to the station, and handed them over to the ladies and reporters. He then refilled the ammunition pouch and again went out distributing cartridges.

After this trip, Rawlins decided to find Tom Curnow, who had spent a lot of time in the hotel the previous day and seemed also to be a good observer. Curnow possibly had knowledge which could be of use to the police, and so Rawlins set off down the road to Benalla.

Earlier, the outbreak of shooting at Jones's hotel was clearly heard at the Curnow house. Tom, Isobel and Tom's sister went outside and looked north but could not see anything. An old man who lived opposite joined them in the roadway. He felt that the Kelly Gang were either destroyed or trapped and facing imminent destruction. Defying his wife's expressed wishes once again, Tom Curnow and his neighbour headed towards the gunfire.

Isobel Curnow and her sister-in-law sat inside, no doubt waiting anxiously for the wandering schoolteacher, and heard a knock on the door. At first, the women refused to answer it; Isobel could not shake her conviction that it was Ned Kelly. Charles Rawlins identified himself, however, and said that he needed their assistance. Soon afterwards, Curnow returned and told the others that he had approached the hotel from several angles to see what was going on but each time was warned off by police in the cordon. Rawlins explained why he was there and asked the schoolteacher to draw up a floor plan of the hotel, noting any obstructions or barricades that the outlaws may have put in place. The methodical Curnow took his time and was not quite finished when they heard the sound of a steam train beginning the gradual ascent up the incline to Glenrowan station. Rawlins thanked Curnow for his work, grabbed the map and ran towards the station.

* * *

When Ned staggered away from the hotel after the initial gunfight, he was badly wounded, in a lot of pain and bleeding profusely. He guessed that none of the wounds would prove fatal, but they were debilitating and he knew he needed time and space to deal with the injuries and adjust his grand plan to address the changed circumstances they now all found themselves in. Joe had chosen not to accompany him, so Ned set off alone, uphill, looking for somewhere quiet and protected where, like a hunted animal, he could examine and lick his wounds. He was hurt, badly hurt, but guessed that none of his wounds would be fatal. He needed time – and space – to come up with a new plan. He had done it before and he could do it again.

Ned found a small copse of young gum trees grouped alongside a larger, older tree and there he lowered himself gently to the ground before removing his helmet and carrying out a careful self-examination. Probably the worst of his injuries was the gunshot wound to the foot. His larrikin boots may have been good for riding and impressing the ladies, but they gave no protection in a gunfight. The bullet that had traversed his foot from front to rear smashed several bones as it passed through and Ned understood that, if he survived all this, he would probably limp for the rest of his life. His right hand, too, suggested future problems. A bullet had passed clean through the ball of his thumb, although it seemed to have missed the bones in his hand. While he knew he could still fire a pistol, he also knew that, unsupported, his injured right hand would probably not be able to carry the weight of that pistol.

Finally, there was the double wound from the single bullet in his left arm. It looked bad and felt worse, but Ned knew it may have been the least important of the wounds. He took off the skullcap he had been wearing to cushion his helmet and used it to soak up the blood from his arm, noting that the flow was sluggish, confirming his assessment that no major blood vessels had been ruptured. As he completed his stocktake of wounds, Ned heard movement downhill and to his right, on the Benalla side of the hotel. He knew that if he stayed where he was, he would be killed or captured. Slowly, painfully, he put his helmet back on and climbed the slight slope, half-walking and half-dragging his shot right foot. He left behind his rifle and skullcap. He knew where they were, though, and would come back for them later.

Ned found another spot, further back from the hotel and again in a small copse of trees and saplings. He lowered himself to the ground, leaned back against a tree and closed his eyes . . . and then was awake again, wondering how long he had dozed and what might have happened while he was asleep.

Slowly, stiffly, and painfully, he stood, donned his helmet and headed back down the hill. The rifle fire was clear and crisp in the still air and he could hear the policemen in their firing positions calling to one another and issuing challenges to the outlaws

Contemporary sketch by Tom Carrington of the site of the Glenrowan siege. 1. Ann Jones's Glenrowan Inn. 2. Outhouse. 3. Railway station. 4. Stationmaster's house. 5. McDonnell's house. 6. Platelayers' tents. 7. Positions taken by the police. 8. Trench occupied by Lieutenant O'Connor and the Queensland Native Police. 9. Spot where Mr. Hare was shot. 10. Paddock where horses were shot. 11. Tree where Ned Kelly was captured. 12. Road to Bracken's station. 13. Half a mile from here the rails were taken up.

Photograph of the siege site in the early afternoon, Monday 28 June 1880.

The only known photograph of the Kelly Gang at large. *From left:* Steve Hart, Dan Kelly and Ned Kelly.

Constable Hugh Bracken.

Sergeant Arthur Steele. Personally affronted by the Kellys, Steele flew into a deadly rage at Glenrowan.

A crowd starts to gather at Glenrowan station in the early afternoon, Monday 28 June 1880.

Tom Curnow, arguably the bravest man in Glenrowan that weekend.

A dance was held at Jones's hotel on the Sunday evening of the siege. Ned is in the foreground, dustcoat over his armour and knitted skullcap on head. Alongside him is Jane Jones.

The Kelly Hunters. Post-siege photograph of the Benalla contingent, who first confronted the Kelly Gang at Glenrowan. *From left:* Daniel Barry, Hugh Bracken, William Phillips, James Arthur, John Kelly, Charles Gascoigne and William Canny.

Police pose for a staged photograph after the siege.

Monday, midafternoon: Jones's hotel begins to burn.

A close-up of the hotel as the fire takes hold.

The precise spot where Ned was taken.

After the siege, a policeman poses in Ned's armour, holding his revolving rifle.

The morning after. Prominent locals pose outside McDonnell's Tavern while the coffins made for Dan Kelly and Steve Hart rest on the undertaker's wagon in the background.

A group photograph of the police at Glenrowan, including the Queensland Native Police and their commander, Stanhope O'Connor (seated centre right).

Joe Byrne's body being posed for photographers.

Shackled and still incapacitated by the wounds he suffered at Glenrowan, Ned poses for a photograph in the exercise yard of Melbourne Gaol on the eve of his execution. The portrait was his last request.

A contemporary sketch of Ned's final moments.

they knew were skulking in the hotel in front of them. For a bushman like Ned, even with his wounds, the police cordon was more a minor inconvenience than a major obstacle. He moved very slowly but he also moved very quietly, sticking to the shadows until he was able to use the cover of the stables and then the kitchen until he reached the back door. There he called out, 'It's me boys. It's Ned.'

* * *

Joe was the first to respond, making his way to the back door where he spoke to Ned in a low voice that no-one else could hear. Whatever he said, Ned's response was, 'I'm shot. You can lick them. Keep your pluck up.' Joe stood quietly for a moment, then turned and walked down the passage towards the front of the hotel.

* * *

On the way, Joe stopped at the large bedroom near the back door and told the prisoners huddled inside to stay where they were because they were probably better off than him. He walked to the front of the hotel, and turned into the bar. From there he looked into the parlour and asked the prisoners seeking shelter there how they were getting on. Several of them asked if he could help them get away and again he said, 'Stay where you are; you are a great deal better off than we are.' With that, he poured himself a glass of spirits from a bottle on the counter of the bar. Some recalled it being a nobbler of brandy while others remembered it as a glass of whisky.

Joe placed one foot on the bar rail and said that he wanted to propose a toast. It was an uncomfortable pose, as the armour apron that protected his groin and lower abdomen now dug into his thigh. He lifted the apron with his left hand, raised the glass in his right, and called out sardonically, 'Many a long and happy day still in the bush boys!'

In the drain outside, Stanhope O'Connor had decided that it was time to fire another volley into the hotel, and ordered his Native Police to aim and fire on his command. One of the Queenslanders either saw, or suspected that he saw, movement behind the door to the bar. He took careful aim and then fired on O'Connor's command. His bullet punched through a panel of the door and struck Joe squarely in the groin, just where the top of his leg met the bottom of his trunk. It knocked him against the bar and severed his femoral artery. The glass dropped from Joe's hand and he fell to the floor.

Young Patrick Delaney was the prisoner closest to Joe, seeking cover in a far corner of the bar room. He did not hear Joe utter a word or make a sound. Dave Mortimer, keeping his head down while lying flat in the doorway to the parlour, heard a dull thud and, looking up, saw Joe stretched out on the floor not two metres from where he himself lay. Further back in the parlour, James Reardon couldn't see directly into the bar, but he did hear everything: 'I heard him fall like a log and he never groaned or anything, and I could hear a sound like blood gushing.'

And that was what most of those in earshot would always remember, the sound of Joe's lifeblood pumping out of the gaping wound in his groin. It was a sound that Joe himself did not hear, as he slipped from unconsciousness to death. One moment he was there, the next he was gone.

* * *

One of the other outlaws, either Steve or Dan, heard the thud, investigated, and found Joe's body where it fell. Their friend was obviously dead. He called the others, who came down the passage to look at Joe's body before all three retreated to the back door to discuss what had just happened and what was to happen next. Ned spoke first, telling the younger men, 'We must make the best of it. My best friend is dead. I'll go out in the veranda and challenge them.' He walked to the front door and roared a challenge to the police outside. There was no obvious response. Back inside, he could see neither Dan nor Steve, so he called out to anyone who could hear that he would challenge the police himself and that they should join him when he did so.

With that, Ned left by the back door, again using the moon shadows as cover and making his way into the back paddock where he tried to catch one of the tethered horses. Perhaps he hoped to mount it and make a last futile charge against the police lines. If so, his injuries prevented him from doing anything beyond untying and patting the horse, another of his favourite's, Music. He would now remain alone and on foot. Ned opened the gate to let Music go where it would. He then trudged off, moving from shadow to shadow, once more passing through the police cordon without challenge.

Back in the hotel, Joe's death came close to destroying both the will and the faith of the younger outlaws. Dave Mortimer watched them seek a quiet corner and heard one say to the other, 'What do we do now?' He did not hear the reply but Michael Reardon, alongside him, said he thought the two outlaws intended to commit suicide. Dan and Steve lifted Joe's head and shoulders from the floor and dragged his body down to their bedroom, the smaller of the two, where they lay it on the floor just inside the door. Surrounded as they were by their prisoners, the two young men now felt very, very, alone.

ii. 05:00–07:00 Monday

The police and civilians surrounding and overlooking Jones's hotel had no knowledge of what had taken place inside.

They still thought they were facing four armed outlaws, as well as an unknown number of supporters, some of whom were probably armed (the police consistently overestimated the capacity of the gang). There was also a general expectation that the outlaws would sally out at dawn in an attempt to escape. John Kelly in particular was worried about the strength of the cordon, fearing that the outlaws could burst through without too much difficulty anywhere but the front of the hotel. He did not know that Joe Byrne had died around 5 o'clock and, when the reinforcements from Wangaratta and Benalla arrived between 5.20 and 5.30 am, he was a very relieved man.

Charles Gascoigne was also pleased by their arrival because his was probably the most important – and the most exposed – of all the police firing positions. When he heard the steam train puffing up the incline from Benalla, he actually walked down to the railway gates to watch the arrival of Superintendent Sadleir and his men. There he bumped into one of the Queensland Native Police who told him that he'd heard that both William Canny and trooper Jimmy had been killed. Depressed by the news, Gascoigne returned to his firing position in time to see one of the outlaws in the back yard of the hotel, where the man released one of their horses and shooed it into the bush. Gascoigne then lost sight of both horse and outlaw, but suspected that the reinforced police lines would now have one less outlaw to face.

* * *

There was a lull in the firing about fifteen minutes after Joe was killed. One or two single shots were fired from the police cordon, but there were no volleys or sustained shooting and Margaret Reardon took the opportunity to approach Dan who had now assumed the leadership role left vacant by his brother's absence and Joe's death. She spoke freely to him, saying that she and the other members of her family wanted to leave. Dan replied that any decision to leave was hers but that, if she did leave, he would like her to take a message to Superintendent Hare. Please tell Hare, he said, that if the police would hold fire, the outlaws would release all the prisoners and then fight the lawmen 'fair and square'.

Margaret walked away to talk to her family who were now gathered in the rear bedroom, but in the few minutes between approaching Dan and readying her children to flee, the amount of firing increased markedly. There was a reason for this that those inside were not aware of. Twenty minutes after Joe's last toast, the first of the Wangaratta reinforcements arrived in Glenrowan, followed over the next fifteen minutes by the remainder of the Wangaratta reinforcements and the Benalla police contingent led by John Sadleir. When these police were placed in the cordon, many took the opportunity to fire into the hotel.

Several other prisoners, concerned about the amount of police firing, called out to Dan as he patrolled the hotel, asking if they, too, could leave. Dan's reply to all was, 'You can go, but I am frightened that you will be shot. I do not begrudge your going if you can escape.'

The male prisoners who had planned an escape took Dan at his word, and made for the front door while the Reardons stayed back towards the rear of the hotel, organising themselves for their escape. As soon as the first prisoner appeared at the front door, the police in the drain shot at them. O'Connor immediately ordered them to stop and, standing up in the drain, called out, 'Who comes here?' There was no answer, as the barrage had forced the would-be escapees to retreat into the hotel. Dan had watched the whole thing, and he told Margaret Reardon that if she still planned to escape, she should scream as she left, and have all her children scream as well. He also repeated the message he wanted her to take to Superintendent Hare, adding that he was looking forward to a fair fight when daylight came.

Dan also promised Margaret that he and Steve would hold their fire while the Reardons made their escape, and so Margaret led the way out the back door and away from the breezeway. She carried her baby, Bridget, in her arms while her oldest son Michael followed a few metres behind, leading his little brother by the left hand and with his right hand in the air. A couple of metres further back, James Reardon followed with the last of their children. And a short distance from all this, Arthur Steele watched the family emerge. He had loaded his shotgun with bullets, and slowly took aim.

* * *

As she left the protection of the hotel and its shadows, Margaret Reardon screamed at the top of her voice, calling on all who could hear her to cease firing. The sudden emergence of people from the rear of the hotel, plus the fact that one was screaming, had an instant effect on the police on the Wangaratta side of the hotel, as they alone could see the initial movements. Several of them, fearing that the action presaged a mass escape, fired shots into the hotel. Others, closer to where the Reardon family suddenly appeared, took up firing positions and waited to see what would happen. Arthur Steele, the closest policeman and no more than twenty metres from the back door, would later claim that he called to the woman when he spotted her, saying that she would be safe if she moved quickly.

All the others within earshot would have a different recollection, and one that was remarkably uniform. All recalled Steele calling out loudly, 'Put up your hands and come this way or I'll shoot you like bloody dogs.' And as he finished calling, Steele shot, the bullet passing through the shawl Margaret had wrapped around baby Bridget and miraculously missing both mother and child. Steele had seen that she was not an outlaw but assumed that the woman was probably a Kelly sympathiser and therefore, to him, fair game.

James Arthur was within fifteen metres of Steele and had a clear view of the incident. Arthur did not trust Steele's judgement any more than he trusted the sergeant's temperament. In his own words, Arthur swore that Steele 'seemed like as if he was excited. He fired from the tree when he was first there. He fired when I could see nothing to fire at'. When Margaret emerged from the shadows leading her little group, Arthur had instantly recognised that it was a mother and child and called on the other police to stop shooting. Even Tom Kirkham, some distance away towards the front of the hotel, heard his call, 'Look out for the woman – cease firing – mind the man.'

Steele could hardly have missed the call, but he chose to ignore it and fired directly at Margaret, who called out, 'Oh, you have shot my baby!' A few paces behind Margaret, James Reardon clearly heard a policeman call out, 'If you fire on that woman again, I am damned if I do not shoot you because she is an innocent woman.' The voice may or may not have belonged to James Arthur, as he had a slightly different recollection of what transpired after that first shot. He recalled looking across at Steele, watching as the sergeant reloaded. He called across and when Steele looked up, James Arthur raised his own carbine and said, slowly and deliberately, 'If you fire again, I'll bloody well shoot you myself.'

But Steele was in a zone where he seemed to neither see nor hear anything around him. He had also somehow convinced himself that Margaret Reardon was actually Ann Jones, for he yelled at the top of his voice, 'I've shot Mother Jones in the tits.' Some distance away, William Phillips heard Steele's call and yelled back sarcastically that such shooting at such a target was certainly a feather in the sergeant's cap. Steele probably didn't even hear those words just as he didn't hear Arthur's earlier warning; the bully in uniform was busily sizing up his next target.

* * *

The firing and yelling at the side of the hotel sparked a significant increase in the amount of firing from the Native Police in the drain at the front. This caused the remaining Reardons to hesitate as it meant they would be walking directly into mortal danger. Michael called out to his mother to turn back, but she just called out over her shoulder that, 'We might as well get shot here as in the house.' Still clutching Bridget close, she crossed from the hotel to the fence on the Wangaratta side and there took shelter behind a tree.

Steele's recollections of what came next were again quite specific and deliberate lies. He said that a man appeared from the back door and that he called on that man to put his hands in the air. At the sound of his voice, the man bent over and ran towards the stables. Steele then fired a single shot at the figure, who then turned and retraced his steps towards the back door. Steele then fired again and believed that he had hit the man, who fell screaming back through the door. Steele said he then took cover as shots were fired at him from the hotel.

Time would add further details to Steele's recollections. Decades later, he would claim that he allowed Margaret Reardon to pass through the police lines and that he then noticed a man crawling along a drain at the rear of the hotel. Twice he called on the man to put his hands in the air and, when his orders were ignored, he fired a single shot. The figure then turned and crawled back to the door where Steele's second shot struck him, knocking him back through the doorway. He then heard Dan Kelly, who he knew well, call out, 'You dogs.' Steele said he responded by telling Dan that he and his mates should surrender, as it was all over for them.

And yet again, everyone else who was there recalled the events quite differently. James Arthur also had a clear view of Michael Reardon leaving the rear of the hotel. He recalled that Michael was walking upright and leading a small child by the hand. He put his free hand in the air when Steele called out, but was almost immediately fired upon by Steele. At this, Michael turned back, and was hit just before he reached safety.

Michael himself remembered following his mother out of the hotel and immediately noting the increase in the volume of police firing. He had let go of his little brother's hand as he cleared the building but then heard the boy call out to not leave him as he could not keep up. Michael turned around, picked up his brother and headed towards the rear paddock, away from the heavy firing at the front. As he did so, he heard someone shout, 'Here he is – look out. Here comes a man with a gun.' Straight away, he felt a bullet hit his shoulder. He immediately put his brother down and led him as quickly as possible back to the safety of the hotel. There, he collapsed with his back against an inner wall of the dining room, his calls for both water and assistance ignored. His father, James, lay on the floor nearby with his two smallest children between his knees. After seeing what happened to his wife and son, he had not been prepared to risk any more lives in an escape attempt.

None of the others would ever recall Steele exchanging any words with any of the outlaws. They would, however, remember him shooting young Michael Reardon in the shoulder as the confused young man seemed to be trying to surrender, and then shouting, 'I've wounded Dan Kelly', perhaps attempting to justify his deliberate targeting of an innocent boy.

* * *

After he disembarked at Glenrowan station with the Benalla police reinforcements, railway guard Jesse Dowsett went for a walk around the station and the adjoining paddocks and reserve to familiarise himself with the police positions. At the Wangaratta end of the Railway Reserve, he thought he heard a woman screaming and calling out from the direction of the hotel. Jesse made his way through the bush towards the woman's voice, dropping to his hands and knees for the last part of the journey and crawling to within 40 metres of the hotel. From there he was able to make out the figure of a woman holding a child and sheltering behind a tree. She was crying and calling out to the police not to shoot her baby.

Jesse watched until he was satisfied that it was not a ruse to draw the police into the open, and then called softly to the woman, telling her to walk towards where he was crouching behind the fence. As she started to move towards him, the police at the front fired a solid volley into the hotel and the woman hesitated. Jesse called again softly and she continued. As she got closer, Jesse recognised her as Margaret Reardon, having met her several times in the past. He spoke to her more encouragingly now and, when she reached the fence, he physically lifted her over, telling her that she and the baby were safe. He asked if he could carry baby Bridget, put his other arm around her shoulder, and gently walked her through the scrub to the station.

The reporters on the platform were able to follow all this, although they did not really know what it was they were following. The yells and screams they could hear meant something was happening, while the increased police firing suggested that the outlaws may have made an appearance somewhere outside the hotel. A few minutes after the police in the front drain unleashed a volley, the reporters could clearly hear a woman's voice, crying and sobbing. Moreover, it was a voice that appeared to be coming towards the station.

Two figures then emerged from the gloom of the Railway Reserve; one was Jesse Dowsett and the other Margaret Reardon, now again with baby Bridget in her arms. The reporters met the pair and escorted them to the passenger carriage, still at the station, and to the compartment occupied by Mrs O'Connor and her sister. Jesse then returned to the cordon, but this time to a different place in the bush where there was an obvious gap in the police lines.

It took a few minutes for a distraught Margaret Reardon to regain her composure. At first, the only thing the others could make out from her ramblings was that 'they' were all there and 'they' were all armoured. When she grew relatively calm and rational, Margaret answered questions from the reporters, John McWhirter in particular. She told them that there were four outlaws in the hotel, that they were all well-armed and that there were a lot of people being held in the hotel. She identified some by name; the Delaney boys, Larkins, Reynolds and Gibbons, plus a number of men she did not know. She was exhausted, her child was fretting, and she asked to now be left alone.

* * *

The heavy volley that caused Margaret Reardon to pause and the reporters to sit up smashed into the hotel where those inside again tried to make themselves as small a target as possible. As the echoes of the volley died away, the elderly labourer Martin Cherry called out from one of the children's bedrooms off the skillion kitchen, saying that he had been shot and calling on the farmer John Larkins to come and cover him. Cherry had been lying on one of the children's beds when a bullet struck him in the abdomen; Larkins was determined to keep well out of trouble in the well-protected bunker he had made for himself in the kitchen.

Larkins crawled into the bedroom and eased Cherry onto the floor. He realised that there was little he could do to treat the wound, and so he covered the older man with the mattress from the bed, hoping it would provide some form of protection as well as warmth. As he finished doing this, William Sandercook crawled to the door and asked if he could assist, but Larkins said that he had done all that he could. Both men then crawled back to the bags of oats. They would remain there until they eventually left the hotel.

Inside the hotel itself, Dan and Steve stood in the passageway just before the back door, not returning the police fire and seemingly overwhelmed. Ned, their leader, had disappeared although he had promised to return and stage an attack on the police lines. Ned had appeared to be badly wounded though, and had also seemed very moody when he left. The death of Joe had also hit the younger men hard, as Joe's voice had always been the voice of moderation and caution. Dan and Steve both believed that Joe would have found a solution to their predicament, had he lived. But Joe was dead and Ned was missing.

When the police firing died down a bit, Dan Kelly appeared in the dining room and told those present to stay in the building because the police seemed determined to shoot anyone who tried to leave. Someone in the room called out that the gang should surrender. Dan replied that, 'We will never surrender, but most likely we will leave directly.' While Dan was talking, Steve walked out of the back door and exchanged shots with William Canny and Trooper Barney, who were sharing a firing position. The breezeway at the back would now become the outlaws' favourite firing position as any movement near the front walls attracted a volley from the troopers in the drain. Joe's death had taught them that, at least.

* * *

At the front of the hotel, Sadleir was well aware of the sound and fury that accompanied Margaret Reardon's bid for freedom. He could clearly hear the yells and screams from the rear and the concentration of fire from the Wangaratta side of the cordon. He could also make out calls and taunts – 'Fire away you bastards, you can't hurt us' – and the sound of metal on metal as the outlaws tapped their helmets and breastplates with their guns. When the firing died down and Sadleir had received reports from Jesse Dowsett, James Dwyer, and several others, he realised that he needed to take direct charge and impose order on what was happening. While he had some knowledge of where the police cordon had been put in place, his knowledge of just about everything else was limited. The fact that no-one around him really knew whether there could be other women or children inside the hotel prompted him to action.

Like several other policemen, James Dwyer had arrived at Glenrowan armed with a shotgun and a revolver which he soon realised would be of limited use in the medium range siege that Glenrowan had become. To make himself useful, Dwyer therefore volunteered his services to Sadleir, an offer the superintendent immediately accepted. He issued his instructions to Dwyer crisply, first ordering a ceasefire: 'Tell the men not to fire until they hear a whistle from me and when they hear two whistles it will be a signal to cease firing.' Sadleir was also aware that any prisoners still in the hotel would probably be lying on the floor, so he told Dwyer to pass on the additional message that, 'whenever they would fire, to fire about the height of a man's head'.

Finally, he told Dwyer that he should, if possible, determine the current placements of the police as accurately as possible while also trying to get the names of all the police at Glenrowan. As he sent Dwyer on his way, Sadleir called out to the hotel from his position in the drain, 'All you innocent people, throw yourselves flat on the ground and you will not be shot.'

As he set off, Dwyer felt alone and exposed. He also felt that he was being targeted by the outlaws as several shots were fired in his direction, one of which (he would later claim) knocked his hat off. He also heard someone yell, 'Knock that bastard over', and hoped that it was one of the outlaws calling out. As well as Sadleir's messages, Dwyer carried a bottle of brandy which he offered to share with those he visited. He first stopped at Charles Gascoigne's position, passed on Sadleir's instructions, and continued clockwise around the cordon.

The bush had been cleared more extensively on the Benalla side than on the Wangaratta side and consequently the cordon there was further back. This forced Dwyer back into the bush and, when he next met Patrick Kelly, one of the Benalla reinforcements, the big man told him that there were several police beyond him but that they were all in voice contact, so Dwyer need not go any further. Dwyer was now enjoying his new role, and he continued on, sharing instructions, ammunition, and brandy with James Whelan, but completely missing James Arthur, who did recall seeing Dwyer wander past his post, bottle in hand. When he completed his circuit and returned to the drain, Dwyer reported to Sadleir, telling him that several men were running short of ammunition while some were hungry. Sadleir gave him a note to be taken back to the station and forwarded to Benalla by the next train; it asked for reinforcements and refreshments to be forwarded to Glenrowan.

There was a great deal of speculation among the police in

the cordon after Dwyer's somewhat erratic circuit. Daniel Barry recalled that when he heard of the order to fire high, he thought it must have been because there were outlaws on the roof of the hotel. Others in the cordon interpreted the order quite differently, saying that they believed they were told that one of the outlaws had climbed up the inside of a chimney seeking a better firing position and was now sniping at any movement in the police lines. Still others thought that it was an instruction to increase their rate of fire. Most would also recall the rumour that swept through that the outlaws were about to attempt an escape. When a voice called out to shoot the outlaw's horses in the rear paddock, a volley of shots cut the animals down in a welter of snorts and screams.

When Dwyer returned from his errand to the station, Sadleir asked him to accompany him on a reconnaissance, and the two moved carefully across the open spaces to the Benalla side of the hotel. There, they stopped at Charles Gascoigne's position; Sadleir later said he was surprised by Gascoigne's youth and also thought that the young man seemed a little nervous. Sadleir asked Gascoigne to concentrate his fire at and around the chimney on his side of the building as he suspected the outlaws were using it as a shield. Gascoigne said that he would certainly do so, but he offered the observation that his shots — several of which he believed had struck their intended targets — had caused no apparent discomfort. He added that he believed that the outlaws were wearing armour, a suggestion that seemed to surprise Sadleir.

From just beyond Gascoigne's position, Dwyer was able to point out all the salient features of Jones's hotel: the outbuildings, yards; and the bush beyond. When he felt that he had a good feel for the layout, Sadleir led Dwyer back to the drain; he had made his plans.

* * *

Despite clear evidence to the contrary and the recent personal observations of Margaret Reardon, the two senior police on site – Sadleir and O'Connor – seem to have continued to believe that all four outlaws were still in the hotel and that all four were armed with repeating rifles. Sadleir was satisfied with what he now understood about the situation on the ground. He would not entertain the thought of storming the hotel, and was content to simply maintain the cordon, strengthening it when he could. He would subsequently say, 'When you have got a rat in a trap, you don't put your hand in the trap to pull it out.'

The shooting had again died down. In his firing position, Daniel Barry suddenly realised that he could see that the hotel's walls and corrugated iron roof were thoroughly shot through. He then realised that he could see this because it was starting to grow light. The night was almost over and a new day was about to begin.

iii. The Man in the Mist

The light that allowed Daniel Barry to note the bullet perforations in the hotel also allowed James Arthur to comfortably pack his pipe for a good, relaxing, smoke. Arthur had moved some distance from his original firing position overlooking the hotel's back door. Still angry with Sergeant Steele's behaviour, he had moved away as soon as he was certain that Margaret Reardon was safe. He was now considerably further back in the bush, but he carried a Martini-Henry rifle and thought, 'It was as good at 100 yards as at 20, and I was afraid that if I stopped too near I would hit someone on the other side.'

He was chilled and bored on this cold, misty morning. His new position, like the old, was behind a log, and James Arthur turned over and stretched out with his back resting against the log. He lay his rifle alongside his leg, shaved the tobacco plug, packed the flakes into the bowl of the pipe, and prepared to light up. As he did so, something made him look across towards Morgan's Lookout. He was first shocked and then nonplussed by what he saw coming towards him. Arthur's first thought was that the figure he saw 30 metres or more away was an apparition, but he quickly realised that it was a tall and bulky figure wearing a light grey dustcoat and a nail-tin on its head. He dropped his pipe and called out, 'Go back, you damned fool. You'll be shot.' All he could think was that it was a madman about to storm the hotel.

From those 30 metres away, the figure replied, 'I could shoot you, sonny', and then attempted to do just that. The figure was having some trouble; it had to use its left arm to support its right hand which was holding a revolver. Raising both hands, it took aim and fired; the bullet fell well short of Arthur but the crack of the pistol alerted all the police in the area that something else was afoot.

Arthur's response was immediate. He rolled to the side, grabbing his rifle and raising himself onto one knee and into a shooter's crouch. He took careful aim at the figure's helmet, hoping to knock it off. He fired and the bullet struck home, but the figure only staggered slightly. Reloading quickly, Arthur took careful aim a second time. He noticed an opening in the helmet that looked like a giant mouth and fired at that. The bullet again struck home and the figure staggered slightly but continued its slow and cumbersome approach to where Arthur crouched. It paused, raised the pistol and fired a second shot, this one also falling short.

Arthur had by then again reloaded and he snapped off a third shot, aiming this time at the figure's body; he heard the bullet hum off into the distance. With this, Arthur realised that his position was rapidly becoming untenable. He moved away from the log where he had been crouching, seeking to move to the side and rear of the figure to have a possible shot at somewhere on the person's body that wasn't covered by armour. He guessed that he would have a better chance if he fired from a different angle. As he moved off, though, Arthur looked back to watch what the figure was doing. It continued to move towards the hotel although its movement was laborious. One leg was obviously injured and could not support the full weight of the body. When moving, the injured leg was thrown to one side and then dragged forward. It may have been slow and laborious, but to Arthur it also appeared to be inexorable.

* * *

James Arthur was not the only one to spot the mysterious figure emerge from the bushland at the rear of the hotel. As the sun began rising behind the mountains to the east, the reporters had again gathered on the platform, looking across to the hotel. One of them spotted something moving in the bush behind the hotel and pointed it out to the others. Looking across, they noticed that first one and then another of the police on the cordon's Wangaratta side, up near the top of the line, turn their backs to the hotel and shoot at something in the thin mist that had formed in the hollows and gullies around the township. The artist Thomas Carrington would use words rather than pencils to describe what he saw:

> Presently we noticed a very tall figure in white, stalking slowly in the direction of the hotel. There was no head visible, and in the dim light of morning, with all the steam rising very heavily from the ground, it looked, for all the world, like the ghost of Hamlet's father with no head, only a very long, thick neck.

THE SIEGE

Jesse Dowsett had been a very busy man in the hour or so since his arrival in Glenrowan. After escorting Margaret Reardon and her daughter to safety at the railway station, he had returned to a position in the cordon on the Wangaratta side of the hotel and there traded shots with the remaining outlaws. He had also joined in the shooting of their horses. He then returned to the station for more ammunition, and after collecting enough to last an hour, he slowly made his way back into the firing line, moving carefully from tree to tree and answering several police challenges on the way. He guessed it was around 6.45 am as it was rapidly becoming light. He also saw a mix of mist and gunsmoke surrounding the hotel.

Jesse's new position again overlooked the side and rear of the hotel; John Kelly was to his left, closer to the station, while Arthur Steele was in front, between Jesse and the hotel. He had just settled in when he sensed, rather than heard, a disturbance behind him. Some 100 metres away, he spotted a figure that at first blush seemed to be a giant, 'a tremendous big black fellow with something like a blanket on him'.

Dowsett called across to John Kelly, 'My God, what is that?' Kelly, too, was uncertain about what he was looking at, but called to the police who were closer to challenge whomever it was and to shoot him down if he did not answer. As he watched the figure's lumbering advance, Jesse heard a policeman call out to the man – for that was what it was – to stop, and then watched the man slowly raised a pistol and fire. He heard someone else shout for the police to scatter and take cover. Although he knew that he was out of range, Jesse fired several shots at the figure as it stopped at a clump of saplings just 50 metres from where he stood.

Ten metres from Jesse, Arthur Steele had been enjoying the brief interval between daybreak and full light when he noticed the distant disturbance at about the same time as Jesse and John Kelly. The figure, when he first saw it, was over 100 metres from Steele's position, and in the half-light and mist Steele thought that he was looking at a tall man with a blanket over his shoulders and thin black legs. His immediate thought was that it was a well-known local Aborigine named Tommy Reid, and he called out to the other police to be careful. As the figure advanced, Steele realised that the blanket was in fact a light-coloured dustcoat, that the figure's trousers were criss-crossed with dark black leggings and that the height was due to the figure wearing a large helmet.

Steele saw the figure raise a revolver and shoot at James Arthur. He saw Arthur return fire: 'I could see the bullets hitting him and staggering him for a moment, with no further effect.' The ringing Arthur's bullets made when they struck made Steele realise that the figure was wearing armour. He saw it fire a second shot at Arthur, and believed he heard it laugh aloud. By then, though, he was up and moving towards the advancing armoured man.

*　*　*

The shouting and shooting from the scrub beyond the hotel had drawn a small crowd onto the platform at the station. With day dawning over the thin scrub, visibility was good and the doctors and ladies joined reporters who were busy trying to make sense of the bizarre drama that they must soon describe to multitudes of readers. The *Argus*'s Joe Melvin watched the distant figure lurching towards the hotel, and would later write:

> . . . it was seen that he was armed only with a revolver. He, however, walked coolly from tree to tree, and received the fire of the police with the utmost indifference, returning a shot from his revolver when a good opportunity presented itself.

Thomas Carrington, who first thought the figure was someone trying to create a diversion so that the outlaws could escape, watched the events through an artist's eyes:

> The figure continued gradually to advance, stopping every now and then, and moving what looked like its headless neck slowly and mechanically around, and then raising one foot on a log and aiming and firing a revolver. Shot after shot was fired at it, but without effect, the figure generally replying by tapping the butt end of its revolver against its neck, the blows ringing out with the clearness and distinctness of a bell in the morning.

As he sought out a new firing position, James Arthur heard someone yell, 'He is a mad man', and recognised Dowsett's response: 'He is the devil', while Steele's contribution was, 'Look out boys, he is a bunyip'. And as he moved, Arthur shouted to all the police within earshot, warning them about the armour and signalling to the three nearest – Phillips, Healey and Montfort – to join him.

This small group then watched the iron titan, now just 30 metres away, stop at the trees where Arthur and John Kelly found the bloodstained skullcap and rifle. It peered at the ground and then, finding nothing, turned and again walked towards the hotel. As the figure moved, flanking fire from Steele and police near him threatened James Arthur's group, who in turn retreated towards the hotel. When the armoured man continued his advance, the police on the Wangaratta side of the hotel moved in without any apparent direction and formed a circle around the man.

Jesse Dowsett also saw the figure stopping at the saplings and initially believed that whoever it was would simply sit down there. Jesse decided to move closer and crawled towards another fallen tree. Once there, he emptied his revolver at the crouching figure, but without any noticeable effect. As he turned aside to reload,

Jesse noticed that John Kelly, armed with a carbine, had followed him and stopped just a short distance behind. He called out to Kelly to fire. John Kelly did just that, but narrowly missed and hit a large tree instead. Kelly then reloaded and fired a second shot which may have struck home as the figure was slowly rising. But if it did, it seemed to do nothing; the armoured man lumbered on into a clearing he would have to cross to reach the hotel.

Everyone could now clearly see that the figure was a man clad in armour, and he was semi-staggering towards several police who had taken cover, occasionally pausing to shoot his revolver and taking police fire in return. At intervals, the man would hit his helmet with the butt of the revolver, making a noise that reminded Jesse of a cracked bell ringing – hollow and tinny. The man started calling out and taunting the police: 'You can't shoot me you bloody dogs!' Perhaps in defiance, or maybe to embolden himself as much as the others, little Jesse called out, 'He must be mad; he is ringing a bell to let us know where he is'.

Nearby, Arthur Steele had watched the armoured man fire several shots as he moved down the slight incline and also saw him pause at a group of saplings, where he seemed to concentrate on reloading. Steele tried to move closer, but he was seen and the man turned and fired. At the same time, the figure tapped the breastplate of his armour with the barrel of his gun and shouted, 'Come out boys and we'll whip the lot of them.' Steele then called out a warning to the other police, saying that the man was wearing armour and that they would have to rush him. Steele then moved off to find a better position from which to fire.

* * *

When he left the hotel after the death of Joe, Ned had promised his mates that he would return and that when he did, they would

THE SIEGE

crush the police between them. That had been more than an hour ago, but Ned had found that everything was taking longer than it should, and there were now many things that his wounds prevented him from doing. His plan had been to attack the police from the rear and on horseback. He had been able to unhitch his mare, Mirth, but not to mount.

If he couldn't ride into attack, at least he could walk. Yet, with a shattered foot and heavy armour, even this was torturously slow. He would have to rely on firepower rather than mobility, but Ned had left his repeating rifle at his first resting place in the small copse of trees. He would return to the hotel via that place to recover the rifle. He still had his three revolvers and these he loaded before slinging his ammunition pouch over his shoulder, draping a dustcoat over his armour and moving very stiffly towards the hotel.

It was relatively easy going at first, slightly downhill, through lightly timbered bushland and in gradually increasing light. He had probably travelled around 50 metres before being spotted, and several metres more before the shooting started. Ned's helmet limited his vision so much that he could only fight one policeman at a time. Those policemen fell back before him – which was good – but he was taking punishment in return. Every time a bullet struck his armour, Ned staggered as the impact was like being punched by a powerful man. The shots that struck his helmet were particularly painful without the skullcap that had absorbed some of the impact before.

Returning fire was also an issue. He could shoot back, but needed both hands to do so. Through trial and error, Ned quickly learned that by placing his left leg on a log, he could then rest his left elbow on that leg and use his left hand to brace his right hand and fire with a fair degree of stability; unfortunately, he could not be certain about the accuracy. He easily found the copse where he had left his rifle and skullcap, but they were no longer there. He stopped in the saplings for a couple of minutes though, as his revolver was empty. He had neither the time nor the inclination to make more than one attempt to reload it, so after one unsuccessful attempt, he tossed it aside, drew a second revolver from his belt and walked on.

Ahead of him now was an open space about twenty metres across with an enormous old white tree trunk lying on the ground on the other side. Ned took several paces into the clearing, stopped, and called out to the hotel, 'Come out, come out boys and we'll whip the beggars.' He had, just before, thought that he'd heard both Dan and Steve calling out to him and he could now see both, standing just in front of the breezeway, firing at the policemen who were flitting between trees and shouting challenges to them. Ned moved slowly towards the dead tree, laughing aloud and yelling, 'Come on you bastards, you dogs. You can't hurt me!'

* * *

Jesse Dowsett was stunned to see his and John Kelly's bullets bouncing off the man's armour, 'like parched peas', and again had the fleeting thought that he might be facing Satan himself. He watched the figure stoop at the small copse of saplings – he, too, thought it was to reload a revolver – and then move slowly out into the clearing. He and John Kelly had moved apart and now Jesse stepped out from behind a tree and fired four shots in rapid succession, all of which appeared to hit the figure in the middle of the chest.

Jesse realised that the man was making for a huge fallen tree trunk at the other end of the clearing with two, thick, cut-off branches forming a fork some fifteen metres from its butt, which pointed at the hotel. Jesse thought it would make excellent cover, and he dodged from tree to tree to get there before the armoured man. He succeeded and, arriving at the butt end of the log, looked over the rim to see the man about twelve metres away, near the fork in the tree. Again, the figure was leaning over, closely examining the revolver it held. Resting the revolver on the tree, Jesse fired and hit the target, calling as he did so, 'How do you like it, old man?' Answering, 'And how do you like that?' the man straightened, aimed, and shot back. The bullet cracked past Jesse's head.

Two of the Wangaratta reinforcements, Moore and Causey, had taken up firing positions level with the hotel stables, and had a clear shot at the armoured man as he moved into the clearing. Their shots did not slow the figure's progress, but did cause several of the circling policemen to change positions. James Arthur and John Kelly were now no more than thirty metres from where Dowsett and the armoured figure exchanged pistol shots. Both policemen fired and believed their shots struck home, while Arthur Steele approached the figure from the blind spot to its rear.

Across at the railway station, James Dwyer had returned to the platform after running messages between Superintendent Sadleir and the engine set to depart with messages for Benalla. Just as Dwyer walked down the platform, one of the reporters pointed at the clearing, the armoured man, and the police closing in, telling Dwyer what had taken place in the last few minutes. Dwyer ran across the Railway Reserve and into the light scrub by the hotel.

As Dwyer ran, he heard someone call out, 'Boys, let's rush him', while someone else called out, 'Look out Dwyer, he has you covered!' Looking ahead, Dwyer saw the armoured man pointing a revolver at him from 50 metres away. As he turned his head, a bullet whizzed past his right ear. Then, as Dwyer and the other police closed in, the armoured man yelled, 'Come on, you bastards. I don't care for you.'

As the figure fired at Dwyer, Arthur Steele stepped out from the cover of a tree and raised his shotgun, now loaded with swan shot, pellets the size of small ball-bearings. As he did this the figure, now just ten metres away, turned and started raising its revolver. Steele fired the first barrel at the man's legs, clearly visible below the armour. The figure staggered under the impact and, as it did so, spread his legs apart to stop from falling over. In doing so, it presented Steele with a clear shot at both unprotected legs. As the man again tried to raise the revolver, Steele fired the second barrel. The man staggered and fell backwards, almost gracefully, and finished on the ground but in a semi-upright position. The helmet had become partially dislodged and he was propped up by one of the dead branches of the white tree. His breath was coming in huge gulps. 'I'm done, I'm done.' he said.

Steele and Jesse Dowsett arrived at the fallen figure at almost exactly the same time. The downed man made an attempt to lift his revolver, but Steele seized his arm while Dowsett grabbed the hand and pistol. The gun discharged, with the bullet clipping Steele's deerstalker hat and knocking it off his head. The side of Steele's face was also blackened by gunpowder. Dowsett wrenched the pistol free just as John Kelly arrived and grabbed the helmet of the fallen man. Within seconds Montfort, Healey and Hugh Bracken had also burst onto the scene, knocking Steele into the figure on the ground. He yelled as the edge of the armour dug into his ribs. As the men struggled, Ned's grey mare, Mirth, trotted through the clearing and disappeared into the bush.

John Kelly had trouble removing the helmet, at one stage holding the man's beard to keep his head still as he pulled the helmet back. When it was off, Steele growled, 'It's Ned himself!' before spitting out, 'You bloody wretch. I swore I would be in at your death.' Ned simply looked up and said phlegmatically,

'I have got my gruel,' – indicating he knew he had just got what he deserved. This infuriated Steele, who pulled his revolver, put it in Ned's face, and seemed to be about to shoot him. But a shotgun-wielding Hugh Bracken stepped in and stood over Ned. Looking directly at Steele, he said, 'You shoot him and I'll shoot you. Take him alive.' He looked at the others still gripping the outlaw and said, 'I'll shoot any bloody man that dares touch him.' And then, more gently, 'Do not shoot him; he never did me any harm. I am going to take his part.'

* * *

Just as Bracken finished his little speech, James Dwyer rushed in with what several others later described as a 'war whoop' and kicked Ned in the groin. It was a good kick, a powerful kick, but Dwyer had not made allowance for the apron-armour that Ned was wearing. Dwyer reeled back, his shin badly bruised.

Reporters George Allen and John McWhirter were following Dr John Nicholson across the Railway Reserve to the bush clearing where most of the action was now taking place. Nicholson's decision to leave the relative safety of the platform had been spontaneous; he had seen the armoured man fire two or three times disappearing behind some fallen timber. At that, he just decided to go, thinking that there would probably be some work for him to do when he arrived.

It took no more than two minutes for Nicholson to reach the clearing. While he was doing so, Arthur Steele and John Kelly tried to remove Ned's armour. That armour was held together with what appeared to be a complicated system of nuts, bolts and straps. Steele borrowed a pocket knife from one of the other policemen and started cutting the straps. John Kelly concentrated on the metal fastenings, but it was slow work and he had only succeeded in separating one side when Nicholson arrived.

The doctor was quickly asked for his assistance, and the three of them were able to force the plates wide enough to slide the chest and back armour up and over Ned's head.

Interviewed many years later, John Nicholson had no difficulties remembering the scene. McWhirter and Allen, plus the ubiquitous Charles Rawlins, had all followed him from the station, but were standing back from the outlaw who had just been captured, the infamous Ned Kelly. Nicholson recalled how, 'he [Ned] was in a sitting position on the ground, his helmet lying near him. His feet and hands were smeared with blood. He was shivering with cold and ghostly white and smelt strongly of brandy'. It was a dramatic and even painful moment for Nicholson; as he was helping remove Ned's armour, a bullet fired from the hotel struck the fallen tree, driving a splinter into his calf.

Watching from the hotel, Dan suddenly realised what had happened to Ned and flew into a rage, cursing and raving at the police. He rushed through the back door, stepped out from the breezeway and fired several shots at the group around Ned, narrowly missing them. While those who had started removing Ned's armour continued to do so, several others shot back at Dan. Dan was forced back into the hotel, a bullet slicing through his calf as he retreated.

* * *

When Dan started firing from the rear of the hotel, John Kelly asked the reporters for their assistance. He told John McWhirter that it was important that the outlaws were kept confined in the hotel and suggested that he take Kelly's carbine and make use of it if necessary. He also asked George Allen to keep an eye on the outlaws' movements while he returned to the task of trying to remove Ned's armour. At one point, Ned either recognised

Dr Nicholson or realised that he was a doctor, for he said to him, 'This is the first time you had me as a patient, doctor.' Nicholson did not respond.

Ned's armour was eventually removed, and the next step was to get the wounded man back to the station. Hugh Bracken and Arthur Steele took responsibility for this and after lifting Ned to his feet, half-carried and half-dragged him away from the clearing in which he had been captured. The pain from his wounds was apparently excruciating, and Ned complained whenever his injured limbs were moved or jolted. As they left the clearing, John Kelly, Dr Nicholson and Charles Rawlins all carried pieces of Ned's armour, while Jesse Dowsett still held tight to the pistol he had wrenched from Ned's grasp.

The journey back to the station was not without incident. The first problem was the Railway Reserve fence; Ned was obviously in no condition to climb, so John Kelly and Nicholson helped Bracken and Steele to lift the outlaw over it. When they arrived at the station, Ned was taken directly to the guard's van that had travelled from Melbourne; once there, though, he fainted from blood loss. A drop of medicinal brandy from Dr Nicholson quickly revived him, but when a bullet fired from the hotel struck the van, John Kelly insisted Ned be moved to the relative safety of the stationmaster's office.

In that office, Ned was allowed to lie down on the floor and drift off to sleep. John Kelly sent one of the junior constables to the Stanistreet house to borrow a mattress for Ned to lie on while he was examined by the doctors. He also ordered that a detail of six troopers be placed to guard the prisoner. Arthur Steele was not one of those six, yet he had not left Ned's side since the outlaw's capture, and showed no inclination to do so now. Steele believed that it was he – and he alone – who had captured the feared and fearsome Ned Kelly. He also believed that other, lesser figures might try to steal some of the limelight that was owed to him. For Steele, this belief would grow into an immutable truth about Glenrowan.

* * *

Police on the Benalla side of the hotel or in the drain at the front did not know what was happening behind the hotel on the Wangaratta side. They could hear shouting and shooting, and most assumed that one or more of the outlaws had ventured out the back door to challenge the police on that side of the hotel. Some suspected that there may even have been another escape attempt. John Kelly knew there would be speculation and when James Dwyer asked if he could return to the drain to tell Sadleir what had taken place, Kelly sent him on his way.

Sadleir listened to Dwyer's report with growing excitement, and wrote down the raw details in his notebook, including the time of Ned's capture. That time was recorded as 7.17 am; Ned had walked out of the mist just 30 minutes earlier.

iv. The Trophy

Superintendent John Sadleir and several other policemen at Glenrowan had spent the best part of two years trying to track down and kill Ned Kelly. Now that he had Ned in his hands, Sadleir was determined to keep the outlaw alive as long as he could in the hope that Kelly would one day be called to answer for the crimes he had committed. After they first arrived at the stationmaster's office, and before a mattress could be brought from Stanistreet's, Ned was placed on the floor only until a stretcher was found elsewhere at the station. He was assisted onto that and a loose rope was looped around his arms. A pile of cotton waste was brought in to support his shattered left wrist, and reporter John McWhirter cut off his boots. Someone else found a pillow and placed it under Ned's head. John Kelly then undertook a quick search of Ned's clothes, but all this revealed was 'threepence in silver and a small Geneva watch of little value'. Kelly also found several cartridges in Ned's pockets.

Dr John Nicholson took over and prepared to undertake a thorough medical examination. He asked Hutchison, his Benalla colleague, to assist and also asked that everyone else except Jesse Dowsett leave the room, perhaps because he believed that Dowsett was the only one he could trust not to try to kill Ned. Nicholson started by removing – either partially or fully – Ned's outer clothing so he could actually assess all the wounds that Ned had suffered. One of the first items he removed was a bloodstained green silk cummerbund, Ned's good luck charm. Nicholson kept it as a souvenir. Before a detailed examination, Nicholson noted that both Ned's eyes were blackened and his body covered in bruises. Yet, overall, his skin was remarkably smooth, supple, and clean, almost as if he had just stepped out of a Turkish bath.

Nicholson then identified a number of serious bullet wounds and approximately 25 shotgun pellet injuries. Most serious of all was the damage to his left arm, where it appeared that a single bullet had passed through as he had it bent, with entry and exit holes both above and below the elbow. The trauma to Ned's right foot was also very serious, as the projectile had broken several bones as it passed through from front to rear. Nicholson also removed a large shotgun pellet from the base of Ned's right thumb and looked closely at several pellet wounds to his right groin, thigh and calf. None were particularly serious, and several he categorised as mere grazes.

As he examined Ned, John Nicholson also talked to him

about his injuries and just how incapacitating they would have been had Ned escaped. The more serious wounds would have left Ned unable to remove his armour without help and he would not have been able to mount a horse unassisted. The foot wound was so severe that walking would have been agony, and it was doubtful he could have travelled much further than he did without collapsing from blood loss and shock. His shot-up hand and arm would have prevented him from firing accurately or reloading quickly.

Despite all this, Nicholson did not consider Ned's injuries to be life-threatening, although he did concede that there was a chance that shock and all the blood-loss might cost Ned his life. Such was his professional assessment and that was what he told John Sadleir.

* * *

While Ned's health was being carefully checked by the doctors, the police were paying close attention to his armour and armaments. Jesse Dowsett and the others had left Ned's armour on the platform where someone, probably a reporter, spotted a set of official railway scales and organised a weighing. The total for all the pieces was 97 pounds (45 kilograms), but what was equally impressive was the number of dents in the armour, well in excess of twenty. All of these were from bullets, as shotgun pellets only left a small shiny spot. The police estimated that nine separate people had engaged Ned at or near the clearing, and that all believed they had hit him at least once each.

When captured, Ned had been carrying a revolver and had an ammunition pouch slung over his shoulder. The pouch had disappeared but Jesse Dowsett still had the revolver. It was a Webley, and it had 'N.S.W.G' stamped into the bottom of its grip. Those on the platform surmised correctly that Ned had taken it from the local police during the Jerilderie bank raid. A closer inspection revealed that three shots had been fired and three remained in the chambers.

What Ned was wearing under his armour and dustcoat also attracted a lot of interest. John Kelly would simply say that, 'Kelly was dressed like a bush dandy'. As he thought he was writing for a wider audience than the other reporters, Tom Carrington had the last word:

> He was dressed in the dandy bushman style – yellow cord pants, strapped [reinforced on the inside] with slate, cross-barred pattern cloth, riding boots with very thin soles and very high heels indeed; white Crimean shirt with large black spots; waistcoat same material as trousers; hair, jet black, inclined to curl, reddish beard and moustache, and very heavy black eyebrows – altogether a fine figure of a man, the only bad part about his face being his mouth, which is a cruel and wicked one.

John Sadleir was not yet particularly interested in what Ned wore or what Ned carried; he wanted to know more about the man and about those who had followed him into Jones's hotel twelve hours earlier. When Nicholson and Hutchison had finished with their patient, Sadleir enquired about his health and asked if Ned was well enough to answer questions. The answer was affirmative. Sadleir, Arthur Steele, and James Dwyer were the first police to spend time alone with the newly captured outlaw, and they were not certain about what to expect: defiance, probably; silence, possibly; cooperation, unlikely.

What they got was the essential Ned, the young man in his prime who was a physical match for anyone, and who responded to an audience as well as any of the actors who had graced the great theatres of Melbourne. He was the honest man wronged, the unwilling rebel who had succeeded because his cause was just and his arm was strong. They thought they may get either the malcontent or the penitent; what they got was Ned.

Sadleir opened the formalities by telling Ned that he wanted him to give some kind of signal to the hotel telling the outlaws who remained inside that their time was up and they should now surrender. And how, asked Ned, do you know that there are still members of my gang inside? Sadleir's response was that it was obvious as there was still firing from the rear of the building. To this, Ned replied, 'They will not mind what I say . . . The heart's gone out of them. They won't come out fighting like men . . . they're only boys . . . they'll stay in there until they're finished.'

Ned continued in a similar vein for a minute or more, adding words like 'curs' and 'cowards' which Sadleir understood to mean that the remaining outlaws would not be prepared to stand up to the police. To Sadleir, this observation could open up several possibilities. He thought he should pursue this subject but before he could, Ned continued what was becoming a monologue. The police were lucky, he continued, that the other outlaws were all obviously occupied when he himself was captured, otherwise the police would all have been 'shot down like rotten sheep' when they rushed him. And, he added, the others in the gang were wearing much better armour than his.

Visibly tired from his exertions, Ned asked Sadleir for a nip of brandy, but there was none in the room, so Sadleir sent Dwyer to McDonnell's to bring back a bottle of brandy and some scones for Ned. As he was about to leave, Ned said that he recognised Dwyer and accused the policeman of trying to kick him when he was down. Dwyer owned up to the offence but said that Ned should consider it payback for Ned having killed his friend Tom Lonigan at Stringybark Creek.

When Dwyer returned a few minutes later, Ned sipped a brandy and perked up to become positively voluble. He had always saved his best for an audience, he loved the use and the power of words, and now that he was relieved of the pressures and complications of command, he could lie back and speak out freely. The others had chosen to take control of their own destinies. He was no longer responsible for them; he was just responsible for himself. There were people who wanted to hear from him and he would give them what he, and not they, wanted. A succession of people now called in to simply see Ned, and with most he shared words, sometimes light banter but generally a serious conversation.

He told John Kelly that he had set off that morning to attack the police carrying three revolvers but his injuries made it difficult to reload and he had discarded two before he was captured. Forever the braggart, he then added that, 'If Byrne came out to load my rifle I would be able to pick any of you off at 600 yards.' He said that James Arthur had been a 'splendid shot', and when he then saw Arthur looking in at him through the door, Ned shook his fist and swore at him. And when little Jesse Dowsett asked the question that many had considered – why didn't Ned keep going after he left the hotel – the reply was a gentle, 'A man would have been a nice sort of dingo to walk out on his mates.'

The reporters also joined in what, at times, must have resembled a formal press conference. As he jotted things down in his notebook, John McWhirter thought that Ned had a 'wasted' look, while Tom Carrington watched and sketched and also took notes. Ned complained several times about having cold feet – cutting off his boots had left him barefoot – and two of the reporters fetched a tin of warm water for Ned to soak his feet in. At times Ned appeared to almost faint away, but not once did anyone hear him complain about his wounds or his treatment.

The reporters also asked Ned a wider range of questions than those put forward by his police interrogators. To the pressmen, Ned said that he was sick of the life he'd been leading, hunted like a dog and getting no rest, and that he really didn't give a damn what became of him. Ned told Tom Carrington that the armour they all wore had been made specifically for a final shoot-out with the police, and that the gang had planned 'to paste as many of the traps' (kill as many of the police) as they could in that shoot-out. They had also planned to be fighting from cover which was why they did not manufacture leg armour.

Dr Nicholson had remained in the room and he expressed an interest in what Ned had done when he had been alone in the bush earlier. Ned said that he'd been lying in one spot for a long time. He had been cold and cramped, and was unable to lift his revolver in case it clanged on his armour and gave his position away. He added though, that he could have shot some of the policemen during the night. While he might have been telling the truth in that instance, Ned also told some quite blatant lies, probably in an attempt to mislead the police. He said several times, for instance, that Byrne, Hart, and Dan Kelly had all escaped and that the only people now left in the hotel were those that the Kelly Gang had imprisoned there. As Ned made his observations and answered questions, Tom Carrington catalogued and illustrated his injuries, describing, 'his whole face bruised and swollen, both eyes blackened from the impact of the bullets, the bridge of his nose chopped by the top edge of the face plate, his cheek torn by a helmet bolt'. Despite the injuries, Carrington thought Ned looked calm and almost peaceful.

Sadleir watched the same scene, but saw it through different eyes:

All those who saw Ned Kelly while he lay helpless on a mattress were struck with the gentle expression on his face. It was hard to think that he was a callous and cruel murderer. But the old spirit, half-savage, half-insane, was there notwithstanding.

By now, Ned seemed close to collapse. It was probably around 9 o'clock in the morning, and Dr Nicholson signalled to the police and reporters in the room that it was time for his patient to rest. He checked Ned's wounds once more and, when he had finished, Ned simply turned on his side and within seconds was fast asleep. A surprise awaited the others when they left the stationmaster's office. With the coming of dawn had also come the people. By the time they left Ned alone to sleep in the stationmaster's office, there were more than 100 people occupying vantage points around the site of the siege with more arriving every minute. They had come to watch the drama's final act.

v. 07:00–11:00 Monday

By the time Ned had been shot down and carried off in triumph, the sun was above the horizon and the day was shaping up to be a typical north-eastern winter's day – clear and bright, cold in the morning but turning into a beautiful, mild day. For the next two hours, very little happened. While Ned held court in the stationmaster's office, the police in the cordon were mostly on high alert, waiting to see if the outlaws still in the hotel would try to escape. On occasion, one of those officers would wander off to the station to catch up on the news and have a look at Ned, but in the main they just continued to do what they had been doing for several hours: sit and wait for something to happen. The exception, again, was Tom Kirkham, officially stationed at the Wangaratta end, but spending most of his time making social calls on friends.

Once it was daylight, those inside the hotel could clearly see the police moving about in the distance, at the station and in the bush. Every window in the building had been shot out, which was as helpful for looking in as it was for looking out. Any obvious movement within the hotel continued to attract police fire, so Dan and Steve remained well back in the shadows. One or the other would occasionally show themselves at a window in a gesture of defiance, but both seemed happy to remain in the relative safety of the interior of the hotel. When they did shoot at the police, they would fire from well back in the room. It was quite easy to recognise their firing as their shots made a duller, more muted sound than those fired outside.

Elsewhere in and around Glenrowan, a number of developments were occurring. There had been almost a rail shuttle-run between Glenrowan and Benalla, with messages going down the line for transmission to Melbourne, and supplies travelling up. The engine and van that arrived from Benalla shortly after 7 am carried ammunition, provisions, and two railway line repairers. These two collected tools from the Glenrowan station tool shed and walked to the spot where Ned had directed the destruction of the line. Within two hours, they had repaired the breach and the north-east railway line was again intact.

The opening of the line allowed reinforcements to be sent from the north as well as the south, and the first group arrived at 9 o'clock. It was a party of eleven policemen from up north at Beechworth, led by Sergeant Mullane and including Mounted Constables Glenny, Armstrong, Meager, McHugh, McColl, Dowling, Duross, Alexander and Wickham. Robert Alexander, Thomas Dowling, William Duross and Harry Armstrong had been the four policemen 'guarding' Aaron Sherrit's hut the previous

THE SIEGE

Saturday night. Their actions that night were already generating talk of cowardice, and Glenrowan would perhaps offer them an opportunity for redemption.

The train that brought the Beechworth reinforcements also brought three civilians named Osborne, Sherrit and Cheshire. Nothing else is known about Osborne, but the second passenger was Jack Sherrit, the late Aaron's younger brother, who was brought to Glenrowan partly for protection and possibly to identify the individual gang members. The most important passenger was the third, Mr HE Cheshire, Beechworth's acting postmaster. While there was no telegraph station at Glenrowan, the main telegraph line to the north-east and beyond ran past the railway station. Shortly after he arrived, Cheshire had that line cut. He then spliced in an extension and connected a small, portable telegraph key. He set himself up at the station and opened a direct link to Melbourne and Sydney. In the coming hours, Cheshire would send tens of thousands of words using that link.

Shortly before the Beechworth reinforcements arrived, the Benalla shuttle train dropped off four more policemen, all called in from stations or barracks further down the line. With the additional lawmen from Beechworth, there were now 46 policemen besieging Jones's hotel. When the Benalla shuttle pulled out again, it took three civilians with it; Mrs O'Connor and Mrs Prout Webb were going back to Melbourne, while Jesse Dowsett was just going home to bed.

Around the hotel, the best firing positions had already been occupied so many of the daylight reinforcements were used to fill gaps, establish a second cordon further out on the main roads, or act as a reserve. Those detailed to reserve duties were based at the station, where many found an opportunity to look at Ned and to pass on the latest rumours, the most popular of which was that Joe Byrne had been shot dead during the night while drinking a glass of whisky. The reserve police were also involved in crowd control, as the number of people coming to watch the siege kept growing. Before any of this, most took the opportunity to shoot a round or two at the hotel. The significant increase in firing immediately affected the prisoners, with Robert Gibbons noting, 'We all lay down on the floor for safety... we were packed so close we had to lie on our sides.'

* * *

John Sadleir thought he had a major problem. His men had captured the Kelly Gang's leader, but its other three members and an unknown number of supporters were still barricaded in the hotel just across the reserve from where he stood. When Dr Nicholson left Ned to doze in the stationmaster's office, Sadleir took the opportunity to ask for his advice. Ned, he explained to the doctor, had straight-out refused to call on the others to surrender. Sadleir was therefore compelled to force their submission, and thought that storming the hotel was a possibility. What did Nicholson think?

Nicholson said that doing nothing may well be the best response, prompting Sadleir to think out loud. He pondered what manner of action could bring about the capture of all the remaining gang members and their supporters. However, he and others had come to believe that the outlaws had built a redoubt, a stronghold within the hotel. This was believed to be centred around the dining room chimney, and constructed with pieces of furniture and bags of grain. Because of this, he was wary of ordering the rushing of the hotel, for fear that lives would be lost to no good end.

Furthermore, he said that he had ordered his police to attempt to bring down both chimneys with rifle fire. His men had concentrated on trying to do just that, but without apparent effect.

Sadleir said that he had also considered using ropes to topple the chimneys; he had brought rope with him and had just sent a request to Benalla for more. However, daylight observation of the hotel had revealed that all the windows had been shot out and all the walls shot through. It would thus be impossible for a man to approach any part of the building without being seen. The rope trick was now no longer viable.

When it was his turn to speak, Nicholson advised against any police assault on the hotel, saying that the armoured outlaws would certainly kill several attackers before being subdued. He said that the outlaws were trapped in the hotel with no possibility of escape. If the police had a field piece or cannon to knock over the chimneys and punch holes through the walls, the remaining outlaws would have just one alternative to surrendering, and that was to be blown apart.

Sadleir seized on the idea, and once postmaster Cheshire had completed setting up his telegraph station, Sadleir dashed off a request to Commissioner Standish, asking about the possibility of having a field piece sent to Glenrowan to end the siege. Almost immediately, he sent another telegram in an attempt to explain the background to the request.

> Glenrowan, June 28, 1880. Weatherboard, brick chimney, slab kitchen. The difficulty we feel is that our shots have no effect on the corner, and that there are so many windows we would be under fire all the way. We must get the gun before night or rush the place.

When Standish received the request, he was in the process of organising his own travel to Glenrowan as he felt his presence there was now necessary. As a former officer of the Royal Artillery, Standish knew what a field gun could do, and he supported the request. However, to cover his position, he first asked the approval of the Colonial Secretary, Robert Ramsay, and, when that was given, Standish sent a note to the Garrison Artillery asking about the availability of a small field piece and ammunition for immediate despatch to action in north-east Victoria. There was a quick response, and within the hour a twelve-pounder cannon and enough ammunition to suppress a small insurrection were on their way to Spencer Street station.

The opening of direct telegraphic communication between Glenrowan and Melbourne also seemed to energise Secretary Ramsay. After discussing the provision of artillery support to Superintendent Sadleir, Ramsay instructed Commissioner Standish to proceed to Glenrowan to take command of the siege. He also sent a note to Dr Charles Ryan, a prominent Melbourne surgeon, asking him to travel to Glenrowan with the commissioner; Dr Ryan's specialty was gunshot wounds.

Ramsay's imagination did not stop there. In one of a stream of telegrams he would send to Sadleir, he advised the superintendent that a bullet-proof shield should be constructed – perhaps based on a wagon's chassis – to allow the field piece to be pushed towards the hotel and then fired at point-blank range. The Chief Secretary also made contact with the Government Astronomer. In August 1879, the Melbourne and Carlton football clubs had played an evening match under electric lights at the Melbourne Cricket Ground; the event was considered a sporting success, and a clear indication of what an electric sporting future might look like.

The electric lights that lit up the football match had been designed by the Government Astronomer who had also supervised their planning and construction. Ramsay thought that similar electric lights could be crucial if the siege at Glenrowan went into a second night. That was the proposal Ramsay put to the Astronomer – a proposal the Astronomer quickly rejected. It would take several weeks to organise what the secretary wanted, he explained, and the best advice he could therefore offer was for the police to light large bonfires every 40 metres or so around the hotel. This was duly noted by Ramsay who passed the advice on to Sadleir by telegram.

By the time he received this advice, Sadleir must have come to realise that direct contact with Melbourne could be something of a double-edged sword. While they could support his ideas, they could also generate ideas of their own. And what seemed a good idea in Melbourne was not necessarily a good idea in Glenrowan.

* * *

It was around this point that Sadleir suggested to Stanhope O'Connor that the two of them inspect the police cordon to reassure the men, carry out a reconnaissance and make plans. As they circumnavigated the hotel the two senior officers sought their men's thoughts on how to bring the siege to an end. By the time they returned to the drain at the front of the hotel, Sadleir had an idea. He was still not prepared to order an assault, fearing excessive casualties among his own men and the prisoners he knew were inside. Without their leader though, he also believed the remaining outlaws would be confused and, possibly, vulnerable. If he could orchestrate the release of the remaining prisoners, the only people left in the hotel would be outlaws, and they could either be blasted out by cannon or starved out. Sadleir and O'Connor stood in the drain, about to put the plan into effect.

John Sadleir then climbed out of the drain and called across to the hotel, saying all those inside who were innocent should now leave the building with their hands in the air. He added that any who remained in the hotel were liable to be shot. There was no obvious or immediate response. As diplomatically as possible, it was suggested to Sadleir that his voice may not have carried clearly all the way to the hotel. Charles Rawlins, who occasionally acted as an auctioneer, repeated Sadleir's call, again without any result. Finally, Constable Harry Armstrong, a large man with a deep voice, climbed out of the drain and shouted, 'All those inside there had better surrender at once. We will give you ten minutes to do so; after that time we shall fire volleys into the house.' A short time later, a white handkerchief fluttered at the front door.

Around 30 minutes earlier, at 9.30 am, another white handkerchief had been waved out of the front door. That earlier handkerchief had been held by John Lowe, who did so to see if it would be safe to leave. The bullet that thudded into the door frame next to his hand answered the question. The incident had further demoralised a group that was already very anxious and almost fatalistic. During the early hours of daylight, Dan had told them that Ned had been shot and captured; he and Steve had then just mentally withdrawn and pretty much ignored what was going on around them.

All three voices calling out for the prisoners to leave were clearly heard inside the hotel. The calls prompted a vigorous discussion among the prisoners. Several said that they were too scared to leave, given what had happened during earlier attempts. Dave Mortimer stood up and said that he, for one, was willing to take the chance. Dan Kelly said that neither he nor Steve would fire until all those who wanted to leave were safe. And with that, Mortimer crossed to the front door, opened it slightly and waved his white handkerchief outside. When no-one shot at it, he opened the door wide, put his hands in the air and strode outside.

THE SIEGE

John Sadleir would later testify that, following the waving of the handkerchief and the opening of the door, 'the prisoners came bouncing out like bees, running out of the front door in great confusion'. It was almost a crush as the remaining prisoners bolted for freedom, and some 25 young and older men and children moved as fast as they could. Behind Dave Mortimer came Louis Piazzi and his labourers, John Lowe, the three Delaney brothers and two McAuliffe brothers, along with Edward Reynolds, Dennis Sullivan, Robert Gibbons, John Larkins – finally leaving his cubby in the bags of oats – and young Tom Cameron. Last to leave were the Reardons, the wounded Michael, followed by his father James, the last prisoner to leave, holding the hands of two of his children, three-year-old William and five-year-old Helena.

When the prisoners burst out of the hotel, the Native Police in the drain became quite agitated and O'Connor had to speak firmly to prevent one or two of them firing at the escapees. Luckiest of all was undoubtedly Dave Mortimer who knew the area well and had decided that the deep drain was the safest place to be. In his enthusiasm and relief, that drain was his sole focus. Most of the police had emerged from their firing positions as the men made their escape, and were calling on the prisoners to stop and put their hands in the air. Ignoring all their calls, Mortimer ran straight to the drain and jumped in, landing alongside some startled Native Police, who instantly covered him with their carbines. It was probably only O'Connor's direct intervention that prevented them from shooting him where he stood.

As they left the hotel, most of the escaping prisoners did indeed put their hands in the air and called out to the police to hold their fire. Their cries carried clearly to the reporters at the station who jotted down what they heard: 'Don't fire', 'For God's sake, don't shoot us; don't, pray don't.' As they ran or walked briskly, they were confronted by numerous armed policemen who had moved to the front of the hotel from their firing positions or from the railway station. When they were twenty metres short of O'Connor's drain, the prisoners were ordered to stop and kneel down with their hands in the air. Any who moved forward were bailed up by O'Connor's troopers and forced to the ground. All were then told to lie flat on the ground, face down, and then again raise their hands in the air.

At the station, the *Argus*'s Joe Melvin wrote down what he could see: 'The scene presented when they were all lying on the ground, and demonstrated the respectability of their characters was unique and in some degree, amusing.' Amusing it might have been for a reporter 50 metres from the scene, but for many of those directly involved it merely added to the ongoing trauma. Lying on the ground, hands in the air, John Lowe heard a 'big burly' policeman call out, 'We will shoot this lot first. They are all sympathisers.' Lowe glanced up and noted that at least a dozen police had their rifles aimed at the prisoners.

When those prisoners had aligned themselves on the ground to the satisfaction of the police, they were allowed to sit up but, children excepted, they were also required to keep their hands in the air. They were then inspected and questioned by Sadleir and John Kelly. Kelly recognised the McAuliffe brothers – two young men in their twenties – and knew they were Kelly sympathisers; both were handcuffed and escorted to the station. Kelly was also suspicious of John Delaney until he established that he was from the 'other' Delaney family. All the released prisoners were questioned closely by the police, and were only released when their identities had been established and confirmed. Sadleir had organised a mobile kitchen at the station, and the released prisoners were directed to it.

There were some exceptions to this general treatment. The

first of these was Michael Reardon, who was quickly identified as being wounded, and who was taken aside and escorted to the station for medical treatment. A second exception was made for the McAuliffe brothers (Dennis and Patrick), under guard at the station. Close questioning of them, with their answers being verified by other prisoners, revealed that they had not provided direct material support to the gang during the siege. Their handcuffs were removed and they were let go, but were told to leave the area immediately. The third exception was Dave Mortimer who was personally escorted to the station by Stanhope O'Connor. This was not because Mortimer had attracted any suspicion, but because he was a keen observer and O'Connor wanted to question him closely about what had happened in the hotel.

Again, the reporters jotted down their observations and thoughts: 'The faces of the poor fellows [the prisoners] were blanched with fear, and some of them looked as if they were out of their minds'. Most of those released were not particularly interested in talking to the reporters, or to the police for that matter, and after having something to eat, headed home to be with family and friends. Dave Mortimer seems to have been the one most prepared to speak of his experiences. He noted that Dan Kelly and Steve Hart had seemed to struggle after Joe's death, while Ned's capture had really flattened them. When Mortimer had last seen the two, they had looked 'for all the world like two condemned criminals waiting for the bolt to be drawn'. Mortimer answered the questions, then wandered off to see if he could find something to eat. He also wanted to see if he could have a chat with Ned.

* * *

With the release of the prisoners, Sadleir sent out instructions that the 'Fire High' order had now been revoked. He replaced it with an order that all police fire would now be in volleys and that it should be fired at where the outlaws appeared to be. However, troopers would be allowed to fire if they had a clear shot at an outlaw. Almost immediately, several volleys were fired into the hotel; with up to 50 policemen now in position at Glenrowan, these volleys were heavy indeed. When the last of the prisoners had left, the front door of the hotel had remained open behind them. The outlaws had not bothered to close it and those who now looked through it, albeit at a distance, could see absolutely no sign of life.

vi. 11:00–15:00 Monday

The open door at the front of the hotel beckoned to the police, but Superintendent Sadleir had absolutely no intention of authorising a direct assault. He had the main prize – Ned Kelly – and knew that the remaining outlaws had nowhere to go; he would simply wait them out. The last two outlaws did begin to appear regularly at the back door – one of them exchanged several shots with Daniel Barry – but they showed no inclination to leave the building for a direct confrontation with his troopers. Rather than force the situation, Sadleir seemed content to spend most of his time with or near Ned, mostly in the room where Ned was held, 'cutting up tobacco and smoking, standing by the fire and talking to others'. Like a sheep dog, Arthur Steele was always somewhere nearby in the background.

Just as when he was free, in captivity Ned remained the centre of attention. After his extended interview with Sadleir and O'Connor was over, Dave Mortimer's search for Ned was successful when he found Ned in his small room, lying on his back on a mattress, apparently asleep, and surrounded by armed troopers.

THE SIEGE

To Mortimer, Ned seemed covered in blood and bruises, and appeared to be defeated and downhearted. Mortimer stood and looked down at the sad figure for a while before turning to leave. As he did so, Ned opened his eyes and said directly to Mortimer, 'Well, I'm done for now, old man. My race is run.' He then fell back on his mattress, turned on his side and closed his eyes.

Joe Melvin also visited Ned, but as part of small group and a little while after Mortimer's visit. Ned always saved his best for the larger audiences, and he put on a performance for Melvin and the other reporters:

> He is very reserved as to anything connected with his comrades, but answered questions freely when his individual case was alone concerned. He appeared to be suffering from severe shock and exhaustion, and trembled in every limb. Now and again he seemed to faint away, but restoratives brought him around.

After he and the other reporters were ushered out, Joe Melvin joined Dave Mortimer in the crowd that had gathered to watch what was turning to an inevitable end.

* * *

The noon train from Melbourne arrived, and a number of passengers quickly disembarked. Five were policemen ordered to Glenrowan as reinforcements. Four of those five were mounted constables from the Violet Town barracks, and the fifth, Senior Constable Charles Johnston, had travelled from Tatura. Johnston, married with several children, was a restless and active man whose wife had once worked for the Sadleir family. It was later revealed that a succession of senior officers had regarded Johnston as being, 'somewhat impetuous and hot-headed', but he got things done, which was exactly why he had been placed in charge of the Violet Town reinforcements. Shortly after they disembarked, Johnston and his men were taken to a storeroom at the station and shown Ned's armour. They were told that the other outlaws were wearing similar outfits.

Also disembarking at Glenrowan was the Very Reverend Dean Matthew Gibney, Vicar-General of the Catholic Church in Western Australia. Gibney, who had boarded the train at Kilmore East, had several years earlier established both boys' and girls' orphanages in Perth. When the boys' facility was severely damaged by lightning, he set off on a fundraising tour that brought him to the eastern states in June 1880. When informed of what was happening in Glenrowan, and that a badly wounded Ned Kelly had been captured, Dean Gibney immediately asked if he could see the outlaw to offer spiritual succour. It was a selfless gesture typical of the man and characteristic of the priest.

Several other passengers also left the train, Benalla people drawn to Glenrowan by news of the siege and who wanted to either volunteer their services or simply look at what was happening. The would-be volunteers included a Benalla bootmaker named Dixon and a fully armed Robert McBean, who happened to be a Justice of the Peace, prominent grazier, and close friend of Commissioner Standish.

The spectators included three teenagers from Benalla whose names would never be known. While seeking the best vantage point from which to observe the siege, the three noticed a grey horse on the rising ground behind McDonnell's Hotel, with something covered in cloth hanging from the saddle. Robert McHugh, one of the Beechworth reinforcements, had also spotted the horse and the four made their ways through the bush to where it stood. The horse was one of the Kelly's pack horses, wearing a saddle and carrying a pack covered by a blanket. An examination of the pack revealed a small oil drum

THE SIEGE

containing blasting powder, about ten metres of fuse, and a complete kit of horse-shoeing tools. McHugh rushed off to report his find.

* * *

Dean Gibney was a senior official of his church, and he had learned that a member of that church was lying nearby, possibly dying; the knowledge brought out the parish priest in him. There was a crowd on the platform, and Gibney was not familiar with the layout, and so it took him around fifteen minutes to find where Ned was being held and then navigate his way through the crowd to the stationmaster's office. Once there, he identified himself and was ushered inside; the police guarding the wounded outlaw discreetly left after the priest entered, although they kept a close watch from the door.

Like several others before him, Gibney felt that Ned's appearance was ghastly and, on looks alone, felt that Ned may indeed be dying. The priest's immediate duty was obvious, and he gave Ned the last rites. As he did so, Ned responded appropriately: 'When I asked him to say, "Lord Jesus have mercy on me", he said it and added, "It is not today I began to say that".' Gibney then spoke to Ned about life and death, and the role of the Catholic church in the life of true believers. To the Vicar-General, Ned seemed genuinely penitent, and so he agreed to hear Ned's confession.

Afterwards, the two spoke quietly together. They talked about what had taken place at Stringybark Creek; Dean Gibney asked Ned about Sergeant Kennedy's watch, saying that he would like to be able to return it to Kennedy's widow. Ned replied, 'I can't tell you; I would not like to tell you about it.' He then added, 'I had to shoot Sergeant Kennedy and Scanlan, and I can't tell you anymore.' It was obviously a painful subject for Ned, and so Gibney moved on, asking Ned's opinion as to whether he

(Gibney) would be able to go to the hotel to ask the other outlaws to surrender. Ned's reply was blunt: 'I wouldn't advise you to go. Thinking you are a policeman in disguise, they will surely shoot you.'

With Ned again visibly tiring, Dean Gibney said he would take his leave, and left Ned with his blessing. The two had been left alone for 45 minutes.

* * *

The period covering the late morning and early afternoon resembled nothing more than a phoney war, an extended period of time when each side sat around waiting for the other to initiate something. At Glenrowan, doing something was only ever a real option for one side after the sun had risen, and that side showed little or no inclination to make a move, at least at the senior level.

During the morning, several people reported that they had seen Paddy McDonnell, licensee of the other hotel, skulking around the station, with most suspecting that he was doing something on behalf of the Kellys. In hindsight, it seems more likely that he was doing something for himself, touting for business. Late in the morning, Tom Carrington walked across to McDonnell's where he had a glass of beer and some bread and cheese. He may have mentioned his visit to Joe Melvin, as the *Argus* reporter walked to McDonnell's at lunchtime. Melvin stayed a lot longer than Carrington, eating and having a drink while writing reports to be telegraphed as soon as possible to Melbourne.

Dean Gibney, too, crossed the tracks to McDonnell's after his meeting with Ned had concluded. He spent a few minutes there, talking to strangers and also meeting up with another clergyman, the Reverend Mr Rodda of the Church of England. The two men of the cloth left the hotel and walked along the railway line to where it had been torn up by the outlaws. There was very little to see, as the track had been repaired, so they walked back to the station where they parted company. In his relatively short time at Glenrowan, Gibney had been looking for some kind of pattern or organisation in what the police were doing, – using his own observations and taking the views of others. By 2 pm, he concluded that the only consistency he could find in the police approach was that they consistently fired at the hotel for no apparent reason.

To the reporters, probably the keenest observers of all, it seemed that no-one was in charge at Glenrowan, and most of the police appeared to be waiting for directions. During an especially quiet time early in the afternoon, John Sadleir and Stanhope O'Connor could be seen relaxing in the cover of a large eucalypt, sharing a copy of the *Argus*. At other times, Sadleir spent time in the stationmaster's office with Ned or standing with a group of people at the Benalla end of the platform, looking across at the hotel. The reporters took advantage of the leadership vacuum; one of them, probably Joe Melvin, wandered across to the cordon and fired a few shots at the hotel, while another souvenired one of the boots cut off Ned's feet.

At least two of the policemen present also took advantage of the situation. Constable Robert McHugh followed up his earlier discovery of the Kelly pack horse and explosives by searching alone the area well back from the hotel where he thought Ned might have begun his ill-fated walk towards the hotel and police lines. His search was successful; he found a blood-covered pistol. It had the number 730 stamped on it, a number that would later be used to identify it as the revolver carried by Constable Thomas Lonigan at Stringybark Creek. The pistol had been in a holster attached to the belt Ned was wearing as he started his final march, but which had been knocked off when struck by a bullet.

James Dwyer was also on the move. As Daniel Barry was sitting quietly, watching the hotel, he heard his name called from behind. Turning, he saw a smiling James Dwyer who said he'd been doing the rounds. 'Have a drink, son,' said Dwyer, producing a bottle of brandy.

* * *

The slight rise on which Glenrowan was situated meant that those on the eastern side of the railway line had a good view of the hotel and the police lines, and it was along that rise that most of the spectators gathered. From the noise they made – cheering anything that seemed to originate in the hotel, and booing or harrumphing any action taken by the police – it was obvious which side most of the spectators supported.

One group stood apart from the main body of spectators, and it took up a position at the railway gates not far from Stanistreet's house. The police knew them for what they were, and pointed out individuals to other policemen who may not have served in the north-east. That big man, they would say, is Isaiah Wright, although everyone here calls him by his nickname, 'Wild'. That's his brother Tom, alongside him; he's a deaf mute, so we all call him 'Dummy'. The solid man in the fancy boots and hat is Dick Hart, Steve's older brother, and that little group there are all cousins of the Kellys. They're the Lloyds, from the King valley.

All eyes were drawn to the group shortly after 2 pm when two women rode in on horseback down the Greta road. They were instantly recognised and recognisable as Ned and Dan's sisters, Maggie and Kate, Mrs Skillian and Miss Kelly. As was usual, Maggie was straightaway the centre of attention, and some present suspected the appearance of the young women at Glenrowan was not entirely spontaneous but calculated to give heart to Ned and his followers. All eyes, though, were drawn to Maggie, who looked simply magnificent. Several of the reporters would go into exquisite detail about her outfit: 'a handsome black riding habit, trimmed with scarlet and a scarlet underskirt . . . a jaunty Gainsborough hat adorned with a conspicuous white feather.'

The Kelly sisters hadn't ridden to Glenrowan just to put on a show for the reporters and spectators, and after a brief interlude at the railway gates, Maggie set off to walk across the Railway Reserve and, perhaps, to Jones's hotel itself. She was intercepted by John Kelly long before she got near the wicket gate. The policeman asked her where she thought she was going; Maggie said she was going to the hotel to see her brother Dan. John Kelly said that, if she was going there, she should invite her brother to surrender. Maggie's response was almost spat out: 'Surrender to you damned dogs?' she snapped. 'I would sooner see him burned alive.'

At that, Kelly told Maggie that she could come no closer, and to go back to her sister and her friends at the railway gates. This Maggie did, and on her way she called out to the crowd that some police wanted her to go to the hotel while others told her to stop. John Kelly was approached by Dean Gibney, who asked him who that young woman was. Kelly told said she was Maggie Skillian, the sister of Ned and Dan, and that she too had declined to ask her brother and his mates to surrender. The priest suggested that perhaps she could be convinced to talk to Dan from a distance, and suggest to him that the time might be appropriate for him to speak to a priest.

Dean Gibney then sought out Maggie in the crowd, and when he met her, introduced himself and outlined what he hoped to do. Maggie did not dismiss his suggestion out of hand this time, instead suggesting that if they both approached the hotel, Dan would have his suspicions allayed and some sort of negotiations may be possible. This was the proposal they then took to John

Kelly, now at the station, and it was a proposal he suggested all three of them present to Superintendent Sadleir. Heavy firing at the hotel front and on the Benalla side had broken out while they were talking. As they sought out Sadleir, standing with several others near the Wangaratta end of the cordon, they were forced to scurry from tree to tree as the firing continued.

Before they could put their proposal to Sadleir, a shout went up from the crowd. Someone had spotted smoke. The hotel was on fire!

CHAPTER 11

Last Rites

After the concentrated activity around the escape of the last prisoners and the arrival of the Melbourne train, everything seemed to slow down and then stop. John Sadleir was happy with his decision to do nothing. Others would later criticise his policy of sitting and waiting, suggesting it was typical of an ambitious man who believes that if you do nothing, you can therefore do nothing wrong. That is probably too harsh an assessment; the best advice that Sadleir could draw on suggested that a direct assault on a reinforced building containing well-armed and armoured opponents would result in police casualties. It was a risk that Sadleir was not prepared to take, and so he sat and waited. He knew that Commissioner Standish would be there later in the day; if he had a better idea, let him authorise it.

There was very little action on the ground after 11 am, and even less after midday. By the early afternoon, the firing had died away to a single shot every now and then, plus an occasional flurry of three or four shots. The police had very much accepted the view that Dan and Steve were using the hotel's chimneys for protection and would probably wait until dark before attempting to escape. The front door was open, but no-one appeared there and the police in the cordon began to wonder what was going on inside the minds of those inside the hotel. Some also wondered what was going on in Sadleir's.

Some idea of the outlaws' intentions could be guessed at when they could be seen or when they were shooting at police, but activity in the hotel seemed to have dwindled to just about nothing. Tom Carrington did not believe that either Dan or Steve fired a shot after the prisoners were released, and that police bullets passing through the hotel confused those who believed they did. His fellow reporter, Joe Melvin, would later state his belief that the outlaws' last shot was fired at 1 pm, and that it was fired from the breezeway between the buildings. Carrington and Melvin were over 100 metres away, though, and those closer were able to recall some specific incidents.

Tom Kirkham at last settled in one place long enough to be able to later testify that he saw an outlaw firing from a window at noon, but that he did not see or hear any activity after that. A number of police at the front and on the Benalla side stated that they did not hear a shot from inside after 1 pm. Perhaps the closest observer of the action was Charles Johnston who would clearly recall three shots being fired from the hotel shortly after he arrived at noon, with a further two shots fired at 1 pm. He believed they were the last fired by the outlaws.

Sightings of the outlaws were also rare. One policeman in the cordon – Mounted Constable Wilson – reported seeing an outlaw at a rear window around 2 pm. Standing close to Wilson at the rear of the hotel at that time was Charles Johnston, whose recollections were more specific. He would clearly recall one of the outlaws – wearing armour – appear at the back door, peering out for what seemed a long time.

Johnston recalled something else. His position gave him a clear view of the rear of the hotel, and a short while after he saw the outlaw at the back door – five minutes, no more – he heard a thud reverberating from inside the hotel, the sound of heavy metal falling onto wooden floorboards. His immediate thought was that both outlaws had taken off their armour and were using it to erect some kind of barricade inside the hotel. Several other troopers in that part of the cordon also heard the thuds around 2 pm. Some believed that one of the outlaws had just been shot, and the sound was that of an armoured body hitting the floor. However, most were unsure what, if anything, the sound signified.

* * *

The newspaper reporters continued to take notes and draw sketches, all the while looking for people to interview and for actions to describe. They were not in the front line and could only observe and speculate from back at the station. This they did. As the time since the last confirmed shot from inside the hotel lengthened, both the reporters and the police speculated on what the silence could mean. Opinion was pretty much evenly divided. Half thought that Dan and Steve were conserving ammunition for either a police assault or a possible breakout after dusk; the other half thought that both outlaws were dead.

* * *

From the time the last of the prisoners ran out into the sunshine, Dan and Steve were alone. More alone than they had perhaps ever been in their lives. They kept their armour on, but didn't move far from the Kelly Room at the rear of the hotel, where one or both would sit on the bed and talk. Occasionally, one of the young outlaws would stand up and walk to either the front or the rear of the building to peer out. There was no hope or expectation in their looking; they knew any chance of rescue – by Ned or anyone else for that matter – had long gone. They just looked to reassure themselves that nothing had changed and that the police had not given up once they had Ned in their grasp. They looked, too, because their homes were just over the hills in the deep valleys at the foot of the ranges, and they knew they would never be going home again.

The talking the two young men did was peremptory chat about what had led them to this: the days in the bush when it seemed that all the world was theirs; the time when they walked and rode through the northeast like giants. But ultimately the talking died away as each retreated into his own little world of thoughts about what had been and what was to come.

Their future was assured and both knew just what was coming to pass. Not one of them, not Ned nor Joe or either of the two younger outlaws, had been prepared to submit voluntarily to capture by the police with the inevitable circus of trial, sentence and execution undoubtedly to follow. Instead they would all die. Perhaps not like Joe, with a glass of whisky in the hand and a toast on the lips, but equally not like Ned, shattered and bleeding to death a short distance from where they sat. They would die though, at a time and place of their own choosing, and that time and place had come.

Shortly after one o'clock, Steve went to the back door for a last look out at the police. He raised his pistol, aimed at nothing in particular and fired once. As he did so, Dan went to the bar, chose two unbroken glasses from behind it, and tipped a small portion of whisky into each. He carried the glasses carefully back

LAST RITES

to the Kelly room and there poured half the contents of a small packet into each. It was that packet that Steve thought he had mislaid at the Stanistreets's the previous day, but which had later been found by Dan amongst their personal belongings at the hotel. The packet contained laudanum, a drug that promised a soporific high in normal quantities but death if too much was taken.

The two young men removed their armour and helmets and laid the pieces carefully on the floor. They rolled the hessian bags that had carried that armour into small pillows which they placed on the floor between the door and the bed. Toasting each other silently, they swallowed the laudanum-laced whisky and tossed the glasses into the corner. They then lay down, each resting his head on a makeshift pillow. As the drug took effect, Dan reached out to place his arm under Steve's head. Steve was already asleep and, before he could say what he really wanted to say, Dan was asleep too.

* * *

By that time many of the rank and file policemen at Glenrowan had only a marginal interest in the strategy behind what was, or was not, happening, and even less interest in what the silence from the hotel might mean. They were there to confront and destroy the Kelly Gang, and that was something that was difficult to achieve if you hid behind a tree or lay flat down in a ditch. It was something that required action, but action did not seem to be a priority for their officers.

Sometime before the arrival of the Melbourne train at noon, James Dwyer, Harry Armstrong, and Mounted Constable Montfort approached Superintendent Sadleir and volunteered to rush the hotel. Dwyer explained that they had thought the proposal through, and that he himself would wear Ned Kelly's armour as he led the assault. The proposal failed on two counts. When Dwyer – widely regarded as a very strong man – was able to squeeze into Ned's armour, he found that could barely move. The second count was that Sadleir was simply not prepared to authorise a direct assault, again for fear of casualties.

Mr Dixon, the Benalla bootmaker, approached Sadleir several times during the early afternoon, volunteering to try to save the wounded Martin Cherry. Again, Sadleir was not prepared to countenance let alone authorise such action. Instead, those in the cordon and on the ground anywhere near the siege were restricted to cleaning their weapons, reloading, and calling on the outlaws to surrender.

* * *

Charles Johnston was nothing if not a man of action, and the sound of the outlaws discarding their armour – which was what he believed he heard – prompted him to seek an active alternative to simply sitting and waiting for something to happen. He left his position at the rear of the hotel and made his way carefully down and around to the drain at the front where he found both Sadleir and O'Connor engaged in doing not too much at all. To those commissioned officers, the senior constable from Tatura outlined the way forward as he saw it.

The outlaws who remained in the hotel had shown no inclination to comply with any of the dozens of calls to them to surrender, Johnston observed, and he agreed with Superintendent Sadleir's assessment that storming the hotel would probably result in unnecessary police casualties. Johnston also surmised that the outlaws were waiting until dark to make a dash for freedom. If the outlaws were not prepared to leave the hotel willingly in the daylight hours, then they must be forced out. The best and easiest way to do just that was to burn down the hotel;

those inside would either leave or die in the flames, and it was a solution that presented relatively few risks to the police.

Johnston went on to explain how the plan could be put into effect. The wall on the Benalla side of the main building was blank; there were no windows looking out from either the parlour or the bedroom located on that side. If the police on that side kept up a steady fire, the outlaws would be forced to remain under cover inside and would be unaware of anyone approaching. A policeman carrying combustible materials could approach the hotel, set and light a fire, and be back in the cordon before the outlaws even knew that the hotel was burning. In conclusion, Johnston pointed out that there was a light south-westerly breeze blowing and that this would push the flames into the hotel rather than away from it.

Both Sadleir and O'Connor agreed with the plan. Their only concerns were about who would set the fire. O'Connor felt that one of the younger constables should be delegated to be the arsonist, but Johnston disagreed. It was his plan, he said, he knew what was involved and he had already been through it a couple of times in his head. He used the same argument with Sadleir when the superintendent suggested that a single man, rather than the married Johnston, might be a more appropriate choice. It was less an argument and more of a discussion, however, and all three soon agreed to proceed with Johnston's plan, and moreover to proceed with Johnston starting the fire.

Sadleir sent runners to reorganise the cordon while Johnston set off in another direction to collect the materials he would need to burn down the hotel. Before they parted, the three agreed to only let others know those parts of the plan that would enable them to fulfil whatever role was required of them. Knowledge of the full plan was to be restricted for fear of Kelly sympathisers learning of it. Sadleir organised for Daniel Barry to take charge of the Benalla side of the cordon and for John Kelly to replace Barry in the dominant firing position in the south-western quadrant; both were instructed to direct volley-firing when Sadleir gave the order.

Charles Johnston, meanwhile, walked to a stable at one of the nearest houses down the Benalla road and grabbed a double armful of hay. As he left, he passed four heavily armed horsemen who had appeared from nowhere and who were sitting quietly and staring across at the hotel. He did not recognise any of them and none seemed to recognise him, so he walked past them without any exchange. He did feel nervous with his back to them, though. He dumped the hay in the middle of the cordon on the Benalla side, and said to several people who asked that he was making food dumps for police horses in case they were needed for a pursuit. Johnston then went to the station to collect kerosene, which he found there in a storeroom. He filled a small lamp and carried it back to where he had dumped the hay.

Shortly before 3 o'clock, one of the policemen at the front of the building called out to those remaining inside the hotel to surrender or face certain destruction. When there was no reply, a heavy volley was fired into the building by the police at the front and on the Benalla side. After a pause to reload, a second volley was fired with a third following after a slightly longer pause.

After collecting his armful of straw and kerosene lamp, Johnston made a wide detour around the rear of the cordon on the Benalla side so that no-one in the hotel could possibly see either him or the load that he carried. When he saw that he was level with the mid-point of the windowless wall, he strode directly towards it, pausing while the three volleys were discharged, and then running the final few metres. He dropped the straw at the base of the wall and shaped it into something he hoped would catch fire quickly, and then splashed kerosene on the pile. He carried matches to set the straw alight, but the first match he struck blew out almost as soon as it was lit. The second stayed alight and within seconds small yellow flames were eating their way towards the heart of the straw.

One or two shots were fired to cover Johnston's retreat to the police lines, but the earlier volleys had already alerted all those watching that something had either just happened or was about to happen. The reporters had watched Johnston run across to the hotel and set what was obviously designed to ignite a conflagration. They watched him strike a couple of matches and they watched him run back to the cover of the trees, and wondered if he had run out of matches, if the hay was too green to light or whether other problems had emerged. Then one of them pointed out two or three thin wisps of smoke that had begun to emerge from the boards at the front of the hotel. As the others started to watch, the wisps became thicker and more appeared elsewhere. And then, with an audible whoosh, the wisps all seemed to run together and, as they did so, became a solid sheet of flame.

*　*　*

The sight of the flames reenergised the reporters, who again realised that they were witnessing history and started jotting down their observations accordingly. Joe Melvin wrote that:

> . . . not very many minutes elapsed . . . before smoke was seen coming out of the roof, and flames were discerned through the front window on the western side. A light westerly wind was blowing at the time, and this carried the flame from the straw underneath the wall and into the house, and as the building was lined with calico, the fire spread rapidly.

There was an immediate reaction among the onlookers. The Kelly sisters were among the first to react. Maggie rushed forward to the police lines, calling out loudly, 'I will see my brother before he dies!' However, the police refused to let her through and insisted she return to her friends at the railway gates. There she was joined by Kate, who was crying out, 'My poor brother. My poor brother.' The sisters embraced. Elsewhere, one of the spectators, possibly one of the released prisoners, called out, 'Where is Martin Cherry?' One voice replied that he was still in the building, while others called out for the police to rescue him.

It may have been those calls that finally convinced Dean Gibney where his duty really lay.

* * *

The Very Reverend Dean Matthew Gibney had been just one of many spectators on and around the platform at the station when he heard the calls about the police setting fire to the hotel and saw the first wisps of smoke. As he stood watching, he thought through what he now believed would happen:

> My feelings revolted and I was wishing in my heart that it might not take fire. I said to myself, 'These men have not five minutes to live. If they stop in they will be burned, and if they come out they will be shot.' That was what decided me and I thought then they will be glad to get my services now – they will be glad to see anyone coming to them.

The reporter John McWhirter was standing near Gibney and the priest asked him if he thought the outlaws would be likely to shoot him; McWhirter said he doubted it. Now determined to enter the hotel, Gibney looked for someone who could authorise this action. He could not find a commissioned officer but one of the policemen pointed to John Kelly, in position halfway between the railway gates and the hotel. Gibney crossed to Kelly's position and asked the policeman for permission to enter the hotel. Kelly told him (again) that only Superintendent Sadleir could authorise that, and pointed to where Sadleir was now observing the hotel from the deep drain at the front.

By now, there were many in the crowd who understood just what it was that Dean Gibney was proposing to do, and as he strode from John Kelly's position across the Railway Reserve towards the drain, pockets of the crowd applauded. When Gibney reached the drain he asked Sadleir directly for permission to enter the hotel, by now clearly alight on the Benalla side. Sadleir refused the request. Gibney did not respond; the time for talk was over. He turned and set off across the reserve towards the wicket gate and the hotel beyond. As he did so, Sadleir called out, ordering him to stop. Gibney snapped back, 'I am not in the police service. I am going to do my duty!' As he continued walking the crowd again clapped and cheered. Pausing before he stepped onto the veranda, Gibney held his crucifix in the air and called out as he stepped through the open door, 'I am a Catholic priest come to offer you your life.'

* * *

Back on the platform, the reporters' pencils flew across their notebooks as Dean Gibney entered the hotel. Tom Carrington noted that it was almost precisely ten minutes between when he first noticed wisps of smoke rising from the building until the time all of the roof was ablaze. Joe Melvin concentrated on watching the police in the cordon, noting how Gibney's disappearance into the building had prompted a general movement in the police lines.

All eyes were now fixed on the silent building, and the circle of besiegers began to close in on it, some dodging from tree to tree and many, fully persuaded that everyone in the hotel must be *hors de combat,* coming out boldly into the open.

As he stepped through the door into the hallway, Gibney again called out, identifying himself and adding, 'For God's sake, speak to me.' He entered the dining room, but it was empty. Retracing his steps the priest noted that the bar room, too, was empty and that the bar itself was burning. He did not even try to approach the parlour, by now a mass of fire, and he noted how, in the blink of an eye, the entire front of the hotel seemed to explode in flames, with a section of the roof above the front door collapsing, and effectively preventing anyone else from entering the hotel via that route.

Although it was now filling with smoke, the hallway towards the rear of the building was still free of flames. Gibney moved down it slowly, feeling the temperature rising rapidly. Looking through a doorway on his right, he saw a body on the floor just inside a bedroom. It was Joe Byrne, and to Dean Gibney it seemed that the young man had only just recently fallen over and was now just lying quietly on his side, almost as if asleep. When he knelt and touched the body though, he found it cold and stiff.

Joe Byrne had been dead for almost twelve hours and rigor mortis had set in. His right arm was folded comfortably across his body while the left was angled out and away, almost as if he was reaching out for something. He was clearly beyond any physical or spiritual assistance, so Gibney rose and looked around the room. There was no-one else there, living or dead. Gibney crossed the hallway to another door he could see through the thickening smoke.

Before he entered that room, Gibney again called out to identify himself. Looking down and into the room, he could see two bodies on the floor, and knew that he was gazing at the earthly remains of Dan Kelly and Steve Hart. The bodies were lying side by side, on their backs with their heads close to an iron-framed bed and their feet towards the door. Alongside the wall next to one of the bodies were the outlaws' suits of armour; on the other side, between the second body and the back wall, was a dead dog; Gibney thought it had been shot through the head. The outlaws' heads rested on pillows they had made by rolling up the calico sacks they had used to carry their armour.

Dean Gibney knelt down and lifted the hand of the nearest body; it was cold and limp. He leaned across and looked into the eyes of the second body, and thought it seemed as though both young men had been dead for an hour at least. When he stood and glanced back down at the dead outlaws, he was struck initially by their youth and then by how 'settled' they seemed to be. They lay stretched out as if asleep, and Gibney could not shake the feeling that they had only recently removed their armour then lain down and committed suicide.

The priest was a little puzzled as well. Because he could see no signs of violence on the bodies, Gibney guessed that they may have held their pistols underneath their jackets and fired directly into their hearts. There was no real evidence of even that, though. He also had the impression that he was looking at something almost contrived, a scene set up as some kind of macabre tableau. The armour neatly laid out against one wall half a metre from the bodies; the dog laid out on its side. The pillows under the head suggested an almost formal pose, and Gibney would later testify, 'They lay so calm together, as if laid out by design.'

Before he could do anything more than muse about the contents of the room, the smoke thickened and the heat increased suddenly. Gibney knew he could do no more and that it was now time to leave. He hurried into the hallway and out the back door.

As he rushed through the breezeway and into the open air, he held his hands up high and called out loudly that all inside were dead.

* * *

As Gibney walked out into the open, he checked his watch and noted that it was between eight and ten minutes since he had entered the hotel. The second thing he did was speak to a policeman who had rushed towards him holding a pistol drawn and cocked. That policeman was probably James Dwyer, and Gibney told him that the weapon would not be necessary as all the outlaws inside were dead. Dwyer was joined by James Arthur and Harry Armstrong, and the three policemen entered the burning building through the back door.

Once inside, it was obvious to the three that there was only a short time left before the building was totally consumed by flames which were now reaching towards the back walls. Dwyer and Arthur both glanced into the smaller bedroom and saw the bodies of the two younger outlaws. Both knew and instantly recognised Dan Kelly, and Dwyer noted a bullet wound in the calf of one leg. The rear and inside walls of the bedroom were now alight, as was the ceiling, and the heat and flames prevented them from doing anything but look into the room.

Armstrong called to them from the other bedroom, where he was attempting to drag Joe Byrne's body through the door and into the hallway. The inner wall and the ceiling of the larger bedroom were now ablaze and it was obvious that the end was now seconds rather than minutes away. Between them, the three policemen were able to drag and carry Joe's armoured body from the bedroom and down the short distance to the back door. From there, they dragged it a further twenty metres into the back yard. Within seconds, flames burst through the doorway they had just exited. As

Dwyer and Arthur caught their breath, Harry Armstrong began to cut the straps that bound the armour to Joe's body.

As Armstrong, Arthur and Dwyer entered the main hotel building, Mr Dixon – the Benalla bootmaker – led two policemen into the skillion kitchen at the rear. The three went straight to the bedroom where Martin Cherry lay on the floor. When they found him, Cherry was still alive but unconscious and it was clear that his stomach wound would prove fatal. The three men carried him from the bedroom and placed him gently on the ground some distance from the burning buildings; the kitchen had now caught fire. Dean Gibney, who had watched the rescue take place, now walked across and knelt alongside the wounded man. He gave the last rites, and Martin Cherry died soon afterwards without ever regaining consciousness.

The rest of the cordon had been closing in on the hotel and not too far behind them came the reporters, followed in turn by spectators converging on the spot where the flames were just beginning to die down. Tom Carrington had been one of the first to move, his notes recording that, 'at a quarter past three the roof fell in, and the flames whirled up to heaven, and myriads of sparks danced through the air'.

By the time he had covered the distance to the rear of the hotel, the skillion kitchen was starting to smoulder, but the newspaperman only had eyes for the drama's central characters:

> The first thing we saw was two or three men dragging out the dead body of Byrne, who still wore his breastplate ... he had a number of rings on his hand, and had boots made after the style of Ned Kelly's.

Then, for a few moments at least, the body of the dead outlaw was the only thing that people wanted to look at. One subsequent report was both graphic and basic. 'Joe's body,' it stated, 'presented a dreadful appearance. It looked as if it had been ill-nourished. The face was black with smoke and the arms were bent at right angles at the elbows.' Others were less graphic. Most noted that Joe's face had indeed been blackened by smoke and that the right side of the body appeared to be slightly scorched by flames. Many noted that Joe was dressed in a blue sack coat, with tweed striped trousers and a Crimean shirt. Some suggested that his boots were ill-fitting while others concentrated on his bushy beard. And a few made a special mention of one of the rings that Joe was wearing when he died. It was quite distinctive, and it had previously belonged to Mounted Constable Thomas Scanlan, long dead at Stringybark Creek.

As the fire burnt itself out, police and civilians gathered in little groups, watching the flames consume Ann Jones's pride and joy, and talking about what they had seen and heard and felt since they came together in Glenrowan. Several small explosions were heard as unfired cartridges exploded in the heat. A small group of police went to the hotel's rear yard to look at the horses that had been shot just before dawn. Not all had been killed outright, and any still alive were shot again to put them out of their misery. A number of police and reporters stood near what had been the rear of the main building, staring at one particular spot until 'the bodies of Dan Kelly and Steve Hart could now be plainly seen amongst the flames, lying at nearly right angles to each other, their arms drawn up and their knees bent'.

* * *

The roof of the hotel collapsed at 3.15 pm, the walls fell onto it, and within fifteen minutes the building was completely destroyed. There were still pockets of fire in the wreckage and it was not until 4 o'clock that the ruins had cooled sufficiently to allow an examination to begin. Appropriately, the first policeman to search the wreckage was the man who had set the fire, Senior Constable Charles Johnston. Armed with a forked stick, he made his way carefully to where the smaller bedroom had once stood, and there removed several pieces of corrugated roofing iron, throwing them to one side to expose what lay beneath.

It did not take Johnston long to find what he was looking for, the bodies of Dan Kelly and Steve Hart. He would testify that, 'They appeared to me to have laid down in one another's arms – the left arm of one was not as much burnt as the right; that it, it appeared to be underneath the other.' At first, he thought he had also spotted a third person before realising that he was actually looking at the remains of a dog. All three bodies – two human, one canine – were covered by quite a lot of debris and Johnston used his forked stick and a curtain rod he found to clear away the rubble. He had to move bricks, timber, and the iron frame of a double bed before both human bodies were fully exposed. When they were, he called for assistance and, with the help of several other policemen, carefully manoeuvred the remains of the outlaws onto separate sheets of corrugated iron and carried them across to where Joe Byrne and Martin Cherry lay.

The outlaws' bodies attracted instant attention: 'Then a sickening sight presented itself. From the smouldering embers were raked out the two charred skeletons of Dan Kelly and Steve Hart.' All that remained of the two young men were their heads and trunks; the lower extremities of their limbs had been burned off. For the police and reporters there were no doubts about which outlaw was which; the remains were easily differentiated by their size, with the larger corpse being Dan's and the smaller Steve's. As the bodies were removed and then examined, Maggie Skillian and Kate Kelly watched from among the small group of friends and relatives grouped at the railway gates. They were silent at first, but then broke down in tears and were soon 'howling loudly and lustily over the blackened bones'.

The Kelly sisters were not allowed to approach either the hotel or the bodies, with the latter still being examined and carefully searched by the police. There was a fear that another body might be discovered but this fear proved unfounded. At the hotel site there were sheets of corrugated iron everywhere and, when these were removed, not a lot of items of interest were uncovered. One subsequent published inventory included, 'the wrecks of two iron bedsteads, a sewing machine and a few tin cans, some of which bore shot marks, were the only recognisable objects in the debris'. Police searchers also removed several gun barrels, the corpse of the dog, and – just centimetres from the bodies – the outlaws' armour.

By 4.30 pm, there was little more to do at the site. Superintendent Sadleir ordered the bodies removed to the Glenrowan station and several of his men to stand down.

Within two hours the sun would set, but would rise again the next morning. Before then, there was work that needed to be done by all those who had survived Glenrowan. For some, it was preparing to farewell family and friends; for others, tidying up whatever loose ends they felt they had left. For Ned, it was understanding what had come to pass and what waited for him further down the road.

CHAPTER 12

Midwinter Afternoon, Glenrowan

After the fire had burnt itself out, all that recognisably remained of the Glenrowan Inn were the front lamp post and signboard.

Over at the station, the bodies of the three outlaws and Martin Cherry were laid out, with a police guard assigned to keep the general public away from them. Joe Byrne's body was thoroughly searched, and a macabre inventory prepared. On his right hand was a topaz ring, identified as originally belonging to Thomas Scanlan and believed to have been taken from his corpse at Stringybark Creek by Joe. On his left hand, he wore a gold ring with a white seal; its provenance unknown. In one of his coat pockets, police found a Catholic prayer book and in the other, a small, brown-paper packet labelled 'Poison'.

While he was not yet decided on his next course of action, Superintendent Sadleir was almost generous in victory. The Kelly sisters were not yet allowed near the bodies of those killed in the siege, but Sadleir did agree to let them see and talk to Ned, with certain conditions attached. There would be a strong police presence, and the Melbourne reporters would also be allowed to attend and ask questions.

Dummy Wright accompanied Maggie and Kate to the room where Ned was being held, and all three greeted Ned by leaning down and kissing the wounded man on the cheek. Ned lay back, drinking a glass of brandy and water. While he looked terrible – his sisters were at first visibly upset at his appearance – a reporter noted that, 'at times his eyes were quite bright and, although he was of course excessively weak, his remarkably powerful physique enabled him to talk rather freely'.

What followed was again more like a press conference than an intimate family gathering, with Ned speaking freely and at length to the reporters while also answering one or two of his sisters' questions.

Ned also spoke freely about the battle itself and how the wounds he had received in the initial exchange of gunfire limited him afterwards. At this, Maggie asked him if he couldn't have remained hidden behind a tree, to which Ned replied, 'I had a chance at several policemen during the night but declined to fire. I got away into the bush, and found my mare, and could have rushed away, but wanted to see the thing out, and remained in the bush.' He went on to describe how, 'I was at last surrounded by the police, and only had a revolver with which I fired four shots. But it was no good. I had half a mind to shoot myself.'

In answer to one question, Ned said that the outlaws had agreed to shoot each other rather than be captured by the police, but when then asked about the earlier incident at Stringybark

Creek, he replied, 'I do not care what people say about Sergeant Kennedy's death.' That was the end of the meeting.

* * *

While Ned was speaking to his sisters and the reporters, a number of policemen were closely examining the remains of the hotel and the bush to the rear. They found that the trees behind the clearing where Ned was captured were riddled with bullets, and there was a considerable amount of blood on the ground where he had been overpowered. Other police searched further up the rise to the rear of the hotel and found a spot under a fallen tree where Ned had apparently rested, as there were scuff marks caused by boot heels and a lot of dried blood there.

Other police searched through the hotel's still-smoking ruins. When the metal had cooled enough to be handled, the armour that had been worn by Dan and Steve was dragged out and carried to the station where it was laid out alongside Ned's and Joe's. Ned's was in the best condition, and it attracted the most attention from both police and spectators. One reporter recorded that, 'the armour in which each member of the gang was clad was of a most substantial character', and there was a lot of discussion about the strength required to walk and fight while wearing 45 kilograms of iron. A close examination of Ned's armour also revealed five bullet marks on the helmet, three on the breastplate, nine on the back plate and one on the only shoulder plate still attached.

The bodies laid out on the platform also attracted attention. Under Victorian law, they were the property of the colonial authorities until the cause and circumstances of their deaths had been determined through legal processes, usually a coronial inquest. Dick Hart had already asked for his brother's body, but was told that it would not be released until a post-mortem examination had been conducted. Then, after they had spoken to Ned, Maggie and Kate were taken to view the bodies. At first, they were unable to distinguish between the charred remains, but when they realised the larger body was Dan's, the sisters wept and wailed over him.

The bodies of the two younger outlaws were wrapped in blankets and removed from the station and carried across the railway lines to McDonnell's Hotel. While Sadleir did agree to these bodies being handed over to their families for burial, there is uncertainty as to whether this permission was given before the bodies were moved or when he was presented with a fait accompli. At McDonnell's Hotel, Dick Hart said publicly and loudly that if the police wanted the bodies back they would have to fight for them. Later in the evening, when a wagon had been organised for transport, the bodies were taken to Maggie Skillian's home in Greta, where they were laid out on the kitchen table.

* * *

Early on in the siege, Tom Carrington had written:

> No extra rifles were taken up in the special train and the four reporters on the platform were quite at the mercy of any of the outlaws or their pals. We quite expected to be attacked from the rear, as there was a perfect nest of sympathisers on the opposite side of the line, in and about McDonnell's hotel.

If anything, John Sadleir was even more attuned than Carrington to the threat posed by sympathisers and supporters of the outlaws. The superintendent had sources of information not available to newspaper reporters. Charles Johnston had spoken of the four heavily armed horsemen he had seen while out collecting hay, and Sadleir had received other reports about armed Kelly supporters in the area. He was also aware that a bag containing a barrel of gunpowder and fuses had been found near the station.

It may have been these fears which prompted Sadleir to release the bodies of Dan Kelly and Steve Hart to their families, and it was certainly these fears that he reported to Standish when the commissioner's train pulled into Glenrowan station at 5.30 pm. As well as the police commissioner, the train carried his good friend, noted surgeon Dr Charles Ryan, and a twelve-pounder cannon. To operate the cannon, a Captain Anderson was leading twelve members of the Garrison Artillery.

Standish at least, and probably the gunners as well, was disappointed to have arrived after the main action was completed and before he was able to exert any direct influence on the outcome. He was also annoyed at some of the decisions that had been made, particularly allowing relatives of identified outlaws to remove their remains before legal protocols had been followed. He told Sadleir that he disagreed with the decision and intended to do something about it. One issue on which the two men were in complete agreement, however, was the need for both themselves and their notorious prisoner to get out of Glenrowan as soon as possible. Night was falling and neither was certain what the darkness might bring.

There were few substantial and no really secure buildings in Glenrowan, whereas Benalla had both a secure police barracks and a lock-up capable of holding several prisoners. The decision was therefore made to move Ned, a decision that the newly arrived Dr Ryan said was medically authorised. Ned was carried to a mattress in a guard's van. A number of armed policemen were assigned to accompany him. Sadleir and his Benalla troopers, along with O'Connor and his Native troopers, followed

Standish's train in their own, the one that had left Melbourne some eighteen hours and half a lifetime ago.

* * *

After the train arrived in Benalla, a cart carried Ned to a cell in the police barracks. A second carried Joe Byrne's body, which was placed in a cell next to Ned's. After he had been made comfortable, Ned was again examined by Charles Ryan, who believed Ned was now unlikely to die from his wounds. The local hospital was told to remain in readiness, though, just in case anything happened. It had been a big day, a very big day for all involved, but there was one more little act before it was through.

Senior Constable John Kelly entered Ned's cell and asked the outlaw if he could spend a few minutes with him. Ned assented, and the two men who were most responsible for the outcome at Glenrowan, one by planning a murderous ambush, the other by ensuring the would-be ambushers were themselves caught in a trap, spoke quietly for a few minutes. In response to John Kelly's 'Why?' Ned said that everything that he had done had been done under provocation, including his shooting of Constable Fitzpatrick in the Kelly home at Greta. And when the policeman asked whether his good friend Michael Kennedy had said anything before he had been killed at Stringybark Creek, Ned nodded. Their eyes had met, the outlaw said, and just as Ned squeezed the trigger, Sergeant Kennedy had said, 'God forgive you'.

CHAPTER 13

Aftermath

The four reporters who had set off for Beechworth had hoped that they would be able to witness history in the making, even if at a distance. When their train had stopped unexpectedly at Glenrowan and they set themselves up on the platform, looking across at the hotel, their wishes came true. When the telegraph connection to Melbourne was established, they also began to write history. The events surrounding the destruction of the Kelly Gang at Glenrowan captured the public's imagination like few events before or since, and the four Melbourne newspapermen both fed and stimulated the public's demand for news.

The statistics around that news alone are daunting. After Mr Cheshire's temporary telegraph office was established in a spare room at Glenrowan station, more than 300 telegrams – some containing more than 1000 words – were sent from that room. A number of those messages were official police and railway messages concerning the clash at Glenrowan, but the overwhelming majority were detailed accounts of the unfolding events written by the reporters. Some 90,000 words were sent to newspapers in Sydney and probably double that amount were despatched to newspaper head offices in Melbourne.

The reporting of the Glenrowan news itself became news. One report began:

> It would be impossible for the most graphic writer to adequately describe the scene of excitement that prevailed in the streets of Melbourne yesterday from an early hour in the forenoon until nearly midnight. In every direction the streets were thronged with people following the tragic events then being enacted a hundred and thirty miles or so from the metropolis.

Another described how, 'Anxious crowds assembled in the streets, flocking round the offices of the *Age* and other newspapers, awaiting with eagerness the announcement of the intelligence.' Even more serious writers were struck by what was almost a sense of hysteria surrounding the events: 'People were waiting with almost bated breath for the next news from Glenrowan. It was safe to say that never before had there been such a widespread and profound sensation created in the history of the colony.'

Again, the figures tell the story. In Melbourne, the two main newspapers were the liberal-leaning *Age* and the more conservative *Argus*. The *Age* cost a penny and in 1880 had a daily circulation of 30,000. The more expensive *Argus* sold at threepence a copy and had a daily circulation of around 20,000. On the Monday of Glenrowan, both newspapers published five 'special editions', each of which consisted of either two or four pages containing the latest information plus a summary of what had gone before.

AFTERMATH

The special editions were brought out every two or three hours during the afternoon and evening, and even late at night 'throngs' of people remained outside newspaper offices in Collins Street, hoping for more news. Over 100,000 copies of the special editions were sold in addition to the newspapers' normal circulation; in 1880, Melbourne's entire population was 250,000.

The newspaper frenzy was not confined to Melbourne alone. Among the 90,000 words sent to Sydney, 8500 went directly to the waiting presses of the *Evening News*; it, too, would publish five special editions about the siege at Glenrowan. The Adelaide *Advertiser* was another that would bring out regular updates well into the night while its offices were 'besieged' until after midnight. Two days after Joe Melvin sat in McDonnell's Hotel writing his descriptions of the scene across the railway line, those descriptions were on the front page of the Hobart *Mercury*.

The interest would remain high in the days and weeks that followed. The train that brought Mr Cheshire and the police reinforcements from Beechworth also brought Mr. JE Bray of Camp Street, Beechworth. Bray was a photographer, and he took a number of remarkable photographs of the latter part of the Glenrowan siege. Bray was joined by several other enterprising photographers at both Glenrowan and Benalla, and within days a wide range of postcards depicting the end of the Kelly Gang was available. For those who wanted something more realistic, by late afternoon on the Monday, staff at the Melbourne Waxworks planned a new exhibition about the events at Glenrowan. By the end of the week, an effigy of Joe Byrne was on display in the Waxworks' Chamber of Horrors.

* * *

Back on the fringes of Kelly Country, Captain Standish was not a happy man on Tuesday morning. In what should have been one of his finest hours, the law he had sworn to uphold was still being flouted. He was especially disappointed that the bodies of Dan Kelly and Steve Hart had been released without reference to him and he now demanded that they be recovered. Early on Tuesday morning he had the appropriate orders drafted, directing sixteen Mounted Troopers to report to the Glenrowan police barracks later that day. Unfortunately, events continued to conspire against the hapless commissioner.

After the outlaws' bodies had been taken to McDonnell's Hotel, someone there sent a message to a Wangaratta undertaker named John Grant ordering two coffins to be delivered to the Skillian homestead on Tuesday; cost was not a consideration. Grant worked throughout the night on the coffins, attaching a metal plaque to the lid of each when he had finished. One read, 'Daniel Kelly, died 28 June 1880, aged 19 years', and the other, 'Stephen Hart, died 28 June 1880, aged 21 years'. At dawn on Tuesday, Grant loaded the coffins onto the rear of a freight wagon and set off for the Skillian farm. He travelled via Glenrowan, seeing smoke still rising from the ruins of Jones's hotel.

At Skillian's the bodies had been laid out for a viewing, and a steady stream of family, friends and neighbours called in to pay their respects. When Grant and his coffins arrived, the formal funeral process began. A parade of 80 horsemen and eight wagonloads of women and children accompanied the dead from the Skillian farmhouse to the small cemetery at Greta, some fifteen kilometres away. There, a man named Michael Bryan, a local farmer and minor council official, conducted a brief service before the coffins were placed together in a common grave in a remote corner of the cemetery. After the grave was filled, the area around it was ploughed over and then rolled flat to prevent identification of the grave site, which was not recorded in the cemetery's record books.

AFTERMATH

The siege at Glenrowan had been a public event, open to anyone to view, and covered comprehensively by the four reporters who were present. By contrast, Dan and Steve's viewing, funeral, and wake was a private affair, open only to those who had a right to be present through ties of blood or friendship. There were no reporters at any of the various rites and it was only later that the details of what had happened finally emerged. Nevertheless, the lack of direct knowledge did not deter some journalists and commentators. One reporter suggested that, at the viewing of the bodies, family emotions overflowed and Maggie lost her temper, seized a gun and would only allow those who wanted to view the bodies to do so in pairs. Another wrote that, 'After the bodies of Dan Kelly and Steve Hart were given up to the relatives, they were removed to Mrs Skillian's hut, which was rushed by a crowd, and a drunken orgie (sic) ensued.'

Despite some even more flamboyant reporting by those who were not actually there, the circumstances surrounding the burial rites of Dan and Steve seem to have been overwhelmingly sombre. Later estimates put the number at the wake held at the Skillian's at around 200, with many of the men present openly carrying arms. It would have made an interesting scene had the sixteen policemen arrived to claim the bodies, but this was not to be. It took longer than planned to bring the police together at Glenrowan, and they were ordered to stay overnight at the police barracks there before proceeding. On Wednesday morning, they were all recalled to their home barracks when higher authorities recognised how much of a provocation Standish's plan of action would have been.

* * *

Benalla, and especially the town's government facilities, was a hive of activity on that Tuesday. The morning saw a flurry of action as a number of events associated with the end of the siege were held. Some were official and some were not. Standish and Sadleir spent the early hours caught up in official activities, despatching troopers to Glenrowan and beyond, dictating letters and telegrams to the various colonial authorities, and organising the imminent transfer of their valuable prisoner from the Benalla police barracks to the Melbourne gaol. At 11 o'clock, there was also an official police parade at which Commissioner Standish would address those officers who had been engaged at Glenrowan. As Standish was preparing to speak to the assembled troopers, he noticed that O'Connor's Native Police had also lined up. He instructed Sadleir to have them removed before he would continue.

Less formal, and possibly without official sanction, was the presentation of Joe Byrne's body for photographs. A Melbourne photographer asked if he could shoot the body, which was taken from its cell and tied upright to the door. The photographer and his assistant then composed the body in as natural a way as possible. Joe's face and hands were washed and his hair combed and parted. One of the crowd watching described how:

> ... the face was small with a retreating forehead, blue eyes, the upper lip covered with a downy moustache, and a bushy beard covering his chin, whilst his hair had been recently cut. His figure was that of a tall, lithe young man.

Once it was positioned and posed, Joe's body was photographed by several cameramen from different angles and distances. When enough photographs had been taken, the police removed Joe's body. The photographers remained in place, taking group and individual photographs of anyone associated with the siege at Glenrowan. Joe's body had been removed because it was needed elsewhere.

* * *

AFTERMATH

For reasons as unclear today as they were in 1880, Victorian authorities chose not to hold formal coronial inquests into all the deaths that occurred at, or because of, the events at Glenrowan. In the cases of Dan Kelly and Steve Hart the decision was made on the basis of wanting to avoid 'inflaming [the] passions' of the Kelly sympathisers. For the others, expediency seems to have been the guiding principle.

Rather than a coronial inquest, a magisterial inquest was convened at the Benalla Court House, with Mr Robert McBean, JP, as presiding officer, assisted by Commissioner Standish acting in his capacity as a Crown Law Officer. All or part of three inquests were rushed through in what would have been record time. The inquest into the death of Martin Cherry was the simplest and the shortest. Medical evidence was offered showing that Cherry had died as the result of a single bullet wound to the lower left-hand side of his abdomen. McBean found that Martin Cherry had been killed by a bullet fired by the police in the lawful execution of their duties. Cherry's body was then claimed for burial by his sister and interred in Benalla cemetery.

The second and more complicated inquest was that conducted into the death of Aaron Sherrit. The inquest took evidence from Aaron's father, mother-in-law (Mrs Barry) and brother, and also from the doctor who had first examined Aaron's body. The doctor testified that Aaron had been killed when struck by two bullets, one of which remained in his body. This inquest was then adjourned until Wednesday when evidence from the policemen stationed at Sherrit's hut would be offered. In the meantime, the inquest agreed to release Aaron's body to his family for burial.

Finally, an inquest into the death of Joe Byrne was opened. In these proceedings, Joe's body was formally identified by Mounted Constable William Canny, based at the Benalla police barracks, who testified that he had known the deceased for more than eight years at the Woolshed, Beechworth and other places, adding that Joe, 'had always bore [sic] a bad character'. Constable Thomas McIntyre then offered evidence on the events at Stringybark Creek which led to Byrne being declared an outlaw while Louis Piazzi, the quarry contractor, described the circumstances of Joe's death. No other witnesses were called.

Within minutes, the formal finding was handed down – 'justifiable homicide' – accompanied by the formal language which specified that, 'The outlaw Joseph Byrne, whose body was before the Court and in the possession of the police, was shot by them in the execution of their duty.'

There was no-one in court, or probably in Benalla, to claim Joe's body, which was disposed of at the court's discretion. Joe's body was stripped naked, wrapped in a canvas shroud and placed in a plain wooden coffin. Early in the evening, two policemen and an undertaker transported the body to a remote corner of Benalla cemetery where it was buried quietly and without ceremony in a pauper's grave. The rings Joe was wearing when he had been killed, and which are clearly visible in the photographs taken of his body at the police barracks, had disappeared by the time he was buried.

* * *

Joe Byrne was not the only victim of Glenrowan buried in Benalla that week, or even that day. His burial was conducted in the lengthening shadows of evening, and followed two earlier burials. The first was the interment of Martin Cherry, laid in his grave by his sister with just one or two colleagues and one or two policemen present. A short time later, Aaron Sherrit was also buried, again farewelled with little ceremony and only immediate family, including his pregnant fifteen-year-old wife, and a few policemen present. His champion, Superintendent

Frank Hare, was long gone, having more important matters to attend to.

After their early escape from the hotel, Ann Jones and her two wounded children, Jane and John, were assisted firstly to the station and then across to McDonnell's Hotel, where they stayed for nine hours. The midday train that brought Dean Gibney and Charles Johnston and his men to Glenrowan departed for Albury after a short stop. Aboard were all three Joneses. They left the train at Wangaratta and were taken directly to the Wangaratta Hospital where the children were both examined by a Dr Healy. He informed Ann that John's wound would inevitably prove fatal, but that Jane's head wound was 'very slight' and required minimal treatment.

John Jones died soon after midnight, in the early hours of Tuesday, 29 June; he had not regained consciousness since shortly after he was shot. Later that day, the Melbourne *Herald* suggested that, 'the wound itself was not of a serious character, but the effect of the dreadful scene on one so young led to the fatal result'. Young John Jones was buried in the Wangaratta cemetery the next day.

* * *

On that Tuesday, like on so many days before and after, the focus of attention was fixed firmly on Ned. On Tuesday morning, he was helped from his cell and driven slowly in a spring cart from the barracks to the railway station. Ned lay on his stretcher in the back of the cart, which was driven by a policeman and escorted by eight others; all were heavily armed. As well as another strong contingent of police, there were a number of spectators on the platform at Benalla station, one of whom was a cousin of Ned's, a Miss Lloyd.

When the train pulled in, several passengers boarded,

including the wounded Superintendent Frank Hare and some reporters. Ned's stretcher was carried to the guard's van and placed inside. Half a dozen police took up positions in the guard's van, where they were joined by Dr Ryan, who would accompany the wounded prisoner all the way to Melbourne. As the train pulled out, Miss Lloyd burst into tears.

To the reporters, Ned appeared 'reticent and sullen', but this may have been something he put on for effect. At every stop the train made, people crowded around the guard's van hoping to catch a glimpse of the famous outlaw. He told his escorts that he did not mind being an object of curiosity. Between those stops, Ned was almost upbeat and was prepared to talk to the escorts, answering questions and offering explanations. He told the police that, at Glenrowan, he had sent a man armed with a light shotgun known as a fowling piece to a point opposite the police barracks when he realised that Curnow had stopped the train. The man was to tell the Melbourne police that the gang was holed up in the police barracks, which was probably the strongest building in Glenrowan. If the police concentrated there, Ned would have had time to adjust his plans. Again, Ned was being Ned, the teller of tales. He also said that while the Queensland trackers were his greatest fear, he was also very wary of being given food or drink that had been drugged.

Dr Ryan monitored Ned's health throughout the journey to Melbourne. He regularly checked Ned's pulse – it was almost always 125 beats per minute – and gave the wounded man medications and stimulants (brandy) at regular intervals. The two men also spoke. Ned told Ryan that he doubted whether Dan and Steve had shot themselves because they were 'too cowardly', but was full of praise for Joe, whom he described as 'plucky'.

AFTERMATH

The huge crowd that had gathered at Spencer Street station to see the legendary outlaw was to be disappointed, as the train carrying Ned made an unscheduled stop one station early, at North Melbourne. There, Ned was carried from the guard's van to a police wagon which was driven straight up Victoria Street to Melbourne Gaol at the Russell Street intersection. When Ned's wagon arrived, the main gates of the gaol were open, and the wagon drove straight in without pause. The small crowd that had gathered there gave a cheer, although to some it was unclear just who or what they were cheering. The wagon stopped and the gates slammed shut.

Once inside and stationary, the wagon doors were opened and Ned was carried on his stretcher from the van to the gaol hospital where he was placed on a specially prepared water bed. He was also formally placed into the care of Dr Shields, the gaol's medical officer. Before the handover, Drs Ryan and Shields conducted an examination of Ned. Ryan believed that Ned's injuries and travel were catching up with him and that he was in a 'sad' condition. Ned's wounds were again examined, and his pulse and temperature taken; the latter had risen to 102 Fahrenheit (41 Celcius), while the former had dropped to 114 beats per minute. Dr Shields officially described his new patient's condition as 'feverish'.

Part of this admission process also involved a brief chat with one of the prison's chaplains, the Reverend PJ Aylward. The only result of the chat was the chaplain's agreement to visit Ned's mother Ellen, held elsewhere in the gaol. He would inform her of Ned's health and well-being.

After dropping Ned and his escorts off at North Melbourne, the Benalla train continued on to Spencer Street. There was no Ned Kelly to ogle but there was a Frank Hare, and the wounded policeman was given a resounding cheer by the crowd. He walked through them to a waiting carriage, which drove him straight to his home in Richmond.

* * *

Life would never be the same for many of those caught up in the occupation and siege at Glenrowan, nor would the history of the little township on the railway line. The day after the siege ended, one of the Melbourne newspapers reported:

> Glenrowan this morning is the scene of much subdued excitement and evident curiosity. Crowds of people from all parts of the district have flocked in to view the scene . . . The visitors are very eager in their efforts to secure relics of the conflict; and out of the ashes of the hotel burnt knives, forks, cartridge cases, and anything else that could be kept are being carried off. In the stockyard fence a great many bullets are imbedded [sic], and these have been cut out and treasured up.

And that was just the beginning. For several weeks after the siege, Glenrowan was a mecca for sightseers and souvenir hunters. They came on foot, on horseback and in buggies, but mostly they came by rail with up to 50 people hopping off every train that stopped at the township. Anything that could be remotely connected to the siege was taken away. Young John Lowe saw 'bits of iron, saucepans, pots, dishes, pieces of half-burnt furniture, legs and sides of bedsteads, etc.', all disappearing into sacks and kitbags and pockets.

Most popular of all were spent bullets, with locals being paid up to two shillings for each bullet. Specimens were mainly recovered from trees, sometimes from branches well above the ground where digging them out could be perilous. There was only ever going to be a finite supply of spent bullets, although one of the line repairers had a lucrative sideline that involved making his own bullets, firing them into a tree and then digging them out and selling them to unsuspecting souvenir hunters for the discount price of one and sixpence each.

Road builder John Lowe and the quarry workers returned to work on Tuesday morning, the excitement of the weekend already behind them. One of Lowe's first jobs was to burn the bodies of the four horses in the hotel's rear yard. It was a good job as he would be paid seven and sixpence for each carcase; by the time he got around to starting the job on Tuesday afternoon, the hoofs of all the horses had been cut off for souvenirs. At every meal break for several weeks, the labourers' camp would be visited by the curious, who would ask questions about Ned and the siege or simply stand and stare.

And so it went. For days and weeks and months afterwards the sightseers would come. One local newspaper reported that four months after the events, a lady had travelled from Melbourne to Glenrowan to visit Hillmorton Reynolds' house where she simply wanted to sit on the lounge that she believed Ned may also have sat on. They were still coming years after the little township had changed so much that the only features Ned would have recognised were the quarry, the Gap and Morgan's Lookout. They still come today.

* * *

The experiences of just two of the little township's permanent residents that first week also gave a good indication of what was to come. On Wednesday, 30 June, Tom and Isobel Curnow travelled to Melbourne by train and there met with Commissioner Standish and Chief Secretary Robert Ramsay. Both officials thanked Tom for his efforts and assured him that those efforts would be recognised by a grateful government. He also met with Education Department officials. They told Tom that he would be given a week's leave to pack up his family and his possessions; he was to be relocated to a school in a different district as it was considered too dangerous for him to remain in Glenrowan where Kelly supporters might seek revenge for Tom's role in Ned's downfall.

After burying her son in Benalla, Ann Jones returned to Glenrowan with her surviving children, and there, with the assistance of neighbours and the labourers, constructed a crude dwelling on what had been the back yard of the hotel. Little more than a rough lean-to, it was hastily built with local timber, roofing iron, and items scavenged from the ruins of what had been Ann's one big project in life. The family relied on the continuing generosity of neighbours for their food, clothing, and other necessities. It was a situation that couldn't last and it didn't. After just a week of living in the hut, Ann packed up her family and their few possessions and took them all to join her husband and their father, Owen Jones, then living at Bunyip in South Gippsland. In November, Ann was charged in Wangaratta Court with harbouring a felon – Ned – during the Glenrowan siege. She was released on bail, but committed to stand trial at Beechworth in May 1881. When the trial was eventually held, all charges against her were dismissed.

Tom Curnow and Ann Jones were among the first to learn that there would be consequences for all those directly involved in the Glenrowan siege. The heroes and the cowards would all answer for their actions one way or another, and those at the top and the bottom would have to face a day of reckoning.

CHAPTER 14

The Reckoning

Watching Ned at Glenrowan in the hours after he was captured, Joe Melvin was moved to write, 'Ned Kelly after being secured quieted down, and became absolutely tame.' It was a motif that would be repeated many times over in the few months of life that remained to Ned. He and his gang had held large areas of two colonies to ransom for the best part of two years, had shot down innocent policemen undertaking their normal duties and had treated all forms of authority with contempt. Three members of the gang were dead and Ned was in custody, behaving as gently as a lamb. His day of judgement would not be based on his behaviour as a prisoner though, but on his actions as a free man and there was only ever going to be one result of that judgement.

Within a short time of his admission to gaol, Ned was regarded as a model prisoner, a process probably assisted by the proximity of his mother. Ellen Kelly had been informed of the siege and its outcome on Monday. She replied that the news was not surprising as in her sleep on Saturday night she had dreamed that there had been a clash between the gang and the police. In her dream, the police had been victorious.

Two days after his arrival, Ned and his mother met in his cell for 30 minutes in the company of Governor Castieau. Ellen became upset when told she could not stay for longer, but was calmed and reassured when Castieau said they could meet again when Ned's health had improved. Ned and Ellen would have several more meetings in Melbourne Gaol, with Governor Castieau always present. Castieau never revealed what Ned and Ellen spoke about, saying that they were private conversations between a mother and her son.

On most days, a large crowd would gather outside the main gates of the gaol, hoping to catch a glimpse of Ned as he was taken to court to begin the legal processes that would lead directly to what the government wanted – his execution. Early one Monday morning, on the 9th of August, their waiting was rewarded – at least in part – as a prison van swept out through the gates and many thought they saw the outline of a bearded figure inside. It was Ned, but it wasn't the same Ned who had arrived six weeks earlier. One of his homeland's newspapers had earlier reported that, 'The outlaw Ned Kelly is quiet and respectful in demeanour. His wounds are rapidly healing, and his recovery is now a question of time.' By early August, he had generally regained his health, although his hand and foot wounds were a problem for the remainder of his life. He could walk, but only slowly and with crutches. In many ways he was physically and psychologically reduced, but there were still sparks smouldering within. The anger at his family's treatment that helped fuel Glenrowan still provided Ned's motivation to go on.

That Monday morning, Ned was whisked through the gates and taken directly to Newmarket railway station where a special train was waiting. He was then escorted to a private compartment where he met the policemen who would accompany him to Beechworth for his committal hearing. One of those escorts was a familiar figure, Constable Thomas McIntyre, the only police survivor of Stringybark Creek. McIntyre had received an amount of public ridicule over his disclosure that he had crawled into a wombat hole after fleeing the fighting at Stringybark. When Ned saw him sitting in the plush carriage, he quipped, 'This is better than a wombat hole, eh McIntyre?' It did, at least, cause McIntyre to smile.

The committal process opened with Ned's counsel applying for a week's postponement; the application was peremptorily rejected. Some items of interest emerged during the hearing. For a short while, there had been a fifth member of the gang, but when it became apparent that he was not a good fit, he was let go. From what would later emerge, this fifth member was most probably Ned's cousin, Tom Lloyd. It was also revealed that the outlaws made their armour near Greta. The main suspects for providing professional assistance were two blacksmiths, one from Greta and the other from nearby Oxley. When completed, the armour was tested by shooting it from a distance of fifteen metres with a variety of weapons.

The fact that the committal hearing was being held in Beechworth was supposed to be a secret, but the locals soon became aware of Ned's presence, and the Beechworth Court House was packed for his appearance. Extra efforts were made to ensure that there was no physical contact between Ned and his supporters to prevent either weapons or poison being passed to the prisoner. Ned again had an audience, and he quickly reverted to type. At one point he was suspected of exchanging some kind of message with Dick Hart using sign language, and at another point he blew kisses to a young woman in the gallery; she responded in kind. Other females seated closer to Ned were not so lucky. A number who stared openly at Ned received a withering Ned Kelly stare in return, and none were able to hold his gaze.

This was all a sideshow, however, to the actual legal proceedings. To no-one's surprise, Ned was committed to stand trial for the murders of Constables Lonigan and Scanlan at Stringybark Creek. Sergeant Kennedy's death was not included in the committal as the only man who knew what actually occurred to Kennedy was Ned, and he could not be expected to give evidence confirming his own guilt. McIntyre had witnessed the other deaths and would be the main prosecution witness. What was a little bit surprising was that Ned's trial was to be held in Melbourne. The Victorian Attorney General had estimated that there were at least 2000 Kelly sympathisers in the Beechworth district and that it would therefore be impossible to empanel an impartial jury there.

* * *

Ned's trial, before Justice Sir Redmond Barry and a jury of twelve men, began in the Supreme Court in Melbourne on 28 October. Ned was charged with just one count of murder, that of Constable Thomas Lonigan at Stringybark Creek two years earlier. The prosecution called sixteen witnesses, the most critical being Thomas McIntyre. Henry Bindon, Ned's court-appointed barrister, did not call a single witness for the defence, and would not allow Ned to give evidence on his own behalf: dubious legal tactics under the circumstances. Barry instructed the jury that they did not have the option of finding Ned guilty of manslaughter, and the jurymen left the court.

Although one juror apparently expressed some reservations, the jury returned in 25 minutes to announce that they had found the accused guilty of murder.

Because of his foot wound, Ned was allowed to sit rather than stand in the dock, which may have contributed to many observers saying that he seemed listless and dispirited as he watched his destiny being determined by one group of people, while another group looked on with obvious interest. The old Ned returned with a vengeance when he had his celebrated clash with Judge Barry as the stern jurist prepared to announce the death penalty. Ned said that he would meet the judge in a higher court than this, and the rights and truths would be determined there. Some say they heard him declare that he would return from the grave to fight for his name.

After the death sentence had been handed down, Ned was led directly from the dock to the condemned cells in the gaol next door. There his civilian clothing was removed and he was dressed in prison uniform. The gaol blacksmith attached leg irons with rivets. Ned's irons were covered with woollen collars to prevent chafing. His new cell was as Spartan as his previous one. It was in the gaol's old wing and had both inner and outer doors. The outer was of solid iron, while the inner was composed of iron bars. The outer door was left open permanently, the ceiling lamp was never extinguished, and there was always a warder at the door. The state was owed a life and it would not be cheated.

Chief Secretary Ramsay continued his instructions to Governor Castieau; Ned was not to have any visitors without his approval and was not to send or receive any letters without Ramsay's personal authorisation. One of the main reasons for these strictures was the almost paranoid fear that Ned would find a way to cheat the hangman. He had been considered suicidal when first admitted to gaol, and even when he regained most of his normal ebullience, suicide prevention was at the front of the authorities' minds. Joe Byrne had died with a packet of poison in his coat pocket and they wanted to ensure that a similar packet was not slipped to Ned during a routine visit.

Ned rediscovered an interest in religion in the few days remaining to him. He also rediscovered an interest in his own welfare. His injured hand prevented Ned from writing, but he was able to dictate a number of pleas for clemency, signing the finished documents with an 'X'. The most important of these was a long letter to Lord Normanby, the Governor of Victoria, which he dictated in his condemned cell on 5 November. In this letter, while making a plea for clemency, Ned made some further claims about Glenrowan. He said he had deliberately waited for the 9 pm passenger train to pass through on Saturday night before he took over the township, and that he had only bailed up the labourers because he believed there could be some police among them. He also claimed that his plan had been to stop the train at Glenrowan station and then threaten to blow it up if the police aboard would not surrender. The stories sat easily on Ned's conscience. The warder on duty noted that, on that night like most others, Ned sang himself to sleep. One of his favourite songs, 'In the sweet bye and bye', was again included several times in his repertoire.

Outside the confines of the gaol, others were also agitating on Ned's behalf. On the evening of the Normanby letter, as Ned was singing himself to sleep, a public meeting was held at the Hippodrome in Melbourne. Two and a half thousand people squashed into the building while another 6000 waited in the streets outside. The meeting unanimously passed the motion, 'That in the case of Ned Kelly, the prerogative of mercy should be exercised by the Governor in Council.' The Governor in Council met on the following Monday, 8 November. Among other actions, they considered the motion from the Hippodrome meeting and a petition for clemency which had the signatures of 32,000 adult Victorians attached. Both calls for clemency were rejected.

On Wednesday, 10 November, Governor Castieau informed Ned that he should prepare for the worst as there was no longer any hope of a reprieve being granted. At 10 o'clock the next morning, Ned walked the short distance from the holding cell to the gallows and was hanged by the neck until dead. One of his last requests had been that his body be returned to his family for burial. That request, too, was denied.

* * *

The confusion that characterised most of the Kelly hunt and most of the siege at Glenrowan continued unabated in the post-Glenrowan world. A number of incidents occurred, several of which reflected very poorly on the police and on the broader colonial establishment. On 7 July, Inspector Stanhope O'Connor was personally thanked for his efforts by Chief Secretary Ramsay, and was asked to pass the praise on to his Native Police, who had not been invited to the occasion. O'Connor and his troopers departed Melbourne three days later, sailing for Sydney aboard the SS *Wotonga*.

The government Ramsay represented happily paid out £607 in medical expenses for Frank Hare's wrist wound. Most of this money was paid to Dr Charles Ryan, gunshot expert, close friend of Commissioner Standish, prominent member of the Melbourne Club and – allegedly – a cousin of Hare's to boot. The same government chose to question the payment of just over £4 to treat one of the Native Police for a head wound suffered at Glenrowan. Hare also engaged in an unseemly bickering match with John Sadleir over the possession of Ned's armour. Hare eventually got his hands on Ned's revolving rifle and a set of armour, which he then proceeded to present to his patrons, the wealthy Clarke family of Sunbury. Although Hare identified the armour as being Ned's, the suit of armour he presented was actually Joe Byrne's.

The police also seemed to mishandle the case of George Metcalfe, the quarry worker struck in the eye by a police bullet during the siege. The injury proved to be more serious than was first believed and Metcalfe had to travel to Melbourne for treatment as an outpatient at St Vincent's Hospital. The Victoria Police at first accepted responsibility for Metcalfe's injury, and paid his board in Melbourne while he was being treated. Then Metcalfe died suddenly on 15 October, and the police story changed. George Metcalfe, they now suggested, had been accidently shot by Ned Kelly while the outlaw was examining a rifle with which he was not familiar.

Even when the police tried to do the right thing, their plans did not always work out as they hoped. It was felt that Aaron Sherrit's two brothers, Jack and William, were at risk of physical harm if they remained in the Beechworth area, and the decision was made that they would be 'taken into' the Victoria Police. The young men were relocated to the Melbourne suburb of Oakleigh and paid an allowance while undertaking police recruit training. Unfortunately, both proved to be completely unsuitable, and they were dismissed in late October. Both were believed to have returned to the north-east.

At about the same time as the Sherrit brothers were being let go by the police, Ann Jones was arrested and charged with harbouring Ned Kelly for the duration of the siege at Glenrowan. The charge was understandably thrown out when it eventually came before the court.

About the only positive news for those involved was the fate of Mirth, the grey mare that was both Ned and Joe's favourite.

Mirth was found the day after the siege, saddled and bridled and grazing quietly alongside the railway line. She was subsequently sold at auction in Benalla before being sold a final time for the considerable sum of £100. Her owner was the well-known Melbourne actor and entrepreneur George Coppin; she spent her declining years pulling his sulky around the streets of Melbourne.

On 23 November, Judge Redmond Barry died of 'congestion of the lungs and a carbuncle on the neck'.

* * *

Within a few hours of Ned's capture, Sir Henry Parkes, then Premier of New South Wales, sent a telegram of congratulations to Robert Ramsay: 'Honourable the Chief Secretary, great satisfaction in prospect of complete destruction of Kelly Gang. Congratulations to your Government.' A few months later, Parkes followed up his congratulatory letter in a more concrete form by forwarding to the Victorian government the New South Wales government's share of the £8000 reward for those responsible for the destruction of the Kelly Gang.

In December 1880, a Rewards Board was formed and called for applications for a share of the reward money. It took evidence from just five people before announcing the disposition of that money. Ninety-one people had applied for a share of the £8000, and the Board decided that 66 of those applications were worthy of positive consideration. There are glaring anomalies in the payouts, and now – as then – it is difficult to understand the rationale behind the distribution which, notionally at least, should have been proportional to an individual's contribution to the destruction of the gang.

Superintendent Frank Hare headed the rewards list with an individual payment of £800. There are reports that Hare refused the money (wasn't it enough?) but it seems that the money was actually paid out. Next on the list, and awarded £550, was Tom Curnow, who was further recommended for a special reward. Senior Constable John Kelly was awarded £377 and Sergeant Arthur Steele £290; he, too, was nominated for further consideration. Hugh Bracken, with £275, and John Sadleir, with £237, were the only others to receive more than £200. The Board clearly believed that Frank Hare was the person most responsible for the end of the Kellys, an opinion he was believed to share.

Railway guard Jesse Dowsett was awarded £175, although he, Hugh Bracken, and Charles Johnston were deemed to be equally worthy of further recognition. Part of that recognition had already been made, as the police had given Jesse one of Ned's pistols, one of the boots that had been cut from his feet, and Ned's mustard tin, still full of cartridges. Johnston undoubtedly deserved a greater financial reward than the £98 he was awarded.

Thereafter, the amount of money awarded seems to have been determined primarily by the amount of time an individual spent on the ground at Glenrowan, although there were both peculiarities and anomalies in that as well. The police who arrived on the scene as part of Frank Hare's initial party were awarded £137 each – with one notable exception – while those who arrived later with John Sadleir were awarded £115. That notable exception was Stanhope O'Connor's Native Police detachment, members of which were only awarded £50 each. To add insult to injury, the reward money was not paid directly to the troopers, but instead was paid to the Queensland police to be expended on their behalf. O'Connor was so disappointed at this decision that he refused his own reward of £237.

As well as Dowsett and Curnow, a number of other civilians were also rewarded. The driver, fireman, and guard of the first police special were each awarded £104 and the railwaymen who followed them from Benalla on the second train received £84 each. Charles Rawlins was awarded £137 and two 'John Sherrits' were rewarded £47 and £42 respectively; one would have been Aaron's father and the other his brother Jack. It is probable that this represented compensation rather than reward. Mr Cheshire and Mr Osborne were both paid £25, suggesting that Osborne may have been assisting Cheshire in setting up the telegraph at Glenrowan.

Among the more questionable payments were £42 each to the Beechworth reinforcements, the same reward to those who had hidden under the bed at Sherrit's hut as to those who didn't. Detective Michael Ward received £100, although the closest he came to the Glenrowan siege was when he turned up at McDonnell's Hotel the day after it had ended, making enquiries about some horses the Kellys were believed to have stolen. Ward was presumably rewarded for setting up a spy network throughout the north-east. However, no members of that network – including the redoubtable 'Diseased Stock Inspector' – were given any of the reward money. Finally, Constable Thomas McIntyre, whose evidence condemned Ned, was ignored by the board.

* * *

The end of Ned did not mean the end of the controversies that his short life had generated. No sooner had the charges against Ann Jones for harbouring Ned at Glenrowan been dismissed than Ann lodged a compensation claim against the government for loss of property and goods when the police burnt her hotel down. Another board was set up in November 1880; it awarded Ann £305 in compensation, an amount that was later reduced to £265. This case, widely reported in the colonial press, alerted the wider public to alternative outcomes which may have been considered at Glenrowan. Superintendent Charles Nicolson threw fuel on the embers by publishing a highly critical report on the hunt for the Kellys which was described by Commissioner Standish as 'twaddle' and by Frank Hare as 'infernal bosh'. The report further stimulated calls for a Royal Commission, calls that were eventually addressed.

On 7 March 1881, the Victorian Premier announced that the government had approved a Royal Commission into all the circumstances surrounding what had been called the 'Kelly Outbreak'. The Commission sat for the next six months, holding 66 sittings and examining 62 witnesses in some depth. The Commission also visited Greta, Benalla, Glenrowan, Beechworth, Sebastopol, and Wangaratta. As the Commissioners were examining all the events subsequent to the Fitzpatrick incident and focusing particularly on how the police responded to the various Kelly incidents, a number of senior police officers took the opportunity of an appearance at the Commission to embellish their own achievements and – if the occasion arose – take a bit of the gloss off their rivals.

Glenrowan formed only part of the Commission's terms of reference, but when it examined witnesses about the siege, their responses threw a lot of new light on the events of the previous year. Dean Gibney appeared twice before the Commission. In one appearance, the clergyman expressed surprise that he had not been called as a witness in any of the inquests which followed Glenrowan, especially as he was in nearby Albury when they were held. He also repeated his belief, when asked about the younger outlaws, that, 'they had been . . . some considerable time dead'. When recalled for a second appearance, Gibney was asked to expand his earlier comments on uniformity among the police: 'The only uniformity I observed was in the intermittent firing at the house . . . they used to begin at one end of the cordon and fire all round until they reached the other.'

Sergeant Arthur Loftus Maul Steele gave what must have

been one of the more memorable performances by a witness. Early on in his appearance, Steele suggested that he thought there may have been some form of conspiracy formed to downplay his role in the events at Glenrowan. He named John Kelly, James Arthur, and others unknown as the main conspirators. He next went on the counter-attack by accusing James Arthur of cowardice, describing how the unarmoured policeman fell back before the armoured outlaw. Steele then took everything one step further, stating categorically that it was he, and he alone, who was responsible for taking Ned Kelly alive. He said he was forced into that position because all the other police had run away.

There were one or two funny little asides to the process of determining the drivers and charting the course of the Kelly Outbreak. In answer to one very pointed question, Arthur Steele denied that he had suggested to Ann Jones that if she told authorities that Ned had shot her son, he would recommend that she be paid part of the reward money. And in what was the funniest exchange during the six months the Commission sat, one of the commissioners asked James Arthur what weapon James Dwyer had carried at Glenrowan. 'A bottle,' was his reply.

When the last witness had been heard, the Commissioners retired to consider the mass of evidence and opinion they had collected and to determine their findings and recommendations. There were a number of findings of fact. The Commissioners estimated that the total cost to the government of Victoria in addressing the Kelly Outbreak was £150,000. In addressing the Glenrowan siege specifically, they concluded that there was little, if any, firing from the hotel after the prisoners were released at 10 am. The Commissioners then turned their attention to those involved in that siege.

Regarding the positive contributions by the police present at

Glenrowan, the Commissioners singled out John Kelly, Charles Johnston, and Hugh Bracken for praise. All three were recommended for promotion, and certain 'disparaging' remarks that Superintendent Sadleir had placed on their files were to be removed. Individual actions undertaken by all three at various times during the siege were singled out for praise, an accolade extended to Tom Curnow for his foresight and bravery over an extended period.

The Commissioners made the point that, 'The spectators were clearly not that day impressed with a very elevated opinion of police proceedings.' Nor were the Commissioners. Their recommendations included one that Commissioner Standish be retired immediately and that Superintendent Hare be superannuated, but with an additional allowance for his wound. They further recommended that Superintendent Sadleir be placed at the bottom of the promotions list. They regarded Arthur Steele with disdain, and recommended that he be reduced to the ranks. They held Michael Ward in similar regard, and recommended that he be censured and reduced one grade in rank.

The Commissioners spent some time comparing and contrasting the actions of Frank Hare and Ned Kelly at Glenrowan, with the dead outlaw proving a more capable leader than the wounded policeman. From the safety of time and space, the Commissioners considered the quantum of police activities at Glenrowan. For those directed by the senior police on-site, the Commissioners suggested that, 'a dispassionate observer could not fail to couple this activity with a want of capacity, if not of courage, to deal with the difficulties'. Eighteen months after the event, the truth did out.

CHAPTER 15

The Legacy

In the days and weeks and months following Glenrowan, tensions remained high in the north-east. For the best part of two years, the region had been holding its breath, waiting for the next chapter of the Kelly story. That chapter was written at Glenrowan and, apart from the postscript of Ned's execution, it would be the last. At the time though, no-one was certain just what would happen next. The Victorian Attorney General had estimated there were at least 2000 adult Kelly sympathisers in the north-east, and there were legitimate fears that at least a proportion of those supporters would seek to avenge Ned's death and the destruction of his gang.

Bad policing and bad police had made a major contribution to the Kelly Outbreak; good policing and good police would make a similar contribution to healing the wounds that the outbreak caused. A decision was made immediately to reinforce the Glenrowan police barracks, and Hugh Bracken was replaced as officer in charge by John Kelly, who had performed so well there during the siege. In the aftermath of the siege, Superintendent Sadleir had written a very positive note on his file as well as recommending Kelly for promotion. Sadleir was more than happy to now have him in charge of one of the district's most sensitive stations.

To support Kelly, Mounted Constables Harry Armstrong, James Arthur, and Charles Gascoigne were also posted to Glenrowan. Armstrong still carried the stigma of his performance at Sherrit's hut, but he had proved to be both brave and competent at Glenrowan, while Arthur and Gascoigne had been two of the most steadfast policemen throughout the entire Kelly saga. The posting had a little bonus for Gascoigne. Shortly after the siege concluded, he had returned to his firing position and found the shoulder piece he had shot off Ned's armour. He had hidden it in a creek and was now able to return to claim it at his leisure. Armstrong remained at the Glenrowan barracks until February 1881, while the others would remain until the end of that year when the police complement at Glenrowan was reduced due to the declining risk of violence in the district.

A further decision was made to reopen the Greta police station and to again locate it in O'Brien's Hotel, still regarded as a locus for pro-Kelly feeling. Sadleir asked John Kelly to move from Glenrowan to take charge at Greta. Kelly had been married in the weeks following Glenrowan and was not prepared to expose his new wife to the potential dangers which were inherent in the Greta posting. He wrote to Sadleir, pointing out that he had given evidence against Ned during the committal proceedings in Beechworth, and requesting that he not be posted to Greta. An angry Sadleir cancelled the transfer, censured Kelly, and put a note on the senior constable's file questioning his bravery and suitability to continue as a sworn officer of the law. It was an

THE LEGACY

undeserved slur, and one that was quite rightly removed at the direction of the Royal Commission.

John Kelly's replacement as officer in charge of the four policemen who would be posted to Greta proved an inspired choice. Senior Constable Robert Graham had been present at the Glenrowan siege for only its latter stages, but Sadleir had gained a favourable impression of him there. Graham was both a good man and a good policeman, whose attitudes towards the locals and approach to community policing went a long way towards healing the scars of Glenrowan. By the end of his posting, Graham had won the trust of the community and had also gained a deep appreciation of the complex forces that had caused the Kelly Outbreak. Most of the issues revolved around the personal, physical, and financial insecurity of smallholders in a society then dominated by a form of landed gentry. The Kellys, like their relatives the Lloyds and the Quinns and their friends, simply wanted equality of access to the land, literally, a level playing field, where they would have a reasonable chance of succeeding. Ned's uncle, Tom Lloyd, explained it all to Graham by saying simply, 'The Kellys wanted ground.'

The feared north-eastern revolution never came and revenge attacks did not occur. Those considered to have been most at risk were no longer in the district, while sympathetic policing helped assuage fears of an ongoing crackdown by colonial authorities. After Glenrowan there were no more mass arrests. The concentrated violence of Glenrowan appears to have had some kind of cathartic effect. There were one or two incidents afterwards, but these may have been driven by personalities rather than circumstances. Arthur Steele, the self-proclaimed hero of Glenrowan, was presented a commemorative sword by the local Stock Protection Society. He also had his greyhound poisoned by a person or persons unknown.

* * *

The hereafters of most of those involved at Glenrowan fell somewhere between public presentations and private poisonings, but the siege did leave its mark on all whose lives it touched.

Ann Jones and her children stayed with Owen Jones at Bunyip for almost a year before returning to the north-east, a return prompted partly by concerns that the cool, damp climate of South Gippsland was harming Jane Jones's health. Ann and her children lived first at Barnawartha and then in Wangaratta while a new house was being built on their now vacant land in Glenrowan. It was in Wangaratta that Jane Jones died on 16 April 1882 of what the local doctor, Dr McFarlane, called 'an inflammation of the lungs', but which was probably tuberculosis. Jane was buried alongside her brother and sister, John and Ann, in the family plot.

For several years afterwards, Ann campaigned actively and extensively for compensation for the loss of both John and Jane; to her, both deaths were the direct results of police actions at Glenrowan. Eventually, in August 1886, the Victorian government paid Ann £100 to compensate her for the loss of her children.

With the earlier monies paid as compensation for the loss of the hotel and its contents, Ann had a large weatherboard house built on the block at Glenrowan. She was unable to regain her publican's licence, but she was granted a wine seller's licence. At least once, in 1888, she was charged with selling whisky without a licence. For several years, she also leased the house to the Victoria Police for £57 a year. A new police station was built in Glenrowan in 1895, and Ann moved back into the house, converting it into a wine bar and eatery.

As if her life was not already hard enough, Ann was never completely accepted back into the Glenrowan community, as partisans on both sides of the Kelly divide suspected her of

THE LEGACY

being too close to the other side. As well, and perhaps building on some earlier tensions, relations between the Jones and Reardon families soured after the siege. The falling out seems to have been based partly on a combination of Michael Reardon's wounding, John Jones's death, Margaret Reardon's near-death experience, and Ann's accusation that James Reardon had made free with her brandy during the siege, yet failed to pay for it afterwards.

Ann slowly faded from view. Owen Jones died sometime during the 1880s and in 1891, Ann married a Henry Smith. In 1910, the then 77-year-old was interviewed by journalist W Cookson for a series of articles he was writing on the Kelly Outbreak. Ann died shortly afterwards; she was buried in an unmarked grave near the graves of her first husband and four of her children.

Tom Curnow and his wife Isobel (nee Mortimer) were relocated to a secret location, possibly in Gippsland, where he taught for several years under an assumed name. He resumed using his real name when he took up a teaching position in Ballarat. The Curnows may have asked for the Ballarat position, as Dave Mortimer had moved there soon after the siege. Mortimer had been warned off from Glenrowan with threats to shoot him and burn down his parents' homestead.

Tom and Isobel Curnow raised four children. The oldest was Muriel (born 1879), who later married a farmer and moved to Western Australia. Next was Isabella (born 1881), who served with distinction as a nurse during the First World War. Their son, Thomas (born 1883), enlisted for service in that war and was killed in action in France on 8 August 1918. Their youngest child, a son named Leonard (born 1887), also enlisted and was wounded. Tom Curnow retired from teaching in 1915 and died in Ballarat in 1922.

Also choosing to seek a new life in better circumstances was

Joe Byrne's mother, Margaret, who relocated her remaining children from the Woolshed to Albury.

When it was his turn to recall Glenrowan for a newspaper article, Dr John Nicholson would write, 'Little Dowsett, what a plucky fellow he is!' Plucky little Jesse Dowsett was also moved away from the north-east because of concerns about possible reprisals. For a while he was Senior Guard on the Melbourne–Bendigo run, and was awarded a pay increase of one shilling per day. He also worked the Melbourne–Queenscliff run. In 1926, the then 84-year-old was interviewed by the *Victorian Railways* magazine. The years fell away as he recalled the events in Glenrowan on that June morning. 'There he is, behind that tree . . . It must be the Devil . . . Look out, he is going to fire!' rolled easily off his tongue as he gestured towards the figure he could still see clearly, though that iron man had been dead now for 46 years.

Michael Reardon was one of the few casualties to survive his Glenrowan wounds. James Reardon, talking later about his son being wounded, stated categorically:

> . . . my son, he got wounded in the shoulder, and he fell on the jam of the door, and he has got the bullet yet, and he is quite useless to me or himself. I would sooner have seen him killed.

Because of where the bullet finally lodged – in his chest cavity near his heart – it was inoperable and remained in situ for the rest of Michael's life. The Victorian government agreed to pay him compensation for the wound deliberately inflicted by Arthur Steele. Michael Reardon was almost 80 years old when he died in Bendigo in May 1942, shortly after learning of the death of his youngest son in fighting then taking place in North Africa. For 62 of those years, Michael had received £1 per year for the wound he had suffered at Glenrowan.

THE LEGACY

Quarry contractor, Alphonse 'Louis' Piazzi, died suddenly in late 1881 and is buried in Benalla cemetery.

Dean Matthew Gibney rose steadily through the hierarchy of the Catholic Church and was ordained as Bishop of Perth in 1887. He retired from this post in 1910, and passed away on 22 June 1925, aged 88.

The indefatigable Charles Champion Rawlins had been everywhere during the siege, and later named his son after the place where he had experienced his finest moments. That son later went to London to study painting and, when the First World War broke out, was among the first volunteers to enlist for the fight. Private Glenrowan Champion Rawlins died in one of the war's opening battles.

* * *

Both Commissioner Standish and Superintendent Hare were affronted by the findings of the Royal Commission, and both tendered their resignations almost immediately. Frederick Standish stepped back from public view but remained active in his favoured pursuits of Freemasonry and the life that existed in and around the Melbourne Club. He died at the club in March 1883 of what newspapers described as, 'disease of the heart, aided by a general break-up of the system'.

Superintendent Francis Augustus Hare retired from the police but not from public life. In 1882, the Victorian government appointed him to the position of Police Magistrate and other, similar appointments were to follow. Hare also contributed to the growing collection of 'Kellyana'. He was interviewed extensively by writer Charles White who used many of Hare's observations in his two-volume, *History of Australian Bushranging*. Hare also turned his own hand to writing, and in 1891 his memoirs, *The Last of the Bushrangers*, was published in Melbourne. Frank Hare died in that city the following year, probably from complications of the diabetes he had suffered for several years.

Compared to the others, Superintendent John Sadleir took the criticisms of the Royal Commission in relatively good grace. He remained in the Victoria Police – indeed he remained in his position at Benalla – and continued his measured and steady approach to policing. When he retired in 1896, Sadleir was in charge of the Metropolitan Police District, a position second only to the Commissioner in the police hierarchy. John Sadleir retired to his family home in Kooyong Road, Elsternwick, and there wrote his memoirs, *Recollections of a Victorian Police Officer*. His book was published in 1913, and in it Sadleir recalled how he had decided that, had the fire not taken hold at Glenrowan, he was resigned to storming the hotel, but would have done so as late in the day as possible. He said that he had also felt an overwhelming sense of relief when the fires died out at Glenrowan; three years of intense pressure were over. John Sadleir passed away quietly at home in 1919.

Most of the other policemen in the siege at Glenrowan followed Sadleir's example and simply continued to do their jobs as well as they could away from the glare of publicity. Their stories are known primarily to their families. Some others left slightly more permanent entries in the public record. Stanhope O'Connor returned to Victoria in 1881 and joined the Victoria Police as an inspector. At around the same time, Mounted Constable Harry Armstrong resigned from the police, primarily because of the censure he was given by the Royal Commission for his failure of will at Sherrit's hut. Armstrong reportedly left Australia, seeking to redeem both his reputation and his life in the United States.

Charles Johnston, the man who lit the match that ultimately led to the end of the siege, remained with the Victoria Police

THE LEGACY

until 1885, when he retired from the force to take up farming on a property near Ballarat. He passed away in 1936.

Daniel Barry, one of the original policemen in Frank Hare's party, was the same age as Ned Kelly at the time of Glenrowan. He remained in the north-east afterwards, and died in Beechworth in 1915.

James Arthur had been in the police force for a little over two years when he performed so well at Glenrowan. He went on to have a 35-year career with the Victoria Police, much of it spent in Geelong and the south-western districts of Victoria. He died in North Melbourne in 1924.

William Canny resigned from the Victoria Police in 1881 and was a publican in Melbourne for much of the remainder of his life. He maintained an active interest in Australian Rules football and at one stage was vice-president of the Richmond Football Club. Canny, the last surviving policeman from the originals at the siege at Glenrowan, passed away in 1935.

Charles Gascoigne, another of the policemen to emerge with some honour from Glenrowan, found that the siege marked the high point of his career, which ended not too long afterwards. Gascoigne, one of the few native-born troopers, was dismissed from the Victoria Police in 1882, allegedly because of comments he made suggesting the Kelly Outbreak could be explained in part by the behaviours and attitudes of the police themselves. He remained in the north-east, and sometime around 1887 was involved in the discovery of significant deposits of turquoise in the King valley, the first time the gemstone had been discovered in Australia. By the 1890s, several open-cut mines had been established between Edi and Cheshunt, and Charles Gascoigne – 'the field's main prospector and promoter' – dominated the industry until 1921 when the industry declined substantially after the state government refused to back Gascoigne's proposal to develop a new mine. Charles Gascoigne died in 1927, leaving behind a wife, Mary, and five adult children.

John Kelly, who was arguably the most professional policeman at Glenrowan, subsequently transferred to Victoria's Western District, and retired there as a sergeant of police in 1898. The 'other' Kelly at Glenrowan died at his home in St Kilda in 1905.

Tom Kirkham's idiosyncratic police career continued after Glenrowan. In 1886, he applied for official leave so he could travel interstate but actually used his leave to perform with a theatrical troupe in Myrtleford. When this ruse was discovered, Kirkham was asked to resign from the police. The wanderer, Thomas Kirkham, died in the Melbourne suburb of Armadale in 1911.

With Ned's execution in November 1880, Thomas McIntyre became the last survivor of Stringybark Creek, and one of the few policemen who had been involved directly in the Kelly Outbreak for much of its course. McIntyre continued with the police until he retired, and later settled in Ballarat where he died in 1918, aged 72 years. Former Mounted Constable Alexander Fitzpatrick, whose behaviour in the Kelly home at Greta set off the chain of events that led to Glenrowan, died in May 1924. Several years earlier, the journalist Cookson had interviewed him at his home in suburban Hawthorn. In an article published in September 1911, Fitzpatrick spoke of the past and of what could have been:

> Ned Kelly rises before me as I speak. Considering his environment, he was a superior man. He possessed great natural ability, and under favourable circumstances would probably have become a leader of men in good society, instead of the head of a gang of outlaws.

It seems to have been one of the few times in his life that Fitzpatrick made a conscious effort to tell the truth.

* * *

Life's little twists and turns are graphically illustrated by the fates of two of the central police figures at Glenrowan. Fearing for both his own and his family's safety, Constable Hugh Bracken requested a transfer away from the Glenrowan police barracks. He had done his best, and knew that he had played a significant role in the destruction of the Kelly Gang and, moreover, played a role that attracted high praise from the Royal Commission. Bracken's request was granted, and he was posted firstly to the Richmond Training Depot and then to the police barracks at Wallan, not far from where Ned had spent his formative years. In both postings, he was snubbed by a number of officers who thought that he should have let Arthur Steele shoot Ned.

Hugh Bracken suffered a nervous breakdown in 1883 and was discharged from the Victoria Police as being medically unfit for duty. Widowed twice over, and with one son from each of those marriages, Hugh Bracken couldn't escape the demons that followed him as he once imagined Ned might do. Bracken died from a self-inflicted gunshot wound at Wallan in February 1900. His youngest son, James Bracken, was decapitated by a German shell during the Australian advance on the Hindenburg line in September 1918.

Sergeant Arthur Steele, the man Bracken stopped from killing Ned, was rightly censured by the Royal Commission for his behaviour at Glenrowan. He displayed an almost total disregard for anyone other than himself and was clearly derelict in his duty as a sergeant of police; at no stage did he display anything remotely resembling leadership. The Commissioners were quite right in recommending his reduction in rank. A braggart and a blowhard, Steele remained in the Victoria Police and does not seem to have suffered any long-term personal or professional disadvantage from his actions at Glenrowan.

Steele retired in Wangaratta, and in his retirement continued to give interviews to anyone who would listen about what he claimed had really taken place at Glenrowan. One account was published in *Life* magazine in February 1910. The following year he was interviewed by WH Cookson for that journalist's series of articles about the Kellys. During the interview, which went very much as expected, Steele produced his only memento of Glenrowan, Ned's ammunition bag with bloodstains still discernible on the leather. The interview produced a Steele outline of the events and a Steele analysis of the 'real' Glenrowan: 'The actual capture of Ned Kelly was surrounded by a good deal of romance at the time, but the account here given may be relied upon as absolutely correct, and as plainly as I can state it.' He was right on the first count and wrong on everything else as, while the truth and Arthur Steele knew each other, they were never really close. Arthur Steele died in Wangaratta in 1914.

* * *

While many of those involved in the events at Glenrowan would come to regard the siege and its aftermath as some kind of turning point in their fortunes — some for better, some for worse — to the Kelly family the events were nothing short of tragic. Ellen Kelly was released from Melbourne Gaol on 7 February 1881 and straightaway returned to the family farm at Greta. Ellen never spoke publicly about her thoughts and feelings for the various fates that overtook her children. Like several others, she granted the journalist Cookson an interview in 1911 and told him that, at the time of the incident which started it all, Constable Fitzpatrick was drunk and it was his attempt to kiss her daughter Kate that precipitated all that followed. Ellen and her eldest son Jim spent their lives at Greta looking after family and farm. In March 1923, Ellen passed away quietly at home; she was 85 years old.

Maggie was always Ned's favourite sister. Both siblings were forthright and strong-willed, rarely deviating when they had decided on a particular course of action. Shortly after Ned's execution, Maggie left her husband, William Skillian, for her cousin, Tom Lloyd; at the time, Skillian was still in prison serving out a sentence for horse theft. Maggie and Tom had ten children before Maggie died of 'rheumatic gout' in 1896. After Maggie died, Tom Lloyd married Rachel Hart, Steve's younger sister. The couple had six children.

Kate Kelly became somewhat estranged from her family, with one storyline saying it was because she agreed to appear in a somewhat lurid stage play about the family. The story continues that she went to New South Wales where she joined a Wild West troupe as its star female rider. A second story has her simply moving interstate to escape the post-Glenrowan glare of publicity. Both place her eventually in Forbes where she used a pseudonym, worked in several different jobs and, in 1888, married a local named William 'Brickie' Foster. She was now known as Ada Foster.

Again, Kelly folklore has it that, in the 1890s, a touring stage company playing in Forbes included a brief Kelly pantomime in its repertoire. Kate was in the audience and at the conclusion of the sketch a cast member pointed to her and said, 'There's the real heroine of the story.' Kate immediately ran out of the theatre. The incident seemed to trigger a deep melancholy within her. A few days later, her body was found floating in a river.

The truth was a lot less dramatic, but no less tragic. Brickie and Ada Foster had six children, three of whom died in infancy.

The last, a girl they named Catherine, was born in 1889, and Kate was alone for the birth. She developed post-natal depression which was then often diagnosed as 'milk fever', began to drink heavily and disappeared from her home in early October. Her body was found floating in a lagoon nearly a week later. Kate Kelly was buried in Forbes cemetery, not far from the grave of bushranger Ben Hall.

Kate had been Jim Kelly's favourite sister, and when news of her passing reached Greta, Jim harnessed a horse to a buggy and rode the 700 kilometres to Forbes to collect Kate's children and bring them back to Greta. They were Kellys by birth and they would be raised by Kellys. Kate's only son volunteered for service in the First World War, as did both her sons-in-law. They returned home; he did not. In April 1917, Private Frederick Arthur Foster was shot dead during an exchange of rifle and machine-gun fire on the Western Front.

There was another Kelly sister, little Grace, just entering her teens as the tragedy of Glenrowan unfolded. Researching a book on bushranging, the journalist and author Tom Prior interviewed Paddy Kelly, Grace's son and nephew of Ned and Dan, during the early 1960s. Paddy Kelly said to Prior:

> Maybe Ned Kelly is history; maybe you think he was a great man, maybe you don't. I didn't know him. I wasn't born until he was dead. But my mother was alive and she lived a long time. She was the kindest and most wonderful mother a man ever had and until the day she died she grieved over what happened to her brothers. What happened to Ned and Dan spoiled her whole life and I'll never forget it. I can't remember Ned and Dan but I can remember my mother. She didn't do anything to anyone but she suffered and I'll never forget it. There'll be no monuments to my mother's grief.

THE LEGACY

Had he not been in prison at the time, it is almost certain that Jim Kelly would also have ended his days at Glenrowan, fighting alongside his brothers and their friends. It was not to be. On the eve of his execution, Ned told Jim that it was now up to him to look after the family. It was a commitment and an obligation that Jim honoured for the rest of his life. He never married and spent the next 60 years as a semi-recluse, living on the family farm at Greta and interacting primarily with family and close friends. Jim Kelly was 87 years old when he died in 1946, a man whose wild and wilful youth became something else. 'Jim Kelly was one of the most beloved men in the whole of this district. He would help anybody who was down or wanted help.' Jim was the last of Red Kelly's sons and, as much because of what he didn't do as well as what he did, he may just have been the best.

* * *

The story of Glenrowan is actually bigger than the legend of Glenrowan. In the legend, Ned Kelly strides across the stage like a colossus, a literally larger than life figure who takes on all the forces of law and order before falling, like Achilles, to a combination of bad luck and a flaw in his protective shield. In the story of Glenrowan, Ned is still the central figure; after all, it was his plan that was put to the test in the little railway township. But, while Ned may occupy a prominent position, others share the spotlight with him and, at times, even have it all to themselves. In *Glenrowan*, I have tried to more clearly delineate the reality rather than just add to the legend.

The death of Aaron Sherrit triggered the siege at Glenrowan, where another five people – Joe Byrne, Dan Kelly, Steve Hart, Martin Cherry and John Jones – died during or soon after. Two more, Neil Metcalfe and Jane Jones, passed away in circumstances that were linked to Glenrowan. One was a direct linkage;

the other, except to her mother, much more tenuous. Three other people, Michael Reardon, Frank Hare and a Native Policeman named Jimmy suffered wounds of varying degrees of seriousness. Ned himself was badly wounded and may have died if not for the expert treatment that the doctors on the spot were able to administer. The number of casualties alone makes the story of Glenrowan one of significance.

For collectors of statistics, there are also interesting elements to the story. Hundreds of rounds of ammunition were fired from rifles, carbines, shotguns, and pistols and, had the siege continued for another two hours, field artillery would also have been involved. Given the rate at which some of the police fired, the total number of cartridges discharged may well have easily topped 1000. They were also fired at a ratio of more than 20:1 in favour of the police. The casualties reflect this ratio, with seven people killed or seriously wounded by police firing and just two relatively minor injuries from the outlaws' shooting.

There was property damage associated with the siege as well. Ann Jones's hotel, its furnishings and fittings, were all totally destroyed and anything of value on the property was afterwards cut up and carried off as a souvenir. There were also livestock losses. The most reliable figures identified four Kelly horses shot dead by police at the rear of the hotel, while some writers have suggested that up to eight horses were killed and that several others were later found starving in the stables behind McDonnell's Hotel. As well, the station buildings at Glenrowan and several rail carriages and engines suffered damage from either bullets or inappropriate usage.

At another level again were the personal costs of Glenrowan. Individual reputations were both made and lost as the siege unfolded. While he may have remained well-connected with the

Melbourne establishment, Frank Hare's erratic behaviour on the ground meant that few rank and file policemen would ever again trust his judgement. John Kelly's reputation among his peers went the other way; far from being a plodder, he had proved to be a leader of men. For each John Sadleir, there was a Charles Johnston and for each Arthur Steele, a James Arthur.

Men like Tom Curnow, Jesse Dowsett, and Hugh Bracken rose to the occasion, while others – like James Dwyer – retreated to the place where they were most comfortable. Margaret Reardon and John Stanistreet did what they needed to do to protect their families. Two young men, Dan Kelly and Steve Hart, also did what they felt they needed to do when life seemed to offer so little: chose to end them at a time, if not a place, of their choosing.

Ultimately, though, Glenrowan is the story of an incident given historical significance by the actions of a number of individuals responding to a specific set of circumstances. These circumstances were generated partly by social, political and economic inequalities that had grown and festered in colonial Victoria. Ned, through his personality and natural leadership qualities, was the lightning rod that brought a lot of these issues to a head, partly through what he and others read into what were really just a series of criminal events. He did so knowingly and he did so at a time and a place where he was comfortable and where he felt in control. Ned Kelly chose to make his last stand at Glenrowan and then stuck with his plan, knowing it was falling apart and knowing that it was not fully supported by his team. He stayed – and they stayed with him – because he was sick of running. Within a few hours of Ned making that decision, the three who chose to stay with him would all die and Ned himself, wounded and a prisoner, would be a long way down the path to the gallows.

Glenrowan can also be posited as the clash between the old and the new as the 20th century approached with its revolutions in transport and communications. The railways which had opened up much of the hinterland behind the coastal towns and cities were to be used as a weapon by Ned, a weapon directed against the state that was intent on crushing him. When his initial plan failed, those railways brought the reinforcements that sealed his fate, reinforcements summoned and directed by another recent invention, the telegraph. Ned consciously cast himself as the successor to Bold Jack Donahue, Frank Gardiner, Ben Hall, and Dan Morgan. He may well have been their successor, but he was also the last in that line. While the modern world which was emerging would not eliminate criminals, it did force them to be simple criminals rather than criminals with a wider social agenda. Who again would rouse popular sentiment with the likes of the Jerilderie Letter; who again would put on dances for their captives, and who again would dress like medieval knights for their war with the law? There were no more bushrangers worthy of the name after Ned.

The separation of fact and fantasy, story and legend, started to become problematic in the immediate aftermath of Glenrowan. Most people who have written of Glenrowan include references to behaviours and values we all like to associate with 'Australianness' — courage in the face of adversity, resourcefulness and making do with what you have, self-reliance and, above all, mateship: sticking with your mates to see an enterprise through to the end. In itself, such references are neither a problem nor an issue. What may be an issue though, is assigning such values to just one side in a two-sided contest. Partisans on both sides of the argument, those who pitch Ned the Saint against Ned the Sinner, all draw inspiration from Glenrowan, each claiming the moral high ground through different interpretations of the same events.

THE LEGACY

In the end, it may all just be semantics. What was the philosophical difference between Ned walking down from the bush in the pre-dawn mist and Charles Johnston crossing open and exposed ground to set fire to the hotel, clutching his bundle of hay and kerosene? Glenrowan was about people and the interactions – sometimes violent, sometimes tender – between those people. Glenrowan is about Ned and Charles and all the others who were there. Some of them have become larger with the passage of time; Ned, Frank Hare, and Commissioner Standish in particular, although for vastly different reasons. Others who had been previously either unknown or unnoticed, rose to prominence at Glenrowan; Hugh Bracken, Tom Curnow, Jesse Dowsett, John Kelly, James Arthur, Charles Johnston and Charles Rawlins all did what was regarded as 'sterling work' in the fight. As these individuals rose, others fell; Arthur Steele and James Dwyer had every reason to feel embarrassed about their performances at Glenrowan, although I could find no evidence that they did. Still others, like Ann Jones and Dave Mortimer, simply tried to make the best of the circumstances in which they found themselves. All who were there made their mark on Glenrowan just as Glenrowan made its mark on them.

History does not need our approval and, like it or not, Australians will remember Ned Kelly for generations after we have all been and gone. A significant part of that remembrance will be based on what he did (or is alleged to have done) at Glenrowan. Without the others whose lives intersected at Glenrowan and whose stories I have tried to tell, Glenrowan would have been something totally different. Theirs, too, are stories worth telling, not to balance some kind of scorecard, but simply to establish that people like John Kelly, James Arthur, Jesse Dowsett, and Charles Gascoigne – no less than Ned and Dan, Joe, and Steve – fought and fought hard at Glenrowan.

The legend belongs to Ned, but the story belongs to the others, to the Joneses, the Reardons, the Curnows, and the Stanistreets, and to all the people whose lives were changed by the events in that little township in north-eastern Victoria over that winter weekend in 1880.

NOTES

Prologue: The Long Drop
Page
4. A crowd that would grow to 5000 . . .: Ned's family were not part of that crowd, preferring to remain together as a group at the Robert Burns Hotel in nearby Lonsdale Street.
6. A convicted felon named Elijah Upjohn: As well as earning a slight remission of his sentence, Upjohn would be paid for his work.
6. 'Altogether the man's appearance . . .': John McWhirter, *Herald*, 11 November 1880.
7. Several of the other witnesses . . .: See, for example, Wannan, *Tell 'Em I Died Game*, p. 15, and John McWhirter, *Herald*, 11 November 1880.

Chapter 1: Ned Kelly, Son of Red Kelly
Page
16. Land, no matter how poor, she now had: The gradual decline of the alluvial goldfields in Victoria had released thousands of diggers from those fields. One response by governments in Victoria (and elsewhere) was to allow small-scale farm enterprises

through the simple expedient of allowing qualified applicants to 'select' up to 300 hectares of land. These selections were subject to residential and development requirements, while the land available was often far inferior to that already occupied by squatters. Land would become an ongoing source of friction between the two groups of farmers.

17. The necessity of staying together . . .: J.J. Kenneally, *The Complete Inner History of the Kelly Gang and Their Pursuers*, p. 21.
19. The youngest son . . .: To family and friends, Dan was always called 'Dan'; to Ellen Kelly, however, he was always known as 'Danny'.

Chapter 2: Outlaws
Page
28. The senior officer, Sergeant James Whelan: Whelan had been a member of the Royal Irish Constabulary before immigrating to Australia in 1856. A friend of Robert O'Hara Burke, he joined the Victoria Police and was posted to Burke's Beechworth inspectorate, moving from there to Benalla where he would ultimately be stationed for 28 years.
28. The 'attempted murder' of Constable Fitzpatrick: A little over a year later, Fitzpatrick would be dismissed from the Victoria Police, with the Commissioner labelling him 'a liar and a larrikin' (Corfield, *The Ned Kelly Encyclopedia*, p. 165).
28. Sergeant Arthur Steele: Steele was an impetuous and, at times, imperious Englishman who had previously served with the Royal Irish Constabulary. In 1877, he was appointed officer in charge of the Wangaratta barracks.
31. Robert McBean, a wealthy squatter and Justice of the Peace . . .: while McBean had a reputation for fairness among the district's selectors, he would brook no opposition to the law. It was McBean whose reward money led to the capture of Harry Power, and it was McBean who sponsored the formation of a District Stock Protection Society in 1877. It would also be McBean who would lease paddocks to the police for horse agistment during the Kelly hunt.

NOTES

32. 'And, if Catholic . . .': Robert Haldane, *The People's Force*, p. 82. Other proportions were English (10 per cent), Scottish (3.3 per cent), and Australian-born (3 per cent).
37. Mortally wounded . . .: While Ned would always claim that he fired the shot that killed Scanlan, experts believe that it was most probably fired by Joe Byrne.
41. And two unidentified men: The police believed they knew the identity of the other two and named them as Charles Brown and William King. Charlie Brown and Billy King were known associates of the Kellys and lived in the Greta area.

Chapter 3: The Killing of Aaron
Page
44. A flying visit to the area . . .: See Ian Jones, *Ned Kelly: A Short Life*, p. 88.
44. Due to information he supplied: See Charles White, p. 296.
52. Metaphysical bond: With no real evidence to support the supposition, Hare always believed that his admiration of Sherrit was reciprocated and later recalled: 'He expressed himself very pleased at my return [in June 1880] and told me he did not get on very well with the inspecting superintendent [Nicolson] as he did with me, and he would set to work with fresh zeal and endeavour to find out where the outlaws were to be found.' (Evidence given by Hare to the Royal Commission on the Kelly Outbreak.)
53. 'Kate is a girl of medium height . . .': *Benalla Standard*, 21 January 1879.
53. 'The hiding place . . .': Fitchett, *Ned Kelly and his Gang*, pp. 57–58.
57. The notional second in command: As well as keeping an insider's eye on what the Queenslanders were doing, Kirkham also offered some practical value as he knew and could recognise all the members of the gang. He would later go on record as describing Ned as, 'A fine, manly fellow [who] possessed a high moral character.' (Kenneally, p. 17.)
58. 'The tracks . . .': Fitchett, p. 60.

NOTES

61. On Dan Kelly's plans: Kenneally in particular advances Dan's ideas as the better option.
62. Although suspicion fell . . .: One of those who came under suspicion was a man named Culph, a blacksmith from Oxley. Culph was well-known in the district; his sister Margaret was married to Mick Reardon, the ganger in charge of rail maintenance at Glenrowan.
66. 'You'll not blow . . .': Joe Melvin, *Argus*, 28 June 1880.

Chapter 4: Ann Jones's Glenrowan Inn
Page

68. Morgan's Lookout: Named after the 1860s bushranger, 'Mad' Dan Morgan, the closest that Morgan ever actually came to the feature named after him was twenty kilometres, and that was on the day he was killed.
69. 'A courageous and intelligent man': Fitchett, p. 37.
73. Made the right decision: Clare Wright and Alex McDermott, *Meanjin*, p. 116.

Chapter 5: Saturday Night and Sunday, 26/27 June 1880
Page

75. Ammunition of various calibres: When he rode into Glenrowan, Ned carried a .31 calibre Colt pocket revolver, an old .577 calibre carbine with a sawn-off stock and barrel (probably given to him by Harry Power), a Spencer revolving rifle taken at Stringybark Creek and two cap and ball revolvers, one of which was the .36 calibre Colt Navy revolver he had taken from the police at Jerilderie.
77. 'Put a bullet through him Strahan': John Lowe. *John Lowe's Glenrowan Diary*. Then based at Benalla, Senior Constable Strahan had been based in the north-east for several years and knew the Kellys well from their early attempts at horse stealing.
77. John Delaney: John Delaney's father, a blacksmith, was another who was later suspected of involvement in making the Kellys' armour.
79. Stationmaster John Stanistreet: Stanistreet's story was published in the *Argus* on 29 June 1880, written by Joe Melvin.

NOTES

80. On events at the Reardon house: Sourced from an interview conducted by Joe Melvin with Margaret Reardon, published in the *Argus* on 29 June 1880.
81. Bacon, pig's cheek, and bread: Douthie, *I was at the Kelly Gang Round-up*, p. 66.
85. 'Watch his countenance . . .': Joe Melvin, *Argus*, 29 June 1880.
86. Discussion by the Kelly Gang: Based on Joe Melvin's interview with John Stanistreet, *Argus*, 29 June 1880.
87. The second Delaney family: There would later be some confusion because there was another Patrick Delaney among the prisoners. That Patrick Delaney was older, had quite an extensive criminal history and was a known Kelly supporter. He was also one of the Wangaratta Delaneys.
91. Serve food and drink . . .: Hotels in Victoria were not allowed to serve alcohol on the Sabbath, another law the Kellys broke with impunity.
92. His partner in the first dance: At this time, men dancing together were neither unusual nor effeminate. Like riding and shooting, it was just another skill for a young man to master.

Chapter 6: The Dark Hours: 27/28 June 1880
Page
100. Ann Jones locked . . .: In an aside to Ned and Joe, Ann Jones had said: 'I have plenty of bread but I am keeping it for you as I would not give a bite to half of those inside as they treat me like a blackfellow.' (Evidence given by Dave Mortimer to the Royal Commission into the Kelly Outbreak.)
100. Jane Jones to hold one of his pistols: Both Margaret Reardon and Tom Cameron saw this, and would later insist that Jane was actually guarding the prisoners.
100. Dan and Joe found a small table . . .: Margaret Reardon interview, *Benalla Standard*, 10 June 1881.
104. Arming himself: Since Stringybark, police in north-eastern Victoria had been instructed to arm themselves before answering doorknocks after dark.

109. Sullivan: The New Zealand killings involved a number of strangulation murders undertaken by a gang of four, including a man named Sullivan. That Sullivan gave evidence against the other three, who were convicted and hanged. Sullivan was given a Queen's Pardon and free passage to Melbourne. It was widely speculated that Sullivan had not bothered to change his name, and was working as some kind of labourer in the north-east of Victoria.

109. Morgan: Daniel 'Mad Dog' Morgan, a bushranger based in southern New South Wales who had been shot dead just north of Wangaratta some fifteen years earlier.

115. Every time a train whistle blew: White, p. 359. In *The Briars and the Thorns*, chapter 16, Joseph Ashmead claimed that someone on the train gave Tom Curnow a revolver before he left to return home. Curnow was so nervous, he almost used it to shoot a goat he heard grazing near his home, suspecting it was one of the outlaws. No-one else reported this story.

116. This was the first time . . .: Joe Melvin, *Argus*, 29 June 1880.

Chapter 7: The Police Special
Page
128. The time of the collision: John McWhirter, *Age*, 29 June 1880.
132. 'It was a splendid night': Evidence given by Frank Hare to the Royal Commission on the Kelly Outbreak, 1880, Report 1801, (Francis Longmore chairperson), Melbourne, p. 225.

Chapter 8: First Blood
Page
139. 'When I was within': All these recollections are taken from statements made to the subsequent Royal Commission on the Kelly Outbreak. Report of the Royal Commission on the Kelly Outbreak, (Francis Longmore chairperson).
140. Flashes lit up the veranda: Evidence given by John Kelly to the Royal Commission on the Kelly Outbreak, (Francis Longmore chairperson).

NOTES

141. Seemed to originate from one spot: Carrington, *Ned Kelly: The Last Stand*, p. 17.
141. 'The smoke was so thick': Report of the Royal Commission on the Kelly Outbreak, (Francis Longmore chairperson), 11593.
144. Ann screamed: Several police from the cordon would later recall hearing the scream. It was a female voice which several recognised as Ann Jones's. See particularly Joe Melvin's account in *Argus*, 28 June 1880.
149. Tom Carrington, who claimed . . .: For years after the incident, stories circulated that Carrington had got it all wrong. For example, Fitchett (p. 41) wrote: 'The reporters acted as amateur surgeons, and put a ligature on the shattered wrist to arrest the flow of arterial blood. But their knowledge of anatomy was singularly poor, and they put the ligature on the wrong side of the wound, so that the tiny jet of blood continued to run unchecked.' To paraphrase Fitchett, this is 'arrantly wrong'.
151. They had probably been fired off by a Kelly sympathiser . . .: Stanistreet quoted in interview by Joe Melvin, *Argus*, 29 June 1880. The origin and meaning of the firing of the rockets has never been fully explained. The meaning remains open to speculation, but the origin is most probably traced to one of the two Chinese families – friends of Joe Byrne's – who were suspected sympathisers of the gang. There may be a little story in that.
153. 'I left the kitchen . . .': Ibid.
154. 'A strange woman from Benalla': This was undoubtedly the woman who had been sharing a tent (and a bed) with Piazzi. She was never publicly identified and seems to have left the scene as fast as she possibly could. In leaving the scene, she also left the story. Report of the Royal Commission on the Kelly Outbreak, (Francis Longmore chairperson), 11729.
157. 'For God's sake': Evidence given by Rawlins to the Royal Commission on the Kelly Outbreak, (Francis Longmore chairperson), 11729.

NOTES

Chapter 9: Reinforcements
Page
159. Dwyer: Dwyer was a big man, considered by other policemen as courageous and a little bit eccentric. Report of the Royal Commission on the Kelly Outbreak, (Francis Longmore chairperson), 11422.
160. Steele led his party off into the night: If nothing else, Steele certainly looked the part. He was wearing a tweed suit, leggings, and a deerstalker hat. He was armed with a double-barrelled shotgun and a bag of cartridges which included solid shot and swan shot, with 16 small pellets per cartridge.
160. Single file through the scrub: As they moved through the scrub, the police party passed close to where the wounded Ned Kelly lay hidden. He later claimed that, had he been so inclined, he could have killed any of them.
162. To Sadleir's surprise, among the post and telegraph clerks sat Frank Hare: Fitchett (p. 42) paints a funny little tableau of the scene.

Chapter 10: The Siege
i. 03:00–05:00 Monday
Page
172. 'Whistling and pinging': Carrington, p. 18.
175. 'You should see O'Connor . . .': Carroll, *Ned Kelly, Bushranger*, p. 176.

ii. 05:00–07:00 Monday
Page
182. 'I heard him fall . . .': Evidence given by James Reardon to the Royal Commission on the Kelly Outbreak, (Francis Longmore chairperson).
187. 'Seemed like as if . . .': Evidence given by James Arthur to the Royal Commission on the Kelly Outbreak, (Francis Longmore chairperson), 11142.
188. Steele said he responded: Fitchett, p. 53.

NOTES

189. Straight away, he felt . . .: Evidence given by Michael Reardon to the Royal Commission on the Kelly Outbreak, (Francis Longmore chairperson).

iii. The Man in the Mist
Page
196. 'When you have got . . .': Fitchett, p. 44.
196. 'It was as good . . .': Evidence given by James Arthur to the Royal Commission on the Kelly Outbreak, (Francis Longmore chairperson).
198. 'Presently we noticed . . .': Carrington, p. 19.
200. Steele realised that . . .: Fitchett, p. 54.
200. 'It was seen that he . . .': *Argus,* 29 June 1880.
201. 'The figure continued gradually . . .': Carrington, p. 20.
202. 'He must be mad . . .': *Age,* 29 June 1880.
205. As he turned his head . . .: Based on Dwyer's recollections to Fitchett, p. 60.
207. 'Do not shoot him . . .': Evidence given by Hugh Bracken to the Royal Commission on the Kelly Outbreak, (Francis Longmore chairperson), 11277.
208. 'Smelt strongly of brandy': Strangely, Arthur Steele did not think that Ned smelt of alcohol when he was captured. Kenneally, p. 214.
209. 'This is the first time . . .': Carrington, p. 21.

iv. The Trophy
Page
211. Bloodstained green silk cummerbund: Ned's green cummerbund was presented to the Benalla Historical Society in 1973 by descendants of Dr John Nicholson.
213. 'He was dressed . . .': Carrington, p. 21.
216. 'To paste as many of the traps': Carrington, p. 20.
216. He could have shot . . .: Evidence given by Dr John Nicholson to the Royal Commission on the Kelly Outbreak, (Francis Longmore chairperson).

NOTES

216. He said several times . . .: Carrington, p. 21.
216. Despite the injuries . . .: Ibid, p. 20.

v. 07:00–11:00 Monday
Page
217. 'All those who saw . . .': Evidence given by John Sadlier to the Royal Commission on the Kelly Outbreak (Francis Longmore chairperson).
218. Led by Sergeant Mullane: Mullane knew the Kellys well, having been stationed at Greta some years earlier.
219. An opportunity for redemption: Dowling may have assumed that redemption grew out of the barrel of a gun as he would later testify that he fired about 100 rounds during the siege, most of them in the half hour after he arrived at Glenrowan. William Duross would fire 25 rounds over the same period.
220. 'We all lay down . . .': *Argus,* 29 June 1880.
221. 'Glenrowan, June 28, 1880. Weatherboard, brick chimney . . .': Kenneally, p. 212.
223. All those inside . . .: Carrington, p. 21.
225. 'The prisoners came bouncing out . . .': Evidence given by Inspector John Sadleir to the Royal Commission on the Kelly Outbreak, (Francis Longmore chairperson), 2829.
226. 'The scene presented . . .': *Argus,* 29 June 1880.
227. 'The faces of the poor fellows . . .': Carrington, p. 22.
227. 'For all the world . . .': Ibid.

vi. 11:00–15:00 Monday
Page
228. 'Cutting up tobacco . . .': Kenneally, p. 217.
229. 'He is very reserved . . .': Joe Melvin, *Argus,* 29 June 1880.
230. The would-be volunteers . . .: Both offered their services almost immediately they arrived, offers that were declined with thanks.
231. 'When I asked him . . .': *Argus,* 29 June 1880.
231. 'I had to shoot Sergeant Kennedy . . .': Ibid.

NOTES

232. 'I wouldn't advise you to go . . .': Ibid.
233. He found a blood-covered pistol . . .: McHugh would later lodge a claim for the return of the pistol, which he said was no longer usable. His claim was refused.
235. 'A handsome black riding habit . . .': Carrington, p. 22.

Chapter 11: Last Rites
Page
239. The newspaper reporters continued to take notes . . .: See Joe Melvin's reports in the *Argus*, 29 June 1880.
242. Dwyer found he could . . .: Evidence given by John Kelly to the Royal Commission on the Kelly Outbreak.
245. 'Not very many minutes elapsed . . .': Melvin, *Argus*, 29 June 1880.
246. 'I will see my brother . . .': Hunter, *The Origin and Destruction of the Kelly Gang*, p. 52.
246. 'My feelings revolted . . .': Kenneally, p. 226.
247. Tom Carrington noted . . .: Carrington, pp. 22–23.
247. 'All eyes were now fixed . . .': Melvin, *Argus*, 29 June 1880.
249. A dead dog . . .: I have been unable to find anything definitive about the dog, with different observers suggesting it was Dave Mortimer's pet, the Delaney brothers' greyhound, or Dan Kelly's cattle dog.
249. May have held their pistols . . .: Molony (p. 230) claims, somewhat implausibly, that Dan and Steve were killed by police bullets and that, sometime between their deaths and the burning of the hotel, one of their supporters snuck back into the building to lay out their bodies.
249. 'They lay so calm together . . .': Evidence given by The Very Reverend Dean Matthew Gibney to the Royal Commission on the Kelly Outbreak, (Francis Longmore chairperson), 12334. The most likely cause of death was suicide by poisoning, with laudanum being the probable poison.
251. 'At a quarter past three . . .': Carrington, p. 23.
251. 'The first thing we saw . . .': Ibid.

NOTES

252. 'The bodies of Dan Kelly and Steve Hart . . .': Ibid.
253. 'They appeared to me . . .:' Evidence given by Senior Constable Charles Johnston to the Royal Commission on the Kelly Outbreak, (Francis Longmore chairperson).
254. 'Howling loudly . . .': Carrington, p. 23.
254. 'The wrecks of two iron bedsteads . . .': White, p. 373.

Chapter 12: Midwinter Afternoon, Glenrowan
Page
256. 'At times his eyes . . .': Melvin, *Argus,* 29 June 1880.
256. 'I had a chance . . .': Ibid.
256. 'I was at last surrounded . . .': Ibid.
257. 'The armour in which . . .': Ibid.
258. 'No extra rifles . . .': Carrington, p. 24

Chapter 13: Aftermath
Page
262. 'It would be impossible . . .': *Herald,* 29 June 1880.
262. 'Anxious crowds assembled . . .': *Age,* 29 June 1880.
262. 'People were waiting . . .': Hunter, p. 51.
265. 'After the bodies of Dan Kelly and Steve Hart . . .': Frearson, p. 16.
266. 'The face was small . . .': White, p. 375.
267. Cherry's body was then claimed: McBean found that Martin Cherry had been killed by a bullet fired by the police: There were suggestions subsequently floated – primarily from police circles – that Ned himself had shot Martin Cherry after the elderly labourer had been slow to respond to Ned's direction to move away from a window.
268. Joe 'had always bore [sic] a bad character': Frearson, p. 17.
268. Aaron Sherrit was also buried . . .: Sherrit apparently had very few friends, and even Frank Hare suggested that his widow was probably better off without him. (White, p. 324).
269. 'The wound itself . . .': *Herald,* 29 June 1880.
272. 'Glenrowan this morning is the scene . . .': Ibid.

NOTES

272. 'Bits of iron, saucepans . . .': Lowe.
273. A lady had travelled from Melbourne . . .: *Ovens and Murray Advertiser,* 7 October 1880.

Chapter 14: The Reckoning
Page
275. 'Ned Kelly after being secured . . .': *Argus,* 29 June 1880.
276. 'The outlaw Ned Kelly is quiet . . .': *Ovens and Murray Advertiser,* 6 July 1880.
277. There had been a fifth member of the gang . . .: While most people believe that the temporary fifth member was the younger Tom Lloyd, other candidates for the position have included Isaiah 'Wild' Wright and Dick Hart. I think Tom Lloyd is the best fit as the other two always preferred to be leaders themselves.
277. He was suspected of exchanging . . .: White, p. 385.
279. Some say they heard him declare . . .: Wannan, p. 32.
280. During a routine visit . . .: One who was refused permission to visit Ned was Sergeant Michael Kennedy's widow, who wanted to ask Ned about her husband's final moments of existence.
287. 'A bottle': Evidence given by Constable James Arthur to the Royal Commission on the Kelly Outbreak, (Francis Longmore chairperson), 11254.
288. 'The spectators were clearly not . . .': Hunter, p. 53.
288. 'A dispassionate observer . . .': Ibid.

Chapter 15: The Legacy
Page
291. 'The Kellys wanted ground . . .': Ian Jones, *Ned Kelly: A Short Life,* p. 402.
293. Ann's accusation that James Reardon . . .: Judith Douthie, *I was at the Kelly Gang Round-up,* p. 61.
293. Dave Mortimer had moved there . . .: Mortimer would later give the writer Charles White a detailed account of how the events unfolded at Glenrowan.

321

NOTES

294. 'My son, he got wounded . . .:' Evidence given by James Reardon to the Royal Commission on the Kelly Outbreak.
295. 'Disease of the heart . . .': *Argus,* 20 March 1883.
298. 'Ned Kelly rises before me . . .': Quoted in Cookson, 'Sydney *Sun*' articles, published in that newspaper in September 1911.
300. 'The actual capture of Ned Kelly . . .': Fitchett, p. 56.
302. 'Maybe Ned Kelly is history . . .': Tom Prior, *The Bushrangers,* p. 115.
303. 'Jim Kelly was one of . . .': Bate, Weston, 'Tom Kelly and his times', in *Ned Kelly: Man and Myth,* p. 61.

BIBLIOGRAPHY

Writing the story of Glenrowan was made immensely easier than it might otherwise have been because of the presence of four professional eyewitnesses at that siege. The contemporaneous writings of the four Melbourne reporters were critical in working out the who, what, and where of the siege. Even when they were writing about events which occurred before their arrival on the scene or beyond their vision, they were writing from notes taken when interviewing those who had been directly involved. It is also fortunate that, within a reasonable time of the events occurring, a Royal Commission was held, and many of those present gave evidence under oath. That document, too, contains a wealth of interesting information on what occurred under the general rubric of the Kelly Outbreak.

Where possible, I have reconstructed the story based on those contemporaneous accounts, rather than on the secondary stories reported in books published years later. I have also attempted to only describe events and occurrences that were described originally by those present at the time. Where information is from those secondary sources, I have tried to describe it as such. If there are errors, they are mine and they reflect my beliefs about the most likely occurrence or sequence in a particular setting, based on what is happening elsewhere and how the characters behaved previously. There are literally hundreds of books on Ned Kelly and his gang; I have listed only those that gave me something new or significant. Probably the best place for others to start their explorations is the internet, and I would especially recommend the websites I have included in the references. They are labours of love and a treasure trove of information.

Ashmead, Joseph, *The Thorn and the Briars: The True Story of the Kelly Gang*, Glen Rowan Cobb & Co Pty. Ltd., viewed 22 December 2010, www.nedkellysworld.com.au.

Baron, Angeline, *Blood in the Dust,* Network Creative Services, Greensborough, 2004.

Brown, Max, *Ned Kelly, Australian Son*, Angus and Robertson, Sydney, 1980.

Carrington, Thomas, *Ned Kelly: The Last Stand* (Facsimile edition), Lothian Books, South Melbourne, 2003.

Carroll, Brian, *Ned Kelly – Bushranger*, Lansdowne Press, Dee Why West, 1976.

Castles, Alex, *Ned Kelly's Last Days*, Allen and Unwin, Sydney, 2005.

Cave, Colin (Ed.), *Ned Kelly: Man and Myth*, Cassell, North Melbourne, 1968.

Chomley, Charles, *The True Story of the Kelly Gang of Bushrangers*, Wyatt and Watts, Melbourne, 1930.

Clune, Frank, *Ned Kelly's Last Stand*, Pacific Books, Sydney, 1962.

Corfield, Justin, *The Ned Kelly Encyclopaedia*, Lothian Books, South Melbourne, 2005.

BIBLIOGRAPHY

Douthie, Judith, *I was at the Kelly Gang Round-up*, Network Creative Services, Greensborough, 2007.

Dunstan, Keith, *Saint Ned*, Methuen, Sydney, 1980.

Fitchett, W.H., *Ned Kelly and his Gang*, Fitchett Brothers Pty Limited, West Melbourne, 1925.

Haldane, Robert, *The People's Force: A History of the Victoria Police*, Melbourne University Press, Melbourne, 1995.

Hunter, F., *The Origin and Destruction of the Kelly Gang*, A.T. Hodgson, Adelaide, 1900.

Jones, Graham, *Ned Kelly: The Larrikin Years*, Charquin Hill, Wangaratta, 1990.

Jones, Ian, *Ned Kelly, A Short Life*, Hachette, Sydney, 2008.

Joy, William and Prior, Tom, *The Bushrangers*, Seal Books, Adelaide, 1971.

Kenneally, J.J., *The Complete Inner History of the Kelly Gang and Their Pursuers*, Ruskin Press, Melbourne, 1929.

McDermott, Alan (Ed.), *The Jerilderie Letter*, Faber & Faber, London, 2001.

McMenomy, Keith, *Ned Kelly: The Authentic Illustrated History*, Currey O'Neil Ross P/L, South Yarra, 1984.

McQuilton, John, *The Kelly Outbreak, 1878–80*, Melbourne University Press, Melbourne, 1979.

Meredith, John and Scott, Bill, *Ned Kelly after a Century of Acrimony*, Lansdowne Press, Dee Why West, 1986.

Molony, John, *Ned Kelly*, Penguin Books, Ringwood, 1989.

Phillips, David and Davies, Susanna (Eds.), *A Nation of Rogues?*, Melbourne University Press, Melbourne 1994.

Sadleir, John, *Recollections of a Victorian Police Officer*, George Robertson, Melbourne, 1913.

Seal, Graham, *Tell 'Em I Died Game*, Hyland House, Flemington, 2002.

Wannan, Bill, *Tell 'Em I Died Game*, Seal Books, Australia, 1974.

White, Charles, *History of Australian Bushranging*, Lloyd O'Neill P/L, Hawthorn, 1970.

Journals, reports, periodicals and monographs

Burch, Hugh, Letter, National Library of Australia Collection Canberra, 14 March 1881. The incomplete letter is addressed to 'Dear Father and Mother'.
Butel, Elizabeth, 2006, Kate Kelly in the Central West, viewed 1 February 2010, www.katekelly.biz.
Dowsett, Jesse, 'Dowsett Letter', *State Library of Victoria Journal*, No. 11. April 1973.
Ford, Adam, Glenrowan Siege Archaeological Project 2008 – Excavation Report, DIG International Pty Limited, Ocean Grove, 2010.
Frearson, Robert and Frearson, Samuel, *The Kelly Gang: Full and True Account,* pamphlet, Adelaide, 1880.
Hollingsworth, Sharon, 2007, 'Dear Brave Little Woman; Jane Jones at Glenrowan', viewed 6 April 2010, www.nedonthenet.com.
Lowe, John, 1940, *John Lowe's Glenrowan Diary*, Dave White, viewed 22 May 2010, www.glenrowan1880.com.
Morgan, Kevin, *The Particulars of Executions*, Old Melbourne Gaol, Melbourne, undated.
Morley, Joe, 2004, 'A hero at Glenrowan', *Catholic Weekly*, viewed 6 April 2010, www.catholicweekly.com.au.
Morrissey, Doug, 'Ned Kelly's World', *Royal Historical Society of Victoria Journal*, Vol. 55, No. 2, June 1984.
Oldis, Ken, 'The True Story of the Kelly Armour', *The LaTrobe Journal*, No. 66, Spring 2000.
Porter, Trevor, *Executions in the Colony and State of Victoria, 1842–1967*, Aimsetters, Bowden S.A., 2002.

Report of the Royal Commission on the Kelly Outbreak, Report 1801, (Francis Longmore chairperson), Melbourne, 1880.

Wright, Clare, and McDermott, Alex, 'Ned's Women: A Fractured Love Story', *Meanjin*, Vol. 69, No. 2, 2010.

Newspapers

The *Advertiser* (Adelaide)
The *Age* (Melbourne)
The *Argus* (Melbourne)
The *Australasian Sketcher* (Melbourne)
The *Daily Telegraph* (Melbourne)
The *Evening News* (Sydney)
The *Standard* (Benalla)
The *Herald* (Melbourne)
The *Mercury* (Hobart)
The *Ovens and Murray Advertiser* (Wangaratta)
The *Sun* (Sydney)

ACKNOWLEDGEMENTS

Most of the research for this book took place at the National Library of Australia, one of the country's great institutions and a place where the helpfulness of the staff is almost matched by the quality of the coffee. I also experienced both the expertise and the friendliness of a number of people associated with the Old Melbourne Gaol – thanks to Michelle and Stephen Royal and the delightful Sylvia Campbell, and the Victoria Police Museum in Melbourne, where Caroline Oxley led the way. The staff at the State Library of Victoria and sundry persons in the country towns of Wangaratta, Beechworth, Benalla and Glenrowan as well as the big cities of Canberra and Melbourne also assisted my endeavours. For online research, I can thoroughly recommend the National Library of Australia's 'Trove' newspaper site, as well as the websites of the Public Records Office of Victoria and the Australian Archives. A special thank you to Alexander Fax Books in Mawson, ACT, who also seem to have that special little book I have been looking everywhere for. In researching *Glenrowan*,

ACKNOWLEDGEMENTS

I discovered that Ned and I have a several things in common. We both love an audience, we both make plans that sometimes come unstuck and we both are part of families which provide us with more love and support than we sometimes deserve. My family grew while *Glenrowan* was being written. Welcome Eli James Shaw and Billy Winton Fowlie, and may you live long and happy lives with us all.

Thank you especially to Sophie Hamley at Cameron Creswell and to Alex Craig, Samantha Sainsbury and Libby Turner at Pan Macmillan for their ongoing support.

Finally (and again) I would like to thank all my family – and there are quite a few of them – and all my friends for both their sympathetic ears and their good humour, especially when the topic was either Glenrowan or the Sydney Swans.

INDEX

Adams, Edward 4
Adelaide 263
Advertiser 263
Age 123, 262
   special editions 262–3
Ah Fook 17
Alder, Henry 122, 128, 131, 133
Alexander, Mounted Constable Robert 218
Allen, George 123, 207–8
Anderson, Captain 259
Argus 119, 123, 200, 226, 232, 233, 262
   special editions 262–3
armour
   Kelly Gang's 62, 63, 75, 103, 116–17, 139, 148, 151, 159, 169, 177, 181, 195, 200–2, 216, 230, 247, 254, 257, 277, 281–2
   Ned Kelly's 179, 197–8, 200, 201, 203, 206–9, 212, 230, 242, 257, 281
Armstrong, Constable Harry 82, 120, 218, 224, 241, 250–1, 290, 296
arrest warrants 28
Arthur, Mounted Constable James 125, 126, 133, 139–40, 147, 150, 151, 156, 160–161, 164, 167–8, 187–9, 194, 196–8, 200–1, 205, 215, 250–1, 287, 290, 305, 307
Astronomer, The Government 222–3
Attorney-General, Victorian 278, 289
Australasian Sketcher 123
Avenel 13
Aylward, Reverend PJ 271

Baker, Dr Edward 7, 8

INDEX

Bank of New South Wales Jerilderie raid 48–9, 53, 64, 83
Barry, Mounted Constable Daniel 125, 126, 129–30, 133, 134, 135, 155–6, 167, 175, 195–6, 228, 233, 243–4, 296
Barry, Mary 65, 267
Barry, Judge Redmond 29, 278, 283
Beechworth 16, 18, 20, 22, 24, 29, 30, 41, 44, 59, 65, 68, 82, 92, 120, 124
  committal hearing 277
  reinforcements 218–19, 230, 261, 285
Beechworth Prison 69
Benalla 15, 16, 28, 31, 43, 44, 47, 56, 57, 58, 59, 61, 63, 65, 67, 70, 82, 120–1, 124, 150, 158, 161–3, 259, 265, 267
  cemetery 267, 268, 295
  Court House 267
  police barracks 28, 63, 120, 127, 162, 259, 267
  reinforcements 167, 184, 185, 190
  telegraph office 162
Benalla Standard 53
Berry, Premier Graham 108
Beveridge 13
Bindon, Henry 278
Bracken, Constable Hugh 68–9, 92, 97, 102, 103, 104–6, 108–9, 116, 117, 136, 141, 143, 148, 152, 158–160, 206–7, 209, 284, 288, 290, 299, 305, 307
Bracken, James 299
Bray, Mr JE 263
Bryan, Michael 264
Burch, Hugh 123, 131

Byrne, Joe 20–1, 23, 24, 28, 29, 30, 33, 37, 39, 44, 64, 65, 66, 142, 152–3, 179, 182–3, 192–3, 202, 215, 216, 219, 248, 250–253, 263, 270, 280, 294, 303, 307
  body 248, 250–2, 255–7, 260, 266, 268
  death 181–3, 184, 192, 227, 248, 250–1
  declaration as outlaw 41, 43, 268
  see also Kelly Gang
  inquest 267–8
Byrne, Kate 24, 65
Byrne, Margaret 294
Byrne, Patrick 20

Cameron, Tom 90, 94, 101, 116, 225
Canny, Mounted Constable William 125, 126, 133, 134, 167, 184, 192, 267, 296
Carlton football club 222
Carrington, Thomas 123, 134, 149, 172, 198, 201, 215–16, 232, 237, 247, 251, 258
Castieau, Godfrey 3
Castieau, Governor John Buckley 2, 3, 6, 276, 279, 281
Castieau, John 3
Causey, Constable 160, 205
Cherry, Martin 87, 114, 144, 145, 191–2, 242, 246, 251, 253, 255, 303
  burial 267–8
  inquest 267
  last rites 251
Cheshire, Mr HE 219, 221, 261, 263, 285

INDEX

Chiltern 47
Clarke family, Sunbury 282
Coleman, Richard 163
committal hearing 277
Cookson, W 293, 298, 300
Coppin, George 283
Craigieburn 128, 133
Curnow, Isabella 293
Curnow, Jean Isobel (nee Mortimer) 70, 110, 111–12, 115, 178–9, 273, 293
Curnow, Leonard 293
Curnow, Muriel 293
Curnow, Thomas 70, 89–90, 91–2, 94, 96–7, 100, 101–3, 105, 106–7, 109–10, 111–12, 113–15, 132, 178–9, 270, 273–4, 284, 288, 293, 305, 307
Curnow II, Thomas 293

Daily Telegraph 123
Deakin, Prime Minister Alfred 5
Delaney, John 77, 88–9, 191, 225–6
Delaney, Patrick 182, 191, 225
Delaney, William 191, 225
Devine, Constable 48
Dixon, Mr (Benalla bootmaker) 242, 251
Donahue, Bold Jack 306
Doraghy, Chaplain 3, 4
Dowling, Mounted Constable Thomas 218
Dowsett, Jesse 125, 163, 190–1, 193, 199–202, 204–6, 211–12, 215, 219, 284, 294, 305, 307
Duross, Mounted Constable William 218
Dwyer, Mounted Constable James 58, 120, 159–161, 168–9, 193–5, 205–7, 209, 213–15, 234, 241, 250–1, 287, 307

Euroa 45, 46
Evening News 263
execution of Ned Kelly 2, 5–8, 281, 298 *see also* Kelly, Ned (Edward)
official witnesses 5

Felon's Apprehension Act 40, 41, 43
effect 43
Fitzpatrick, Mounted Constable Alexander 26–8, 45, 260, 298, 300
Flood, Ernest 16
Foster, Private Frederick Arthur 302
Foster, William 'Brickie' 301
Freemasons 295

Gardiner, Frank 59, 306
Garrison Artillery 222, 259
Gascoigne, Mounted Constable Patrick Charles 125, 127, 133, 134, 135–7, 140, 146, 150–2, 155, 166, 175, 184, 194–5, 290, 296–307
Gibbons, Robert 69, 101, 103–4, 106, 191, 219, 225
Gibney, Very Reverend Dean Matthew 230–3, 235, 246–50, 251, 269, 286, 295
Gill, Samuel 48
Glenny, Mounted Constable 218
Glenrowan 61, 65, 67–8, 74, 160, 259, 261, 272, 292
ammunition 173, 175, 194, 199
dances 92–3, 100, 111

INDEX

Delaney families 87–8
firefight 139–45, 159, 168–70, 173, 176, 184–93, 199, 204
initial newspaper report 119
legend of 303, 305
newspaper reports of siege 261–2
police barracks 67, 69, 74, 86, 92, 93, 97, 103–5, 290
police cordon 160, 166–7, 169, 173–4, 181, 184, 193–6, 198, 217, 219, 223, 233, 237, 243, 247, 251, 286
police special 119–37
portable telegraph extension installation 219, 261
public officers 68–70
railway station 68, 131, 138, 161, 163–8, 172, 178–9, 190, 199, 200, 209, 254, 259, 261, 304
reporters 161, 165, 171–3, 175, 190–1, 198, 200, 205, 208, 215–16, 225, 227, 233, 237, 245, 247, 251–2, 256, 258, 261–2, 265
siege 171, 177, 193, 217, 219–21, 227–8, 232
spectators 230, 234, 246–7, 251, 253–4, 258
stationmaster's office 167, 175, 209, 210, 217, 219, 233
tents for labourers 73, 77
Glenrowan Inn (Ann Jones's hotel) 67, 69, 70–3, 85, 160, 164–8, 179, 183, 184–93, 199, 204, 208, 218–19, 255, 285, 304
fire 236, 242–52
firefight 143–5, 159, 168–70, 173, 176, 184–93, 199, 204, 235
siege 171, 177, 193, 237–8

Glenrowan siege prisoners 77–118, 143, 166, 169–70, 172, 176–7, 178, 181, 183, 185, 219, 223–4
escapes 154, 169, 188–9
injuries 143, 144–5, 178
release 172, 185, 225, 239
Graham, Senior Constable Robert 291
Grant, John 264
Greta 15–16, 33, 41, 44, 47, 51, 75, 87, 89, 258, 260, 277, 290, 300
cemetery 264
local families 24
police station 290–1
reports of theft 62
Greta Barracks 69
Greta Mob 21–5
Gunn, Alexander 16, 18, 24

Hall, Ben 41, 306
Hall, Constable 18
Hare, Superintendent Francis 31–2, 50–2, 57, 58, 63–4, 82, 120–1, 124–5, 129–31, 132–7, 138–40, 147, 149, 155, 156–7, 159–162, 166, 171, 172, 175, 178, 185–6, 269–72, 281, 283–4, 286, 288, 295–6, 297, 304, 307
injury 139–40, 145–6, 149–50, 158, 303
The Last of the Bushrangers 295
Hart, Dick 22, 23, 234, 257–8, 278
Hart, Ettie 22, 73
Hart, Julia 73
Hart, Rachel 301

333

INDEX

Hart, Steve 22–3, 28, 30, 36, 46–7, 48–9, 60, 73, 75, 94–6, 101, 182–3, 186, 192, 204, 216, 218, 224, 227, 238, 253, 267, 270, 305, 307
   body 249, 252–4, 257–9, 263
   burial and wake 264–5
   death 239–41, 248–50, 252
   declaration as outlaw 41, 43 *see also* Kelly Gang
   recognition by Fanny Shaw 46
Healey, Constable Patrick 160, 201, 206
Healy, Dr 269
Hobart 263
Hutchison, Dr 162, 163, 211, 213

Inquests, magisterial 267
   Byrne, Joe 267–8
   Cherry, Martin 267
   Sherrit, Aaron 267

Jerilderie 48–50
   Bank of New South Wales Jerilderie raid 48–9, 53, 64, 213
Jerilderie Letter 49–50, 60, 306
Johnston, Constable Charles 229–30, 237–8, 242–5, 253–4, 258, 269, 284, 288, 296–7, 305
   Glenrowan Inn fire 242–5, 306
Jones, Ann (nee Kennedy) 70–1, 73, 74, 78–9, 83, 84, 85, 87, 89, 93, 94, 97, 117, 136, 144–5, 152–4, 178, 187, 252, 269, 274, 282, 285, 292–3, 307, 307
Jones, Jane 74, 78–9, 84, 85, 90, 93, 100, 101, 116, 144, 145, 153–4, 178, 269, 292

Jones, John 74, 100, 111, 112, 144–5, 153, 165, 269, 292–3, 303
Jones, Owen 70, 274, 292–3
Jones, Thomas 71
Jones's hotel *see* Glenrowan Inn

Kelly, Annie 12, 16
Kelly, Dan 12, 17, 19, 21–2, 23, 25, 26, 28, 29–30, 33, 36, 38, 41, 48, 61, 64, 65, 182, 184–6, 188–9, 192, 204, 208, 216, 218, 224, 227, 235, 238, 253, 267, 270, 303, 305, 307
   body 249, 252–4, 257–9, 264
   burial and wake 264–5
   death 239–41, 248–50, 252
   declaration as outlaw 41, 43 *see also* Kelly Gang
Kelly, Ellen (Ned's sister) 16, 27
Kelly, Ellen (nee Quinn, Ned's mother) 3, 11–12, 15, 27, 28, 60, 61, 70, 271, 276, 300
   arrest 28–9
Kelly Gang 59–60, 178, 216, 219, 261, 275
   ammunition 63
   armour 62, 63, 75, 103, 116–17, 139, 148, 151, 159, 169, 177, 181, 195, 200–2, 230
   bank raids 46, 48–50, 52, 53
   base camps 45
   capture of Younghusband's Faithfull Creek station 45–7
   disagreements 148
   fifth member 277
   finances 60
   gang names 54
   injuries in Glenrowan firefight 142, 147–8, 203

INDEX

Jerilderie Letter 49–50, 60, 306
legends 47, 50, 303
motivations 291
plans 45, 60–2, 65, 148–9
police raids on families and friends 47–8
publicity 52–4
reaction to Queensland troopers 58–9
reward 43, 50, 283
separation at Glenrowan 152–3, 177, 183, 192, 202
support from families and friends 54, 234, 243, 291
supporters and sympathisers 33, 234, 243, 253–4, 256, 258–9, 278, 289
Kelly, Grace 12, 27, 302
Kelly, James 14
Kelly, Jim 3, 12, 19, 301–3
Kelly, Senior Constable John 27, 34, 37, 51, 124–7, 129, 130, 132–4, 137, 146–7, 155–6, 160, 163–7, 175, 178, 183, 199, 202, 204–6, 207–11, 215, 226, 235–6, 244, 246–7, 284, 287, 290–1, 298, 305, 307
   post-capture interview with Ned 260
Kelly, John 'Red' (Ned's father) 10–12, 14, 70, 303
Kelly, Kate 3, 12, 27, 53, 74, 234, 246, 253, 256, 258, 300–2
Kelly, Maggie *see* Skillian, Maggie (nee Kelly)
Kelly, Mary Jane 12
Kelly, Ned (Edward)
   anti-government and police speech 107–9

armour 179, 197–8, 200, 201, 203, 206–9, 212, 216, 230
attempted murder charge 27–8
capture 203–6, 207–10, 212–13, 224, 227–8, 287
character 17, 19, 49, 61–2, 84
clemency, pleas for 280–1
committal hearing Beechworth 277–8
confession 231
death of father 15
death sentence 279
declaration as outlaw 41, 43 *see also* Kelly Gang
duel with Kennedy 37–8
execution 2, 5–8, 281, 298
family 10–12, 17, 19
final confession 4
first conviction and incarceration 18
friendships 20–5
Glenrowan firefight 182–3, 197
good luck charm 14, 211
horse, Mirth 203, 206, 282–283
horse theft 16, 18, 26
imprisonment Melbourne gaol 275–6, 280
imprisonment of father 14–15
injuries at Glenrowan 142, 147–8, 151, 171, 179–80, 192, 208–12, 216, 256–7
last meal 3
last night 1–2
last requests 2
last rites at Glenrowan 231
medical examination after capture 211–12, 217
medical examination Melbourne Gaol 271

335

INDEX

Kelly, Ned (Edward) (*cont.*)
  motivations 291
  murder of Kennedy 38, 257, 260
  murder of Lonigan 36
  post-capture interview and comments 213–14, 215–16, 217, 228–9, 256, 260, 270
  poverty 13
  reappearance at siege at Glenrowan 197–201, 203–6
  removal from Benalla to Melbourne 269–71
  removal from Glenrowan 259–60
  rescue of Richard Shelton 13–14
  rifle and skull cap 164, 166, 180, 201, 203–4
  separation at Glenrowan 152-3, 177, 183, 184, 192
  supporters and sympathisers 33, 234, 243, 256, 258–9, 278, 289
  trial 278–9
  vital statistics 18
Kelly, Paddy 302
Kelly, Constable Patrick 167
'Kelly Song' 3–4, 111
Kelly supporters and sympathisers 33, 234, 243, 253–4, 256, 258, 259, 278, 289
Kennedy, Sergeant Michael 34–7, 40, 51, 126, 164, 231, 257, 260, 278
  death 38, 260, 278
  discovery of corpse 40–1
  duel with Kelly 37–8
Kenny, Constable 168
Kershaw, James 92
Kilmore East 230
Kilmore Gaol 15

King, Ellen *see* Kelly, Ellen (nee Quinn, Ned's mother)
King, George 16, 23
King River 35, 47
King, Senior Constable Tom 55
King Valley 234, 297
Kirkham, Mounted Constable Thomas 57, 125, 127, 130, 136, 155, 156, 166, 175–6, 178, 187, 217–18, 237, 298

Larkins, John 80, 144, 191–2, 225
laudanum 241
Life magazine 300
Lloyd, Kate 3
Lloyd, Miss 269–70
Lloyd, Tom 3, 23, 63, 277, 291, 301
Lonigan, Thomas 35, 36, 39–40, 233, 278
  murder by Ned Kelly 36, 214
Lowe, John 77–8, 117, 224–5, 226, 272–3

McAuliffe, Dennis 225, 226
McAuliffe, Patrick 225, 226
McBean, Robert 31, 230, 267
McColl, Mounted Constable 218
McDonnell, Hanorah 86–7, 95, 96
McDonnell, Paddy 232
McDonnell's Railway Tavern Hotel 68, 69, 73, 76, 84, 86, 151, 172, 175, 214, 230, 258, 261, 264, 269, 285, 304
McHugh, Jock 77, 116, 153, 165–6
McHugh, Robert 230–1, 233
McIntyre, Constable Thomas 35, 36–8, 39–40, 268, 277–8, 285, 298

INDEX

McPhee, Archibald 123, 128, 130, 132
McWhirter, John 123, 132, 173, 186, 207–8, 211, 215, 246
Maitland, John 77
Maloney, Con 92
Mansfield 33, 34, 39, 47, 164
Mansfield Guardian 51
Mansfield Mob 23
Martini-Henry 177, 196
Meagher, Mounted Constable 218
Melbourne 11, 12, 31, 63, 82, 120–1, 262–3
Melbourne Club 31, 122, 281, 295
Melbourne Cricket Club 222
Melbourne football club 222
Melbourne Gaol 266, 271, 300
　hospital 271
Melbourne Supreme Court 278
　trial of Ned Kelly 278–9
Melbourne waxworks 263
Melvin, Joe 123, 132, 137, 141, 156, 173, 200, 226, 229, 232, 233, 237, 245, 247, 263, 275
Mercury 263
Metcalf, George 77, 143, 282
Metropolitan Gaol 1–2
Milawa 22
Montford, Constable 160, 201, 206, 241
Moore, Constable William 159–161, 205
Morgan, Daniel 'Mad Dog' 41, 109, 306
Morgan, Wangaratta railwayman 160–161
Morgan's Lookout 68, 72, 88, 94, 138, 152, 197, 273
Mortimer, Dave 89–90, 92, 93, 100, 103, 104, 106, 111, 113, 116, 144, 145, 152–3, 182–3, 224–6, 228–9, 293, 307
Mullane, Sergeant 218
Murray River 41, 48

National Bank Euroa raid 46, 52, 83
newspaper reports of siege 261–2
　Melbourne newspapers 262
　Sydney newspapers 262
Nicholson, Dr John 16, 28, 162–163, 207–9, 211–13, 216–17, 220–1, 294
Nicolson, Superintendent Charles 32, 43–4, 47–8, 50, 57, 58, 62, 63, 64, 285
Nolan, Mick 63
Normanby, Lord 55, 280

O'Brien's Hotel Greta 290
O'Brine, Bridget 63
O'Connor, Mrs 165, 175, 191, 219
O'Connor, Inspector Stanhope 55–7, 58, 108, 121, 122, 123–4, 127, 130, 132–3, 135, 137, 146–7, 154, 155–6, 161, 165–9, 175, 178, 181, 185, 196, 223, 225–6, 228, 233, 242–3, 259, 266, 281, 284, 296
O'Dwyer, James 53
O'Hea, Father Charles 3, 4, 13
Osborne, Mr 219, 285
Outlaw Act 40, 41
Ovens and Murray Advertiser 53–4
Ovens River 68, 120

Parkes, Sir Henry 283
Pentridge Prison 13, 17, 18–19

337

INDEX

Phillips, Mounted Constable William 125, 127, 133, 135, 155, 166, 187, 201
photographers 263, 266
Piazzi, Alphonse 'Louis' 77–8, 225, 268, 295
police informants 33, 44, 52, 62, 63–6
  codenames 44, 52
Port Phillip District 11–12
Power, Harry 17, 32, 50
Prior, Tom 302
Prout Webb, Thomas 57

Queensland Native Mounted Police 54–7, 58–9, 121, 122, 123, 135, 146–7, 155, 156, 166, 182, 184, 266, 281, 284
  Trooper Barney 192
  Trooper Jimmy 55, 146, 184, 303
Quinn, Ellen *see* Kelly, Ellen
Quinn, James 11
Quinn, Mary 11
Quinn, Pat 52

Ramsay, Robert 43, 121, 222, 273, 279, 281, 283
Rawlins, Charles 125, 130, 134, 135, 140, 141–2, 146, 147, 149, 156, 157, 161, 178–9, 208–9, 224, 284, 295, 307
Rawlins, Glenrowan Champion 295
Reardon, Ann 154
Reardon, Bridget 80, 154, 186–8, 190–1, 199
Reardon, Helena 225
Reardon, James 80, 81, 88, 90, 96–7, 99, 101, 116, 154, 177, 182, 186–7, 189, 225, 293, 294

Reardon, Margaret 80, 154, 177, 184–8, 190–1, 193, 196, 199, 293, 305
Reardon, Mary 154
Reardon, Michael 80, 144, 154, 183, 186, 188–9, 225–6, 293, 294, 303
Reardon, Thomas 154
Reardon, William 225
Rede, Colonel Robert 6
Reid, Tommy 200
reporters 161, 165, 171–3, 175, 190, 198, 200, 205, 208, 215–16, 225, 227, 233, 237, 245, 247, 251–2, 256, 261–2
reward 43, 50, 283–4
Rewards Board 283–4
Reynolds, Alexander 69, 101, 103–4, 106
Reynolds, Edward 69, 101, 103–4, 106, 191, 225
Reynolds, Hillmorton 69, 97, 101, 273
Rodda, Reverend Mr 232
Royal Commission 286–8, 291, 299
'Rupertswood' property 32
Ryan, Dr Charles 222, 259–60, 270–1, 281
Ryan, Joe 29
Ryan, Matthew 92, 154
Ryan, Mrs 169

Sadleir, Superintendent John 32, 33, 44, 58, 63, 64, 120, 157, 160–163, 165–70, 184–5, 193–6, 205, 209, 212–14, 216–17, 219, 220–8, 233, 236, 237, 241–3, 247, 254, 256, 258–9, 266, 281, 284, 288, 290, 296, 305

INDEX

Recollections of a Victorian Police Officer 296
Sambo, Corporal 55, 56
Sandercook, William 77, 192
Scanlan, Mounted Constable Michael 34–7, 39–40, 51, 126, 231, 252, 255, 278
  death 37
Seymour 129
Shaw, Fanny 46
Shelton, Richard 13–14
Sherrit, Aaron 20, 24–5, 44, 64–5, 82, 152, 219, 303
  burial 268
  codename 44
  delay in reporting death 82
  hut 218, 285
  inquest 267
  Kelly Gang's awareness of police informant role 65–6
  murder of 66, 99, 120, 122
  police protection 66
  recruitment as police informant 44, 52
Sherrit, Jack 219, 282, 285
Sherrit, John 24, 52, 285
Sherrit, William 282
Shields, Dr 271
Simson, James 77
Skillian, Bill 16, 24, 27, 28, 29, 301
Skillian, Maggie (nee Kelly) 3, 12, 16, 27, 54, 63, 69, 74, 234–6, 245–6, 253–4, 256, 258, 301
Smith, Henry 293
Smyth, Constable 167
spectators 270–2, 288
  committal hearing 277
  Glenrowan, at 230, 234, 246–7, 251, 253–4, 258

trial 278–9
Standish, Commissioner Frederick Charles (Captain) 30–1, 43, 44, 50, 52, 55, 56–7, 83, 122, 127, 162, 221–2, 230, 237, 259–60, 263–4, 266, 267, 273, 281, 286, 288, 295, 307
Stanistreet, John 69, 79–81, 83, 85, 89, 90, 94, 96, 98, 101, 107, 110, 116, 134, 144, 153, 154, 305
Stanistreet, Mrs 175
Steele, Sergeant Arthur 22, 28, 34, 120, 159–160, 167, 186–9, 196, 199–202, 205–7, 209–10, 213, 228, 284, 286–8, 291, 294, 299–300, 305, 307
Stevens, Stationmaster 124, 125, 130
Strahan, Senior Constable Michael 34
Strathbogie Ranges 47
Stringybark Creek 35–9, 40, 214, 231, 233, 252, 255, 260, 268, 277
Sullivan, Dennis 79–80, 81, 225
Sydney 263

Tatura 229
telegraph, portable installation Glenrowan 219, 261, 285
Tettleton, Charles 2
trial of Ned Kelly 278–9
turquoise 297

Upjohn, Elijah 6–7

Van Diemen's Land 10
Victoria Native Police 163, 167, 188, 225

Victoria Police 30–2
  Glenrowan firefight 164
  impact of Jerilderie raid 50
  injuries during Glenrowan firefight 139–40, 145–6
  Kelly's opinion of 108
  Native Police 163
  new policing model 43–4
  orders to capture or kill Kellys 44
  personal animosities 57
  police special to Glenrowan 119–37
  Queensland Native Mounted Police and 54–7, 58–9
  tactics 47–8, 51, 57–8
Victorian Railways 294
Violet Town
  reinforcements 229–30

Wallan 11, 13
Walsh, Constable Patrick 167
Wangaratta 15, 22, 28, 30, 47, 50, 59, 67, 70, 71, 76, 87, 124, 130, 141, 158, 159
  cemetery 269
  hospital 269
  police barracks 159
  railway station 159, 161
  reinforcements 184, 185, 205
Warby Ranges 67, 72, 88, 135, 174
Ward, Detective Michael 44, 64, 65, 74, 108, 120, 285, 288
Webb, Mrs Prout 219
Welch, Constable 160–161
Whelan, Sergeant James 28, 163, 167, 194
White, Charles 295
  History of Australian Bushranging 295
White, Henry 7
Wickam, Mounted Constable 218
Wicks, Anton 66
Williamson, William 'Bricky' 24, 27, 28, 29, 52
Wilson, Constable 168, 237
Wodonga 68, 80
Wombat Ranges 56
  gang hideaway 29–30, 33, 35
Wright, Isaiah 'Wild' 18, 23, 24, 51, 234
Wright, Tom 'Dummy' 23, 51, 234, 256
Younghusband's Faithfull Creek Station 45–7